COVINA PUBLIC LIBRARY

NF 941.608 N c.1

W9-BTB-082

COVINA PUBLIC LIBRARY

DO NOT REMOVE
CARDS FROM BOOK

JUN 1988

NORTHERN IRELAND
THE DIVIDED PROVINCE

ALL BRITS MUST DIE!

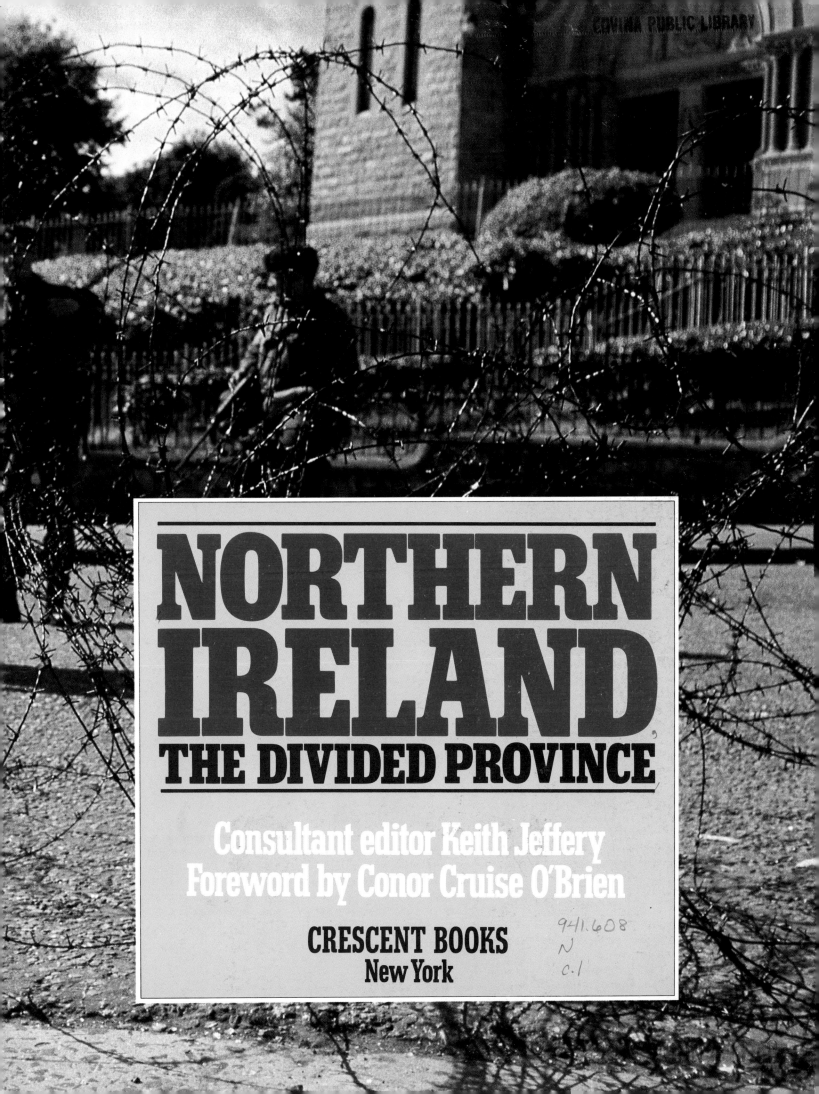

COVINA PUBLIC LIBRARY

NORTHERN IRELAND
THE DIVIDED PROVINCE

Consultant editor Keith Jeffery
Foreword by Conor Cruise O'Brien

CRESCENT BOOKS
New York

941.608
N
c.1

Consultant editor
Keith Jeffery lives in Northern Ireland and teaches at the University of Ulster. A specialist in military and imperial history, he is the author of *The British Army and the Crisis of Empire 1918–1922* and the co-author of *States of Emergency: British Governments and Strikebreaking since 1919.*

The authors
Robin Corbett is a graduate of the Polytechnic of North London, and has contributed articles on international relations and security to a number of publications. He is currently writing a book on guerrilla warfare.

R. G. Grant is a graduate of Trinity College, Oxford. He has written extensively on postwar politics and military history, and was deputy editor of the magazine *War in Peace*.

Arthur Aughey is a lecturer in politics at the University of Ulster. He is co-author of *Conservatives and Conservatism* and has published a number of articles on Conservative politics and Ulster Loyalism.

P. J. Banyard is a former officer in the British Army. He specialises in the relationship between military history and technology.

Acknowledgments
Photographs were supplied by Aerofilms, Associated Press, BBC Hulton Picture Library, *Belfast Telegraph* Newspapers, COI, Camera Press, Crawford Art Gallery, *Daily Telegraph* Colour Library, Carina Dvorak, ET Archive, *Fermanagh Herald*, John Frost Historical Newspaper Service, John Hillelson Picture Library, Robert Hunt Library, Keystone Press Agency, National Library of Ireland, Pacemaker Press, Photographers International, Popperfoto, Press Association, Rex Features, *Soldier* Magazine, Frank Spooner Pictures, Homer Sykes, John Topham Library, Ulster Museum.
The 'Bloody Sunday' box on page 64 is reprinted by permission of Faber and Faber Ltd from *In Holy Terror* by Simon Winchester. The 'Bandit country' box on page 106 is reprinted by permission of Martin Secker and Warburg Ltd from *Contact* by A. F. N. Clarke.

Editor Richard Williams
Designer Michael Moule

© 1985 by Orbis Publishing, London
First published in Great Britain by
Orbis Publishing Limited, London 1985

Published 1985 by Crescent Books
Distributed by Crown Publishers Inc.

All rights reserved. No part of this publication may be reproduced, stored in a retrieval system, or transmitted, in any form or by any means, electronic, mechanical, photocopying, recording or otherwise, without the prior permission of the publisher. Such permission, if granted, is subject to a fee depending on the nature of the use.

ISBN 0–517–473526
Printed and bound in Italy

HGFEDCBA

Contents

Ireland

80 Kilometres
50 Miles

DONEGAL BAY

GALWAY BAY

IRISH SEA

ULSTER

Coleraine
Letterkenny
Londonderry
ANTRIM
DONEGAL
Strabane
DERRY
Ballymena
TYRONE
Omagh
Lough Neagh
Belfast
Dungannon
Lisburn
Comber
Enniskillen
Brookeborough
Armagh
DOWN
FERMANAGH
ARMAGH
Newry
MONAGHAN
Warrenpoint
Crossmaglen

Ballina
SLIGO
MAYO
LEINTRIM
CAVAN
ROSCOMMON
LOUTH
CONNAUGHT
LONGFORD
MEATH
WESTMEATH
GALWAY
DUBLIN
Galway
Dublin
OFFALY
KILDARE
Birr
WICKLOW
LAOIS
Wicklow
Feakle
LEINSTER
CLARE
TIPPERARY
CARLOW
Limerick
Thurles
KILKENNY
LIMERICK
WEXFORD
Clonmel
Wexford
MUNSTER
Tralee
Waterford
KERRY
CORK
WATERFORD
Macroom
Cork
Bantry

Northern Ireland
province borders

Foreword

The great merit of *The Divided Province* is that it gives a good idea of how things appear to the communities on both sides of the divide, not just on one. And by doing so it conveys, better than most accounts, an impression of just how intractable the problem is. So intractable is it, indeed, that it can scarcely be classified as a problem at all. Problems are supposed to have solutions.

In this case, the nearest thing to a 'solution', acceptable to both sides, is probably what Northern Ireland now has: direct rule from Britain. As Mr Jeffery justly observes in his Conclusion: 'Although direct rule is not particularly popular – either with the British government or the local population – opinion polls in the province consistently show that it is among the least unacceptable options. In the circumstances of Northern Ireland today, this amounts to a positive recommendation.'

Nobody likes direct rule much, but there is something that each community dislikes much more than it dislikes direct rule. Most Protestants would probably prefer a restored 'Stormont' (i.e. Protestant-majority rule) to direct rule, but almost all of them vastly prefer direct rule to incorporation in a Catholic-majority united Ireland; or to any 'interim solution' (e.g. joint administration by London and Dublin) which looks like a half-way house on the way to a united Ireland. Most Catholics (though not all of them) would prefer a united Ireland to direct rule from Britain, but almost all of them vastly prefer direct rule to a restored Stormont. So direct rule is in fact the only method of governing the province that is widely tolerable across both communities. To impose any other solution, regarded as *in*tolerable by one or other community, would be likely to bring on higher levels of violence than anything yet experienced.

Generally speaking, *The Divided Province* is an excellent introduction to its subject. The authors have made a consistent effort to be fair to both communities in Northern Ireland, as well as to Britain and the Republic of Ireland. This is commendable, and unusual. They are writing for readers who want to be reliably informed about the facts, and who do *not* want to be beguilingly conned on behalf of one side, as is too often the case with writing on this subject.

In recommending *The Divided Province*, I should, however, like to enter a serious reservation concerning the final sentence in the book, which runs as follows: 'A cynic might be forgiven for believing that, ten years on, nothing short of a resurgence of violence on a similar scale [to that of 1969–74] could once more prompt the politicians in Belfast, London and Dublin to look seriously for effective policies to heal the wounds and bridge the deep divides of Northern Ireland.'

I regret this, not merely for the oblique encouragement it might seem to offer to the IRA, but also because I believe it to be illusory. In my view – which finds a good deal of confirmation in the pages of *The Divided Province* itself – there are no 'effective policies' which would 'bridge the deep divides of Northern Ireland'. Direct rule is in fact the least divisive policy available (as the authors themselves hint in the passage quoted earlier). It follows that any new policies replacing direct rule would be more divisive, not less, than what we have now. And all the more so if the new policies are perceived to have been won by violence. 'What violence can win, violence can reverse' is a proposition well understood in both communities of the divided province.

Neither London nor – perhaps still less – London and Dublin together can 'bridge divides' in Northern Ireland, or unite Ireland. Britain can stay, as now; and face the probability of continuing violence on much the same scale as now, give a little or take a little. Or Britain can cut loose with the result, not of a united Ireland, but of an independent Northern Ireland; a Catholic revolt against that new entity; and civil war engulfing the whole island. Those are the real options, not the nice ones.

In any case, whether you come to agree with that prognosis or not, I recommend you to read *The Divided Province*.

Conor Cruise O'Brien
8 July 1985

Introduction

The Troubles in Northern Ireland have grown out of many different types of division: divisions of loyalty, allegiance and nationality; of economic status and advantage; of history and tradition. Perhaps the most obvious and commonly noted division is that of religion. The conflict in Northern Ireland, it is confidently asserted, is one between Protestants and Catholics. But this is not true in strictly religious terms: the violence of Republican or Loyalist paramilitaries does not stem from theological differences. Yet the population of Northern Ireland is deeply divided along religious lines. Each community – certainly in the towns – largely lives apart. Primary and secondary education is organised along denominational lines so that it is extremely rare for Protestants and Catholics to attend school together. In broad terms each group has different political ambitions. Most Protestants are Unionists and support the maintenance of Northern Ireland as part of the United Kingdom, while most Catholics tend to be nationalists, looking forward to the day when all 32 counties of Ireland will be united in an independent sovereign state. Despite the stalwart attempts of a few brave people – Churchmen and non-believers alike – to remove the religious and sectarian element from Northern Irish politics, the labels Protestant and Catholic continue to reflect important social and political realities in the province. The story is told of an Indian man being stopped by vigilantes in Belfast late one night. On being asked his religion, he said he was a Hindu. 'But', came the reply, 'a Protestant Hindu or a Catholic Hindu?'

Left: The Protestant ascendancy: an Orange Day parade, with flute band leading the procession, marches through a town in Northern Ireland. Such manifestations of Loyalist beliefs, often passing through Catholic areas, act as constant reminders of the deep divisions in society.

Below: Mean streets and an army presence: the Falls Road area of Belfast, 1971. This is the reality of Northern Ireland to many of the poorer inhabitants of the province.

Although religious questions themselves do not contribute much to the contemporary conflict, everyday life in Northern Ireland remains suffused with religious affiliation and religious labels.

The Protestants of Northern Ireland mostly arrived during the 17th century in a process begun in 1607 and known as the 'plantation' of Ulster. This at last established firm English rule upon the whole island of Ireland. English domination over Ireland had begun in the 12th century with the Anglo-Norman invasion and gradually the English administration in Dublin extended its control over more and more of the island. Ulster, the last of the four ancient provinces to be conquered (the other three are Leinster, Munster and Connaught), was not finally subdued until the beginning of the 17th century. By this time Protestantism had become established in Great Britain, but not in Ireland where the Gaelic population clung to their old Catholic faith. Previous attempts in the 16th century to make Ireland secure by 'planting' Protestant settlers throughout the country had met with little success; the plantation of Ulster, however, was more effective, and 170,000 people, including 150,000 Scottish Presbyterians, were permanently settled on land mostly expropriated from the old Irish. The influx of Scottish people was not a complete novelty, since there have always been very close relations between Scotland and the northeast of Ireland, which at its nearest point is only 21 kilometres away. Even today extreme Loyalist groups find allies among Scottish Protestants.

The Protestant ascendancy

The Protestant monarchy in Britain was finally established by the 'Glorious Revolution' of 1688. King William III of Orange defeated King James II and the threat of 'Popery' which he represented to Protestants throughout Great Britain and Ireland. In Ulster the plantation immigrants (known as 'planters') were now securely settled. A Catholic Irish rising in 1641, in which many Protestants were massacred, had been put down, and later in the decade, Cromwell's Puritan army had forcefully and brutally subdued Ireland. By the end of the 17th century the pattern of social and economic power in the island was set for the next 200 years. English administrators ruled the country relying on the support of the 'Protestant ascendancy'. A distinctive community identity was developed by the planters in the North, many of whom, though Protestant, were 'dissenters' from some tenets of the Anglican faith, and so, like the Catholics, barred from taking public office. Ulster tenant farmers, who had brought Scottish

landholding customs with them, were also set apart by having a greater security of tenure than farmers in other parts of Ireland. Commerce and industry developed so that Ulster became the most prosperous part of the island.

In the late 18th century there was political unrest and the ideals of the French Revolution – 'liberty, equality, fraternity' – were adopted by a group of middle-class radicals who called themselves the United Irishmen. Many of these were Northern Presbyterians, who adopted an Irish nationalism which hoped to 'abolish the memory of all past dissensions' and 'substitute the common name of Irishman in place of the denominations of Protestant, Catholic and dissenter'. The United Irishmen, led by Wolfe Tone, a Dublin Protestant, started a rising in 1798 that was an embarrassing failure, but which marks the modern foundation of the Irish nationalist movement. In apparently unifying Irishmen of all creeds – although it actually gained the support of only a tiny fraction of the population – the '98 Rising remains a powerful inspiration for nationalists and Republicans who believe that it is possible to create a genuinely non-sectarian political movement in Ireland.

Following the '98 Rising, Ireland, which had possessed a parliament of its own, although with only very limited powers, was incorporated into the United Kingdom by the Act of Union (1800). Presbyterians abandoned their opposition to the established order as the religious disqualifications excluding dissenters from political power were abolished. Gradually Irish politics began to

divide more strictly along religious lines, with Protestants supporting the Union and Catholics increasingly espousing national aspirations. Enmeshed with the development of political nationalism was a demand for Catholic emancipation. This gave rise to the land agitation whereby landless Irish peasants – almost entirely Catholic – fought for improved tenant rights and ownership of the land they lived on. By the end of the 19th century many of these demands had been met and full civil and political rights had been granted to Catholics. Successive Land Acts passed by the British parliament provided security of tenure and subsidised schemes of land purchase, which together took the steam out of the campaign for land reform. But these reforms were mostly piecemeal and came too little and too late. The political momentum which built up in support of reform frequently escalated the demands so that when the imperial legislators at Westminster finally conceded some Irish improvement it fell far short of what was currently being demanded. Political mobilisation behind Catholic emancipation and land reform, moreover, provided the basis for the growth of Irish nationalism and the call for Home Rule. It came to be believed that the inefficiencies and

Below: The roots of protest: an Irish peasant family in County Donegal, evicted from their stone and turf cottage in the 1860s. The ability of landlords, often Protestant and absentee, to evict their tenants at will was one of the features of Irish rural life in the 19th century, leading to pressures for reform that often took a violent turn.

AT DERRYBEG Co DONEGAL 1567 W. L.

Left: The process of reform: a cartoon of 1881 depicts Liberal prime minister William Gladstone, under pressure from the Irish Land League, drafting a new Land Bill, designed to replace earlier attempts at reform and introduce such basic rights as fixed tenure and fair rents. The Land League, founded in 1879 and led by Charles Stewart Parnell, a Protestant landowner and MP, had its origins in the Fenian movement and was an early example of political pressure combined with selective violence.

Below: The Fenian banner: a popular image of early Irish nationalism; St George lies prostrate beneath the feet of Irish justice as the heroes of reform look on. Note the use of Irish symbols – the Gaelic motto, shamrocks and harp.

THE FENIAN BANNER.

" But the Harp, that so long hath been silent and weeping,
    Resigned by its master in gloom and despair,
Shall again be brought forth from the shrine where 'tis sleeping,
    And with glad notes of freedom enliven the air;

When the voice of the brave with its echoes shall mingle,
    In the clangor of arms, or the transport of glee.
For the millions who love it will shortly assemble,
    To proclaim that their nation again shall be free.

inequities of the administration of Ireland would be removed if only there was once more a parliament in Dublin.

Irish Protestants, especially those in the North, did not share this opinion. Apart from fears of sectarian domination by a Catholic legislature, Protestants believed that their economic position depended on the maintenance of the Union. Ulster was the only part of Ireland to experience an industrial revolution in the 19th century. By the end of the century Belfast was a wealthy industrial and commercial city which, in the opinion of the local merchants and factory-owners, depended on access to British markets for continued prosperity. The links with Scotland, moreover, remained strong, and many Northern Presbyterians looked to Edinburgh or Glasgow for cultural or commercial leadership, rather than to Dublin. When the British Liberal Party under William Gladstone began to respond to the growth of Irish nationalism with proposals for Home Rule, Protestant doubts about the advantage of a Dublin parliament hardened into political opposition with the establishment of a Unionist Party prepared to defend their rights – by force if need be.

The Fenian movement

Violent action has always played a prominent role in Irish politics. Ireland has been denied the comparatively peaceable evolution of parliamentary democracy enjoyed by

England. Irishmen – Protestant and Catholic, Unionist and nationalist – believing that they cannot expect fair treatment at the hands of British politicians in London, have often resorted to the sword and the gun in order to advance their causes. Catholic nationalist risings – all abortive – in the 19th century, especially 1803 and 1848, raised the spectre of violent revolution, as did the Fenian movement under John Devoy in the 1860s. The Fenians, indeed, were prototype nationalist guerrillas: clandestine, organised, armed – and prepared to take action in Britain. In December 1867 they killed 12 people in a bomb attack on Clerkenwell gaol in London in an attempt to free two Fenian prisoners. Focused action such as this, however, is only part of the violent Irish heritage. By the late 19th century sectarian rioting had become commonplace in Belfast. The city had begun as a Protestant town, but as it industrialised

and grew during the century large numbers of poor Catholics moved there in search of work, and a sizable Catholic community became established, especially in the west of the city. This movement off the land was powerfully boosted by the failures of the potato crop, upon which the Irish peasants depended, in the 1840s. These people constituted an abundant supply of cheap labour for the Belfast industrialists, but threatened the jobs of Protestant workers, who responded with violent civil unrest which flared up at intervals during the second half of the century. Belfast thus gained an unenviable reputation for anti-Catholic riots.

By 1912 the battle-lines of political conflict in 20th-century Ireland had been drawn – Unionist against nationalist, Protestant against Catholic – as had the structures providing the framework for political mobilisation. The Irish nationalist movement had

developed a mass following and, as Home Rule became more likely, the Unionists also began to establish a mass organisation. The various types of violence – general revolt, small-scale targeted terrorism, sectarian rioting – which were to characterise much of Irish political life in the 20th century, especially in 1916–23 and from 1969 up to the present day, had also emerged during the 19th century. These provided both precedent and, sadly, inspiration for activists of all kinds, right across the Irish political spectrum.

Below: A soldier of the Royal Regiment of Fusiliers, armed with the standard weapon of the British Army, the L1A1 SLR, peers around the corner of a building in Northern Ireland. Behind him looms the threatening shape of a Humber personnel carrier (commonly known as a 'Pig'), and beside his head are carved the initials of just one of the warring factions.

1. Orange and Green 1912-1962

In April 1912 the British Liberal government introduced an Irish Home Rule Bill in the House of Commons, thus setting off a legislative process which was, ten years later, to lead to Irish partition, the establishment of a semi-independent government in Dublin and the setting up of Northern Ireland as a distinct administrative unit within the United Kingdom. The Home Rule Bill provided for an Irish parliament, subordinate to Westminster, but responsible for specifically Irish affairs. This raised hopes among Irish nationalists and fears among Unionists, who wanted Ireland to remain as an integral part of the United Kingdom, and who constituted a significant proportion of the population of the North of Ireland. The proposed legislation led directly to the 'Ulster Crisis' which dominated British politics until the First World War broke out.

Home Rule had been Liberal Party policy since the mid-1880s. Indeed, the 1912 bill was the third to be put before parliament. But, for the first time, it seemed probable that the proposal might actually become law. Both previous bills had been rejected by the Conservative majority in the House of Lords, but following the two general elections of 1910 the Liberals had been able to limit the power of the Lords with the Parliament Act of 1911, which ensured that the Lords could do no more than delay (for two years) a bill which had been passed by the Commons.

By the time the Home Rule Bill had been introduced, Unionist opposition to the measure had begun to solidify in Ulster under the leadership of two particular men: Sir Edward Carson and Captain James Craig. Carson was a Dublin-born barrister and Unionist MP with a brilliant legal mind – 'the greatest advocate of his day' – and a reputation for striking oratory. Craig was a powerful, businesslike man, son of a wealthy Belfast whiskey distiller, who had served in the Boer War in South Africa. He had been elected a Unionist MP in 1906. In the autumn of 1911, on Craig's invitation, Carson agreed to take

on the leadership of resistance to Home Rule.

The Unionists gained strong support from the British Conservative Party. The Conservative leader, Andrew Bonar Law, came to Ulster – where he had close family ties – at Easter in 1912, and told a meeting of 100,000 Unionists that his party was fully committed to their cause. At a rally in England during the summer Bonar Law declared: 'I can imagine no length of resistance to which Ulster can go in which I should not be prepared to support them.' This blank cheque was reminiscent of the assertion which Winston Churchill's father, Lord Randolph Churchill, had made during an earlier Home Rule crisis, that 'Ulster will fight and Ulster will be right.' Now, however, the young Churchill was a Liberal Cabinet minister and a supporter of Home Rule. Churchill was so hated in Ulster

that when he came to Belfast to speak in favour of the measure in February 1912, seven battalions of infantry and a squadron of cavalry were deployed to protect him.

Faced with the prospect of Home Rule legislation actually passing into law, much of the Ulster Unionists' opposition took the form of extra-parliamentary agitation and organisation. The first need was to marshal Protestant public opinion throughout the North. In the autumn of 1912, therefore, the Unionist leaders organised the ceremonial signing of a 'solemn league and covenant'. The 'Ulster Covenant' contains much that still animates the Loyalists of Northern Ireland. It specifically committed the signatories to use 'all means which may be found necessary to defeat the present conspiracy to set up a Home Rule Parliament in Ireland'.

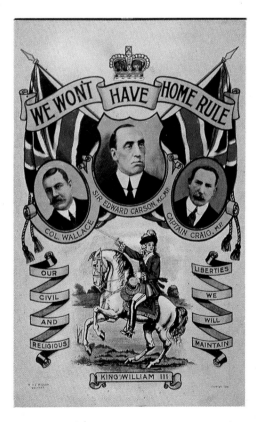

Yet it stressed their loyalty to the British Crown and their commitment to 'civil and religious freedom'. There was a very strong religious impetus behind the agitation. For Northern Irish Protestants, Home Rule meant 'Rome Rule', and they feared the political consequences of a Catholic-dominated Irish parliament in Dublin. The Orange Order, named after King William III (William of Orange) and founded in 1795 after a clash between Protestants and Catholics in County Armagh, provided the initial organisational framework for resistance in Ulster. The 'Loyal Orange Institution' is exclusively Protestant. Its strength and modern survival stem from its role as both a social club and a politically significant institution. In 1912 the Order was unequivocally behind Carson, Craig and the other Unionist leaders.

There could be no doubt about the scale or seriousness of the Unionist opposition to Home Rule. In addition to mass public meetings, 471,414 people – some in their own blood – signed the Covenant. In January 1913 the Ulster Unionist Council formed the Ulster Volunteer Force (UVF) to provide military backing for their campaign. With the help of many retired and reserve army officers – Field Marshal Earl Roberts lent his support – the UVF developed into a formidable organisation. Throughout 1913 100,000 Ulstermen trained and drilled, usually with dummy rifles, and a complete command structure was set up with every contingency provided for. There was an intelligence branch, a transport committee, and the Ulster

Women's Unionist Council recruited 40,000 women for nursing and other duties. A fund of over £1 million was raised to compensate wounded members of the UVF or bereaved dependants. In September 1913 a 'provisional government' was announced, which was to take charge in Ulster should London attempt to enforce Home Rule.

Militant nationalism

Irish nationalists were comparatively slow to respond to the development of militant Unionism in the North. Like the Liberal government in London, they at first underestimated the strength of Craig's resolve, and with the prime minister, Herbert Asquith, they perhaps imagined that the Ulster Unionists would accept Home Rule when they realised that it was at last a certainty. John Redmond, leader of the 84 Irish Nationalist MPs at Westminster, was inclined to belittle the Ulstermen, and was certainly opposed to anything that would interfere with the introduction of a Home Rule parliament. But Redmond and his Westminster colleagues were rapidly losing touch with Irish political opinion, in the South as well as the North. A growing number of Irish nationalists, based round the Irish Republican Brotherhood (IRB), rejected the Home Rule Bill as not going far enough. What they wanted was complete separation from Great Britain.

Among the leaders of this group was Patrick Pearse, a young teacher and romantic poet who stridently called on Irishmen to

accept the mantle of the ancient Celtic warriors and rise up against the English oppressor. Combining sharp realism with mysticism – a heady mixture – he wrote: 'We may make mistakes in the beginning and shoot the wrong people, but bloodshed is a cleansing and a sanctifying thing, and the nation which regards it as the final horror has lost its manhood.' Such was – and is – one of the justifications behind the 'physical-force' tradition in Irish Republicanism.

The 'pure' nationalists rejected Redmond for at best being misguided and at worst being a collaborator, however unwitting, with English imperialists. Unlike Redmond, Pearse and his colleagues appreciated the threat of the Ulster Unionists. 'Personally,' wrote Pearse, 'I think the Orangeman with a rifle a much less ridiculous figure than the nationalist without a rifle.' In November 1913, in direct response to the development of the UVF, the Irish Volunteers was set up as an opposing nationalist force. By 1914 the Volunteers numbered some 200,000 and had become sufficiently important for Redmond to have joined their leadership. Another, much smaller, private army which represented a third strand in Irish political violence was also founded in 1913. This was the 'Citizen Army', a working-class body established by the socialist leaders Jim Larkin and James Connolly. But not all anti-Redmond nationalists supported armed action. Arthur Griffith led a small constitutionalist group called Sinn Fein (Ourselves Alone) consisting mainly of committed intellectuals.

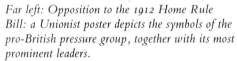

Far left: Opposition to the 1912 Home Rule Bill: a Unionist poster depicts the symbols of the pro-British pressure group, together with its most prominent leaders.
Left: 28 September 1912: Sir Edward Carson is the first to sign the 'solemn league and covenant' opposing Home Rule for Ireland.
Below: Patrick Pearse, nationalist leader during the 1912–14 crisis and in the 1916 Easter Rising.

*Above: Armed men of the 'Citizen Army'
parade beneath their distinctive banner, c. 1916.
Left: James Connolly, founder of the 'Citizen
Army' and driving force behind the nationalist
pressure for a separate Irish state. He was
executed by the British in May 1916.*

the Ulster 'provisional government' as 'a self-elected body composed of persons who, to put it plainly, are engaged in a treasonable conspiracy'. But in March 1914 the deployment of troops to the North was interrupted when nearly 60 cavalry officers at the Curragh Camp in County Kildare resigned their commissions rather than accept orders which they believed were aimed at coercing Ulster into an all-Ireland parliament.

There was considerable sympathy within the army for the Unionist cause. Many officers themselves had Irish family connections. The leader of the revolt at the Curragh, for example, Brigadier-General Hubert Gough, came from Clonmel, County Cork, and in London, the Director of Military Operations, Brigadier-General Henry Wilson (born in County Longford of an Ulster Protestant family) was active behind the scenes and kept Bonar Law fully informed of events in the War Office. The so-called Curragh 'Mutiny' was eventually defused; the War Office did not accept the officers' resignations, and they were told that the government did not intend to take offensive action against Ulster. This assurance was given without Cabinet authority by the secretary for war and the Chief of the Imperial General Staff, both of whom consequently had to resign. But in effect a more accommodating policy towards Craig and his supporters was adopted by the government

The Home Rule Bill actually completed its passage through the House of Commons in January 1913 and under the provisions of the Parliament Act was destined to become law in the summer of 1914. In the meantime the pace of both Unionist and nationalist paramilitary activity accelerated and the authorities began to worry that this might escalate into open violent conflict. Knowing that the UVF were short of weapons, early in 1914 the Cabinet decided to reinforce the garrison in the North of Ireland against a possible Unionist arms raid. Some of Asquith's Cabinet, moreover, were particularly determined that the policy of Home Rule should not be thwarted by the unconstitutional actions of the Ulster Unionists. Winston Churchill cuttingly referred to

during 1914. Indeed, for the first time the serious possibility was raised of a divided Ireland, but only to the extent that the six counties of Ulster with a substantial Protestant population – Antrim, Down, Armagh, Londonderry, Tyrone and Fermanagh – should be allowed to opt out of Home Rule for a period of perhaps six years.

The Curragh affair was an indication of how strong passions were concerning the Irish question. The Unionists signalled their continued resolve with a dramatic gun-running operation. Some 25,000 rifles and 3,000,000 rounds of ammunition purchased in Germany were landed on the night of 24/25 April. The arrangements were masterminded by Major Fred Crawford, the UVF's Director of Ordnance, a swashbuckling figure who had quietly been importing arms in small quantities since early in 1912. For years Crawford had been involved in maverick anti-Home Rule schemes. In the 1890s he had formed a secret Unionist society called Young Ulster, each member of which had to possess either a revolver, a Martini-Henry rifle or a cavalry Winchester carbine, together with 100 rounds of ammunition. When the second Home Rule Bill was before parliament he planned to kidnap the prime minister, William Gladstone, take him to an isolated Pacific island by 'fast steam yacht' and hold him there until the bill had been defeated.

Guns for the Volunteers

The Unionist gun-running encouraged the Irish Volunteers to do likewise. In July 900 rifles and 25,000 rounds of ammunition – again from Germany – were landed at Howth, County Dublin, from a private yacht, the *Asgard*, owned by English novelist and civil servant Erskine Childers. The Dublin authorities sent out soldiers and police to confiscate these arms. They failed to do this, but later in the day three people were killed and 35 wounded at Bachelor's Walk on the Liffey quays when troops fired on a hostile, though unarmed, crowd.

The increasing threat of open violence by activists from both the North and South was a reaction to the political stalemate over Home Rule. The bill as passed provided for the temporary exclusion from the Dublin parliament of those counties which had a majority against Home Rule. But this did not satisfy the Ulster Unionists, who, as Carson put it, were not interested in 'a stay of execution for six years'. Redmond, on the other hand, flatly refused to consider any permanent partition. But at this stage the outbreak of the First World War overtook the consideration of parochial Irish issues and the implementation of Home Rule was postponed for the duration of the hostilities.

The First World War

Most of both Unionist and nationalist Ireland rallied to the British war effort. Redmond immediately pledged the support of the Irish Volunteers, who promptly split over the question. The majority, who styled themselves the 'National Volunteers', supported Redmond, and many joined the 'New Armies' that Lord Kitchener was raising, but some 12,000 pledged themselves to remain in Ireland to secure Home Rule and avert partition. The Citizen Army took a similar stance, adopting the slogan, 'We serve neither King nor Kaiser, but Ireland!' In the North 30,000 UVF men joined up almost *en masse* and effectively became the 36th (Ulster) Division.

At least a quarter of a million Irishmen served in the British forces during the First World War. In addition to the Ulster Division, there were two specifically Irish Divisions – the 10th and the 16th. While the UVF were allowed to join up with their units and organisation virtually unaltered, the War Office carelessly gave offence to the National Volunteers by allowing no such concession to them. Redmond had to protest strongly before the 10th and 16th Divisions were even allowed the official title 'Irish'. He asserted, nevertheless, that for the first time the Irish people had put 'a national army' in the field. Echoing Pearse, he argued that 'no people can be said to have rightly proved their nationhood and their power to maintain it until they have demonstrated their military prowess.'

But while nationalist Irishmen were serving abroad in Flanders or Gallipoli with, for example, the Connaught Rangers or the Royal Munster Fusiliers, other nationalists stayed at home to prove the old adage that 'England's extremity is Ireland's opportunity.' Early in 1916 Pearse and the military council of the IRB, who had assumed control of the Irish Volunteers, decided to stage an armed rising beginning on Easter Sunday, 23 April. James Connolly and the tiny Citizen Army agreed to cooperate. The revolutionaries hoped for assistance from Germany where Sir Roger Casement was pressing the Irish cause. Casement, an Anglo-Irish Protestant, brought up in Ulster, was a former British diplomat who had been knighted for humanitarian work in the Congo and Peru. He was an early supporter of the Volunteers and after his retirement from the British Consular Service in 1913 he devoted himself exclusively to the promotion of the Irish national movement. He went to Germany after the war began in order to obtain arms for the Volunteers. He also attempted, but with very little success, to raise an 'Irish Brigade' from among Irishmen in German prisoner-of-war camps.

The rising, in fact, was launched in circumstances of some confusion. The plans had been kept so secret that even Eoin MacNeill, the Volunteers' chief of staff, learned of them only at the last minute. A German ship carrying a cargo of arms, the *Aud*, was intercepted by the Royal Navy on Good Friday and her captain had no choice but to scuttle her. Casement himself was landed in County Kerry from a submarine, but was quickly captured. He was afterwards convicted of treason and hanged. Eventually the rising began on Easter Monday, 24 April. There was a substantial turnout of Volunteers and the Citizen Army, but only in Dublin. The authorities, however – reassured by the interception of the *Aud* – were caught completely by surprise.

Below: A First World War recruiting poster urges Irishmen to join the British Army. Well over 100,000 enlisted, but the threat to extend conscription to Ireland in April 1918 provided a focus for opposition to British rule.

The Easter Rising

About 1800 insurgents occupied a number of prominent buildings in Dublin. They established a headquarters at the GPO, in what is now O'Connell Street. Here Pearse read out the proclamation establishing 'The Provisional Government of the Irish Republic'. The document placed the rising firmly in the long historic context of Irish nationalism. 'In the name of God and of the dead generations from which she receives her old tradition of nationhood,' it read, 'Ireland, through us, summons her children to her flag and strikes for her freedom.' Yet from the start Pearse and his comrades knew that the insurrection was doomed to fail. They hoped and believed that the gesture – however apparently futile – of striking dramatically against British rule would stir up national sentiment among the general population. At the time this seemed hardly likely.

The rising was certainly not widely supported. It seems only to have been popular among those who seized the opportunity to indulge in extensive looting. There were substantial casualties: 300, moreover, of the 500 killed and 2000 of the 2500 wounded were civilians. Sixty insurgents and 132 troops and police died. The British, embroiled in a savage war on the continent, put down the rebellion with marked severity. The rebels were mostly dislodged with artillery, and much property – up to £2.5 million worth – was destroyed. After a week of intense fighting, with the GPO gutted by fire, the insurgents surrendered. One of the last commanders to give up was the 33-year-old Eamon de Valera, who had held Boland's Mill in the east of the city.

Right: The heavy-handed response to the 1916 Easter Rising in Dublin: a British tank helps in the task of searching suspect premises. Below: The aftermath of the Rising – with Nelson's Pillar in the background and rubble all around, the GPO (with colonnaded front) is back in British hands. The large number of civilian deaths and the scale of destruction alienated many Irish people.

The defeat of the rebels was conducted by Major-General Sir John 'Conky' Maxwell, who was given absolute powers under martial law. After the rising some 2000 people were detained, including many who had taken no active part in the events of Easter week. In a series of secret courts-martial 90 prisoners were sentenced to death. Fifteen, including Pearse and Connolly, were actually executed, over a period of ten days. Here, indeed, was Pearse's 'blood sacrifice'. Although it seemed as if the whole affair had been a failure, the

aftermath of the rising actually vindicated Pearse's views. The insurgents' romantic sacrifice did strike a chord throughout nationalist Ireland, and public disenchantment with the administration was exacerbated by revulsion at the long-drawn-out series of executions. Public support, too, began to ebb away from Redmond's Home Rule Party and to coalesce around Arthur Griffith's more extreme Sinn Fein group.

In 1916 the Ulster Unionists had their own 'blood sacrifice' – not in Ireland but at the battle of the Somme. The battle began on 1 July – the actual date of the battle of the Boyne. (When the calendar was changed in the mid-18th century, 11 days were added on, and Ulster has celebrated the Boyne on 12 July since then.) It was the first large-scale engagement for the close-knit Ulster Division who had been on the Western Front since the autumn of 1915. During the first two days of the battle the division lost some 5500 all ranks, killed, wounded or missing – out of about 15,000 in the formation as a whole. One of the 36th's three brigades – the 107th, drawn entirely from Belfast – had a casualty rate of about two-thirds. Ironically, most of these were caused by British artillery fire because the brigade had advanced too quickly. The sacrifice of the Ulster Division in 1916 has a powerful place in the mythology of Protestant Ulster. It is frequently asserted even today that '50,000 Ulstermen' gave their lives on the Somme, and the battle represents the ultimate test of Ulster's ultimate loyalty to the Crown: the Union sealed with blood.

In the two years after the Easter Rising there were attempts to sort out the political future of Ireland, but even the best efforts of the British prime minister, David Lloyd George, and the establishment of an 'Irish Convention' in 1917–18 failed to reach any agreement. The estrangement of Irish nationalist public opinion from Britain and from Redmondite notions of Home Rule within the United Kingdom was accentuated by the conscription crisis of 1918. Faced with an acute manpower shortage in France, because of the great German spring offensive, London proposed to bring Ireland into line with the rest of the United Kingdom by introducing compulsory military service. This was fiercely resisted by a coalition of nationalist politicians and Catholic Church leaders, much to the disgust of the Ulster Unionists.

The dramatic wartime change in Irish political opinion was graphically demonstrated by the result of the December 1918 general election, when the old Home Rule Party (Redmond himself died in March 1918) was decisively defeated by Sinn Fein candidates standing on a Republican and abstentionist ticket. The Sinn Fein MPs – who included Countess Markievicz, the first woman to be elected to the Westminster parliament – refused to go to London and formed themselves into the first Dail Eireann (parliament of Ireland) in Dublin during January 1919. Eamon de Valera was elected president. The Irish state dates its foundation from this action. The Dail established an administration in parallel to the British system and declared that only complete separation from Great Britain would satisfy their aims. To this end they encouraged both passive resistance and guerrilla warfare.

The Anglo-Irish War 1919–21

The years 1919–21 are known by various names. Historians often use the term the 'Anglo-Irish War'. Nationalists generally prefer to call it the 'Irish War of Independence', although Ireland was quite clearly only semi-independent at the end. Reflecting the involvement of the notorious Black and Tans, it is sometimes known as the 'Tan War'. Many people call it the 'Troubles', but this

Top: The scene in Richmond Barracks, Dublin, as families of the men interned after the Easter Rising are allowed to visit. The treatment of the prisoners, ranging from execution to long prison sentences, attracted attention that did more to spread the nationalist message than the Rising itself.

Above: The Sinn Fein Committee, as constituted in February 1922. In the front row, fourth from left, is Arthur Griffith, then Eamon de Valera and Michael Collins (the 'Big Fellow'). Neither Griffith nor Collins was to see the year out, the former succumbing to illness, the latter to assassination.

epithet is now more generally used for the events in the North since 1969.

The war began in January 1919 at Soloheadbeg in County Tipperary when a group of Irish Volunteers captured a cartload of quarry explosives and killed two policemen escorting it. Throughout the year there was sporadic violence, but gradually a well-organised terror campaign developed. In June, District Inspector Hunt of the Royal Irish Constabulary (RIC) was assassinated in the centre of Thurles, Tipperary, in broad daylight by men who wore no disguise. Those who witnessed the killing gave no assistance to the police afterwards. The Volunteers, who quickly became known as the Irish Republican Army (IRA), launched a series of raids on police barracks for arms. In September a church party of the King's Shropshire Light Infantry in County Cork was attacked and their rifles seized. One soldier was killed and four injured.

In the early days, however, the brunt of the IRA campaign was borne by the police. Originally established under Sir Robert Peel in the first half of the 19th century, the 'Peelers' (a less friendly nickname than the English 'Bobby', but from the same origin), were a semi-military national force. They were armed and operated from barracks. At the beginning of 1919 there were 9000 policemen, all Irishmen living in the local community and all soft targets for the IRA.

The Republican attacks, however, had an odd effect on police recruitment. In the first half of 1919 this fell dramatically, apparently due to the intimidation of relatives. But towards the end of the year, as the terror campaign intensified, local enlistment picked up sharply. Clearly not all Irish people supported Sinn Fein's methods, and many were still prepared to support law and order, even that of the increasingly unpopular British regime based in Dublin Castle. The government were certainly anxious to avoid an overtly military solution to the Irish disorder, and began to expand the RIC. Local recruitment could now not keep up with the demand and at the end of 1919 the RIC for the

first time began to enlist non-Irishmen. Owing to a shortage of police uniforms many of the early British recruits were kitted out with a mixture of RIC bottle-green and service khaki dress. They were first dubbed the 'Black and Tans' in Limerick after a local pack of hounds. The nickname was also generally applied to a further addition to the police strength: the 1500-strong Auxiliary Division which was raised from mid-1920 onwards. Like the Tans, the 'Auxies' were British ex-servicemen who sometimes received only the most cursory of training, and both groups gained a fierce reputation for unflinching severity as they sped around the country in their Crossley Tenders. In keeping with his civil security policy, the British prime minister, Lloyd George, seems to have turned a blind eye to the Tans' policy of counter-terror and their indulgence in sometimes wild reprisals for IRA actions.

Guerrilla tactics

In 1920, 176 police and 54 soldiers were killed, while there were only 43 IRA and civilian fatalities. But as the struggle continued the number of IRA and civilian casualties grew. For the whole period from January 1919 until the truce of July 1921, 751 people were killed and 1212 wounded. Of the dead, 405 were police, 150 military and 196 civilian and IRA. During 1920 the tempo of violence increased. The IRA developed a series of hard-hitting guerrilla tactics. Selected individuals, such as senior police officers and magistrates, were assassinated. In March, for example, a Dublin magistrate, Alan Bell, who had apparently

established a network of undercover agents which threatened IRA operations, was taken off a tram in daylight and shot in the street by men of Michael Collins's squad. Collins – the 'Big Fellow' – was Director of Intelligence for the IRA and emerged during the war as one of the most able and admired Irish leaders. Thirty years old in 1920, he had fought in the GPO in the Easter Rising of 1916. Throughout the Anglo-Irish War he lived a flamboyant, charmed life, evading arrest by moving in disguise from house to house.

Collins's intelligence organisation was particularly good. He even had agents within Dublin Castle. The IRA also had the advantage of widespread, if mostly passive, community support. Collins's most notable success was the simultaneous shooting of a dozen or so British intelligence officers on the morning of Sunday, 21 November 1920. No bout of Irish Troubles passes without at least one 'Bloody Sunday', and this was a dramatic and horrifying operation worthy of the epithet. Some of the men were roused from their beds and shot in front of their families. That afternoon there were more deaths when a squad of Auxiliary police opened fire at Croke Park Gaelic Football Stadium – 12 people were killed and 11 badly injured, many in the panic that followed the shooting.

A week later another dramatic IRA operation marked an intensification of the rural conflict. It was led by the legendary Tom Barry, commandant of the 3rd (West) Cork Brigade. Barry was an ex-British soldier who gained a formidable reputation as one of the most ruthless Republican commanders. On 28 November at Kilmichael, near Macroom,

*Bottom far left: Arming the Dublin
Metropolitan Police, October 1919.
Bottom left: The dreaded 'Auxies', also
generally known as the 'Black and Tans' (some
still wearing British Army cap badges), pose
with their Crossley Tender, January 1921.
Above: 'Men of the South', an idealised
portrayal of the IRA painted by Sean Keating
in the early 1920s.*

County Cork, Barry's force of 36 riflemen
ambushed two lorries carrying Auxiliaries,
killing 15 of the 17 police, and leaving the
others for dead. This particular incident seems
to have persuaded Lloyd George that civil
methods alone could not work in Ireland and
that the army would now have to take a
major role in the security effort.

The shift from civil to military methods
indicated the extent to which general community support was slipping away from the
Dublin Castle administration. Police forces
really only work by consent; armies, on the
other hand, can rely more on coercion. The
growing strength of militant Irish separatism
was boosted by the self-sacrificing example of
Terence MacSwiney, the Lord Mayor of
Cork, who died in Brixton gaol after a
hunger strike of 74 days. This action fulfilled
MacSwiney's aim of provoking national and
international sympathy for Ireland's plight.
Much support – and money – came from the

sizable Irish community in the USA, where
de Valera spent 18 months in 1919 and 1920
arguing the Irish case. From America too
came Thompson sub-machine guns, the
classic IRA weapon.

Many of the features of the Anglo-Irish
War were to be repeated in the post-1969
period. Again there was to be confusion
between civil police and military roles, an
initial lack of coherence to British policy on
the security forces themselves. At the start
intelligence was poor. In both cases there was
an initial reluctance on the part of the British
to recognise the crucial importance of propaganda and public opinion, both at home and
abroad. The hunger strike, as is so often the
case in modern Irish history, turns up as a
potent weapon. As in the 1970s, too, the
earlier period saw moderate constitutional
nationalists continually being outflanked by
more extreme groupings. Both periods,
above all, demonstrate the deep and enduring
tradition of using violence as a legitimate
weapon in the Irish political process.

In December 1920 martial law was proclaimed in four counties in the southwest. At
the beginning of 1921 it was extended to four
more counties in southern Ireland. This gave
the army very wide powers, including that of
trying offenders by court-martial and imposing the death sentence. Although martial law
in only part of the country was a practical

nonsense, it did enable the soldiers to restrict
the activities of IRA 'flying columns'. It is also
true that in 1921 the British finally began to
develop a well-organised and coherent security policy. Hitherto the command of the
security forces had been fatally divided between civil and military authorities. There
were few joint operations and almost no
pooling of intelligence – perhaps the most
vital single factor in the prosecution of a
successful security effort. During 1921 the
army began planning for a major summer
offensive, but in the end the Cabinet drew
back from the brink and decided that some
sort of settlement should be hammered out
with Sinn Fein. Tales of Black and Tan
atrocities had undermined public support for
the government's Irish policy and British
public opinion would not have supported a
new Cromwellian era of repression. The
most dramatic police reprisal occurred in
December 1920 when a unit of Auxiliaries ran
riot in Cork and set fire to a considerable part
of the main shopping street, together with the
City Hall. The Cabinet ordered Major-
General Sir Peter Strickland, the army commander in Cork, to conduct a 'full and
searching' inquiry. When he specifically
blamed the police the government decided to
suppress the report, prompting widespread,
and accurate, jibes of 'cover-up'.

While the security situation deteriorated,

The language of Irish politics

The two political units in the island of Ireland are known by a bewildering variety of different names, each of which may have a particular significance. Under the old British administration, Ireland was divided into four provinces with 32 counties. After partition in 1921 six of the nine counties of Ulster officially became 'Northern Ireland', an integral part of the 'United Kingdom of Great Britain and Northern Ireland'. Although the three counties of Cavan, Monaghan and Donegal are in the Republic, Unionists frequently refer to the North as 'Ulster'. Nationalists on the whole do not use the phrase 'Northern Ireland' in order to avoid conferring legitimacy on what is contemptuously described as a 'statelet' and 'occupied Ireland'. The most common term is 'the six counties', implying that they are indistinguishable from the remaining 26, merely temporarily separated.

According to the Irish constitution the government in Dublin administers a state called 'Eire, or in the English language, Ireland'. Neither Ulster Unionists nor the British government use the latter term, pre-ferring 'the Irish Republic' or 'the Republic of Ireland'. Eire is acceptable since it can be construed as meaning only the Gaelic and nationalist part of the island. One convenient and common solution to the problem of terminology is to refer simply to the two parts of Ireland as 'the North' and 'the South'. This, however, can lead to geographical confusion since the most northerly point of the island – Malin Head in County Donegal – is politically in 'the South'. Other problems arise with the geographical term 'British Isles' which often becomes simply 'these islands' in the Dublin press. Some use the expression 'IONA' (Islands of the North Atlantic).

Irish sport has its own eccentricities. The Irish rugby team is drawn from the whole island and Northern Unionists will happily travel to Dublin to cheer it on against England. Soccer, on the other hand, is divided, with two 'national' teams, a 'league of Ireland' in the South and an 'Irish league' in the North. At the Los Angeles Olympic Games in 1984, Belfast men represented Ireland at boxing and Great Britain at field hockey.

One of the most contentious place-names is Londonderry. In 1613 the prefix 'London' was added to an Anglicisation of the ancient Irish name of 'Doire' to mark the incorporation of the London-based organisation – 'The Honourable the Irish Society' – which colonised the district. The city has tremendous symbolic significance for Ulster Protestants. In 1689 it withstood a 105-day siege by the army of the Catholic King James II. The 'London' confirms the city's Britishness. Nationalists, however, who constitute the majority of the local population, naturally prefer simply to call it Derry. Although virtually all the inhabitants commonly use the more convenient shorter term – at least when speaking – Unionist passions ran high when in 1984 the city council decided to change its official name to Derry. With Solomon-like judgment the government agreed to the *council* changing its own title, but decided that the official name of the municipality would remain as before. Thus, today, Derry City Council presides over the City of Londonderry. Not surprisingly this solution satisfies no one.

Below: Map of Northern Ireland, showing the border established by the partition of 1921 and a bone of contention ever since.
Far right: The outlaws are back in town: anti-Treaty IRA gunmen on the streets of Dublin in July 1922.

the British government cast about for some political solution to the problem. There was no question at the end of the war of implementing the 1914 Home Rule Act. After much discussion a Government of Ireland Act was passed by parliament in 1920. This provided for separate legislatures – still to be subordinate to Westminster – in Dublin and Belfast. The latter was to be responsible for the six most Protestant counties of Ulster. The two governments were to be linked with a quasi-federal 'Council of Ireland', intended to administer matters of common interest.

Elections were held for both parliaments in May 1921. As expected, a Unionist majority was returned in the North, and the first Northern Ireland parliament was ceremonially opened by King George V in June. The King took the opportunity to call for reconciliation, by no means the last British monarch to do this. 'I appeal to all Irishmen to pause,' he said, 'to stretch out the hand of forbearance and conciliation, to forgive and forget.' Belfast, nevertheless, was riven with much bitter sectarian rioting, and the Catholic population suffered. On 10 July 1921 – another 'Bloody Sunday' – Protestant mobs attacked Catholic areas of the city. Fifteen people were killed, 68 seriously injured and 161 homes burnt down. In the South, abstentionist Sinn Fein candidates won all but four of the 128 seats and constituted themselves as the Second Dail Eireann, independent of Westminster. The partition of Ireland, therefore, really dates from the early summer of 1921, when the Belfast parliament was established and began working.

The King's conciliatory speech received a widespread public welcome, both in Great Britain and among the war-weary population

The six counties

IRISH SEA

Ballycastle
Coleraine · Ballymoney
Limavady
Londonderry
LONDONDERRY
ANTRIM
Ballymena · Larne
Swatragh
DONEGAL
Strabane
NORTHERN IRELAND
Ballyclare
Antrim
River Mourne
Cookstown · Lough Neagh
Omagh · Pomeroy
Belfast
Lisburn
TYRONE
Dungannon
Lurgan
DOWN
Portadown
Enniskillen
Newry Canal
LEITRIM
FERMANAGH
Armagh · Banbridge
Rosslea
Downpatrick
ARMAGH
MONAGHAN
Newry
REPUBLIC OF IRELAND

of Ireland. The British government seized the opportunity to invite the two Irish leaders – de Valera and Craig – to take part in negotiations and to declare a truce which began the day after the Belfast riot, on 11 July. Increasingly hard-pressed by the security forces, although by no means beaten, the IRA welcomed the breathing-space, as, indeed, did the British Army. After the truce Lloyd George began a series of talks, at first principally with de Valera and then, towards the end of the year, with a group of Irish plenipotentiaries which included Collins and Arthur Griffith (the head of Sinn Fein), but not de Valera. The threat of renewed hostilities hung over the negotiations and right at the end Lloyd George used this threat to induce the Irishmen to sign a treaty on 6 December 1921. The Anglo-Irish Treaty provided for the establishment of 'Dominion Home Rule', akin to the Canadian constitutional position, in the 26 counties of the South. The Irish Free State, as it became known, retained the British monarch as head of state. Because of the strategic importance of Ireland, especially for the defence of the Western Approaches to Britain, the Irish agreed to allow British retention of naval bases at the so-called 'Treaty Ports', including Queenstown (Cobh) in Cork Harbour, Berehaven in west Cork and Lough Swilly in Donegal. The frontier between Northern Ireland and the Free State was to be reviewed by a Boundary Commission 'in accordance with the wishes of the inhabitants, so far as may be compatible with economic and geographical conditions'. Since there was a majority of nationalists in parts of counties Armagh, Fermanagh, Tyrone and Londonderry, the Irish delegation assumed that the Boundary Commission would reduce the six counties of Northern Ireland to an unworkable rump. The Treaty marked the end of the Anglo-Irish War, though not, sadly, the end of violence in Ireland.

The civil war and the new Northern Ireland state

The Treaty was greeted in Irish nationalist circles with a mixture of relief and recrimination. The great majority of people were simply thankful that, as they thought, the Troubles were over. But a strong Republican element, led by de Valera, bitterly rejected the Treaty since it did not give Ireland complete independence from Great Britain. In addition, it had confirmed the anathema of partition. Michael Collins spoke of 'the freedom we have won to achieve full freedom', but the ultra-Republicans would have none of it. When the Dail voted by a narrow majority to accept the Treaty, de Valera and his colleagues refused to recognise the state, quit the assembly and the country was plunged into civil war which lasted until May 1923. Meanwhile, Griffith and Collins took charge of the new Free State government.

Following the Treaty the British were glad enough to withdraw from southern Ireland. They handed over barracks and munitions to the rapidly organising Free State army, much of which was promptly seized by Republican forces, named 'Irregulars' by the government. In April a body of Irregulars under Rory O'Connor and Liam Mellows occupied the Four Courts – headquarters of the Irish judicial system – in Dublin. Still anxious to avoid a violent split, Collins made great efforts to reconcile the two sides, but events in June destroyed any possibility of this. On the 22nd Sir Henry Wilson, who had retired from the army and become both a Unionist MP for a Northern Ireland constituency and chief military adviser to the Belfast government, was assassinated on his doorstep in London by two IRA men, both British ex-

servicemen. The killing prompted London to press Collins to move against the Irregulars, whom the British thought were behind the murder. The Cabinet even thought of using the remaining British forces in Dublin to reduce the Four Courts. For Collins the final break came when the Irish deputy chief of staff was captured by the Irregulars. At the end of June, using field guns provided by the British, Free State forces shelled the Four Courts garrison into submission.

The Dublin government repressed the Republican Irregulars with rather more violence than the British had shown in the Anglo-Irish War. The new government, of course, had more popular support than the old Castle regime had received. Throughout the civil war over 200 Republican prisoners were killed in official and unofficial reprisals, and an estimated total of 4000 people died during the conflict. The Free Staters had the organisation, the arms and the public sympathy to defeat the Irregulars, who in May 1923 unilaterally called a truce. Their commanders, however, ordered the volunteers not to give up their weapons, but to bury them for possible future use.

Fine Gael and Fianna Fail

The leadership of the Free State changed during the war. In August 1922 Arthur Griffith died of a stroke and ten days later Collins was killed in an ambush at Beal na mBlach in County Cork. William T. Cosgrave took over as leader of the government. The principal political party division in the Irish Republic today stems from the civil war period. Basically the two main groupings, Fine Gael and Fianna Fail, descend from pro- and anti-Treaty factions. In 1920 the pro-Treaty government party took the title Cumann na nGaedheal (League of the Gaels), which a dozen years later was subsumed into a new party called Fine Gael (Tribe of Gaels). In 1926 de Valera, worried about the continued impractical extremism of Sinn Fein, split away from the old party and founded Fianna Fail (Soldiers of Destiny), with the English sub-title of 'the Republican Party'. Sinn Fein remained – and remains – the name adopted by the most extreme and intransigent of Irish Republican separatists.

Despite the bitterness of the civil war, during the 1920s Cosgrave's government was able to establish a stable and acceptable civil administration. For the most part the new rulers of southern Ireland simply took over the old British structure of government unaltered. But there was one significant change. In a brave and imaginative move, the state's new police force, the Garda Siochana (Civic Guard) was established as an unarmed force which soon succeeded, against all expec-

Top: Government forces fire a British-supplied 18-pounder field gun at rebel positions in the Tramway House, Dublin, July 1922. The armoured trucks provide useful protection.

Above: Government troops, uniformed and well equipped, accepting rebels' surrender, O'Connor Street, Dublin, July 1922. Captured Irregulars were not treated lightly.

tations, in becoming widely accepted throughout the country.

The government of Northern Ireland was not so fortunate in the matter of policing. From the very beginning the state was under threat. In 1922 Republican opponents of partition launched an armed offensive against it and there was widespread violence throughout the six counties. In February serious sectarian rioting broke out in Belfast. One particularly bloody incident occurred when a bomb exploded in a group of Catholic

children, killing six of them. The development of the civil war in the South, however, reduced pressure in the North, and a number of meetings between Craig and Collins seemed to offer the prospect of normal relations being established between Belfast and Dublin.

The Belfast authorities nevertheless made an effort to strengthen security by forming the Royal Ulster Constabulary (RUC) in June 1922. The Ulster Special Constabulary which had been formed in November 1920 was gradually reduced, in the end leaving only the B-Specials as a part-time force to support the 3000-strong RUC. The B-Specials, 16,000-strong in 1921, were mostly former UVF men, many of whom had served in the Ulster Division during the war. Exclusively Protestant, their heavy-handedness during the violence of 1922 gained them an enduring reputation for brutality and anti-Catholic bias. The legal basis for stringent security was provided by the Civil Authorities (Special Powers) Act of April 1922, which originated as a temporary measure but became permanent in 1933. It gave the police wide-ranging powers of search and arrest, and for opponents of the Unionist government it came to symbolise what they believed to be the coercive and undemocratic nature of the Northern Ireland state. Unionists, for their part, justified the statute by pointing to the continued (if not always very acute) threat posed to their regime by irreconcilable Republican and anti-partitionist groups.

'A Protestant state'

The Northern Ireland parliament was based on the British Westminster model; it had two chambers, a House of Commons and a Senate. The British monarch was represented by a governor-general. In 1932 the legislature was installed in the magnificent, quasi-imperial Parliament Buildings at Stormont, impressively sited on the eastern outskirts of Belfast. Throughout its 50-year life, Unionists always held a majority of the 52 seats in the House of Commons. The first two elections (1921 and 1925) were conducted on a system of proportional representation (PR), a provision included in the Government of Ireland Act to ensure full representation for the minority community. This also applied in southern Ireland where PR has always been used for Dail elections. But in 1929 the system was abandoned in Northern Ireland and replaced with the British method of single-member constituencies with election on a simple majority. This move was undoubtedly made in order to calm Unionist fears of being outvoted by the nationalists. Yet, throughout the entire life of the Stormont parliament nationalists could never realistically hope to poll more than a third of the votes cast. 'We are', boasted Craig in 1932 (by then Lord Craigavon), 'a Protestant parliament and a Protestant state.'

This was scant comfort for the third of the population who were Roman Catholic. By no means all were Republican, or even nationalist, but the exclusively Protestant tenor of the government, especially in its early days, certainly alienated many Catholics and, if anything, made them more nationalist than hitherto. Indeed, it has been argued that

the minority community in Northern Ireland were not so much anti-British as anti-Unionist.

One particular grievance centred round the question of local government. There had been a PR franchise here, too, at the beginning, but this was abolished in 1922. Electoral areas, moreover, were altered in the Unionists' favour – 'gerrymandered' – as was the franchise between the wars. The worst example of gerrymandering was in Londonderry. Despite the city's Catholic majority, local ward boundaries were drawn to ensure Unionist control.

Catholic resentment at the Unionist domination of much local government festered for 50 years. It was certainly strengthened by the resulting discrimination in the provision of local authority jobs and the allocation of public housing. Job discrimination against Catholics in government service was also reflected in the private sector. This was based not so much on any religious consideration as on a firm belief that all

Catholics were nationalists and thus wished to subvert the constitution of Northern Ireland. 'I recommend those people who are Loyalists', said Sir Basil Brooke, the Northern Ireland minister of agriculture, in 1934, 'not to employ Roman Catholics, 99% of whom are disloyal.'

Between the wars in Northern Ireland jobs were hard enough to find for either Protestants or Catholics. Although agriculture is the most important single industry in Ireland as a whole, Ulster was always the region with the greatest industrial development. Belfast is, above all, a Victorian industrial city and approximately two-thirds of Northern Ireland's 1,500,000 population live within a 50-kilometre radius of the city. At the time of partition two main activities provided the greatest number of jobs in the North: textile production, especially linen, and the engineering industry, dominated by shipbuilding at Belfast. Both depended heavily on export markets which substantially collapsed after the First World War. In the inter-war

Right: An aerial view of the central area of Belfast, taken in the 1930s. The main industries at this time were textiles and engineering. The relative prosperity of the industrialised North, despite its sectarian and employment problems, contrasted with the rural poverty of the South. Below: The Harland and Wolff shipyard, Belfast, in the 1950s.

years the proportion of the population of the North officially unemployed never dropped below 15%. Only the most minimal of welfare support was provided for the jobless. Popular protests against this during the world economic depression included one of Northern Ireland's most unusual disturbances: the 'Outdoor Relief' riots of 1932, when both the Protestant and Catholic working class in Belfast united in violent street protest. The story is told that the only non-sectarian song the demonstrators shared was 'Yes, We Have No Bananas'. But the 1930s were also marked by more traditional sectarian violence. The most serious outbreak occurred in July 1935 when Protestant mobs attacked Catholic areas in Belfast. There were shootings and the British Army was brought in to assist the RUC. Eleven people were killed, nearly 600 injured, and an estimated 514 Catholic families, comprising over 2200 persons, were driven from their homes.

Another major area of complaint was education. Early in the life of the Northern Ireland government the minister of education, Lord Londonderry, introduced an Education Act with the admirable aim of providing a publicly funded, essentially secular system of primary schools. But this offended both Protestant and Catholic Churches which each desired the inclusion of denominational religious teaching within the schools. Under pressure from the Protestants, the Act was amended in 1925 and 1930 so that schools which included distinctively Protestant 'Bible teaching' could qualify for a full government subsidy. Catholic schools, by contrast, remained only partially supported by public funds, a state of affairs which did not change until the late 1960s. Modern Northern Ireland is still characterised by a largely sectarian primary and secondary educational system.

The reluctance of the Stormont parliament to support Catholic schools reflects the continuing fears of Unionists that any encouragement of the minority community would ultimately lead to the undermining of Northern Ireland as a whole. Such worries were, and are, also reflected in equivocal attitudes towards the Dublin government. During the 1920s the threat of the Boundary Commission hung over the possibility of 'normal' relations between North and South. When the commission's proposals were prematurely leaked to the press in 1925 it emerged that only minor modifications of the boundary were to be recommended and, to the horror of the nationalists, the commission actually proposed to transfer some territory from the Free State to Northern Ireland. In the end the two governments agreed to suppress the report and leave the boundary unaltered. Although partition remains an offence in the eyes of Irish nationalists, there have been no serious proposals to alter the frontier since the abortive Boundary Commission report.

The Free State and the IRA in the 1930s

In 1927 de Valera and his Fianna Fail colleagues renounced the policy of violence and decided to take up their seats in the Dail. Their chief aim was to dismantle the Treaty

Below left: William T. Cosgrave, a veteran of the Easter Rising and leader of the Irish Free State in the turbulent 1920s.
Right: Eamon de Valera (right), who became prime minister of the Free State in 1932, emerges from No 10 Downing Street after negotiations with the British government that led to the 1938 agreements over land annuities, trade and defence. In the centre is Sean Lemass, de Valera's successor as leader of Fianna Fail.
Far right: The IRA campaign in England, 1939–40: a shop in Birmingham displays a sign more familiar in the blitz.

settlement and establish an Irish Republic. In the 1932 general election Fianna Fail gained more seats than William T. Cosgrave's party, and with the support of seven Labour members, de Valera formed a government. During the election he had announced that once in power he intended to remove the Oath of Allegiance to the British Crown from the constitution and also to adjust the financial relations between Ireland and the United Kingdom. In particular, he proposed to stop payment of the land annuities which were in consideration of advances made by the British government to Irish tenants under a number of pre-independence land acts.

In 1937 the government introduced a new constitution, which was passed in a referendum by 685,000 votes to 527,000. This constitution is still in force in southern Ireland. It stresses Ireland's sovereign independence, and in de Valera's words made the country 'demonstrably a republic'. Article 2, moreover, claims 'the whole island of Ireland' as the 'national territory'; not an assertion calculated to reassure Northern Unionists. Protestants were also alienated by Article 44 which recognised the 'special position' of the Roman Catholic Church 'as the guardian of the Faith professed by the great majority of the citizens'. (This Article was abolished in 1972.) Divorce, which by this time had become acceptable at least to liberal Protestants, was specifically banned. The constitution, nevertheless, also unequivocally guarantees freedom of conscience to every citizen. To the majority population in the North, however, the new constitution only served to reinforce partition, and the territorial claim in Article 2 simply confirmed Unionist suspicions that the Dublin government sought to enforce its rule on the six

Northern counties. De Valera also distanced himself from the Unionists by disengaging from the British Commonwealth and devising the vague notion of Ireland's 'external association' with it.

The question of land annuities caused a rift in ˌAnglo-Irish relations when in 1932 de Valera suspended their payment. The British retaliated by imposing a 20% customs duty on a large proportion of Ireland's exports to the United Kingdom. This was the start of the so-called 'economic war', which continued for six years – in effect a series of irritating tariff sanctions imposed on the trade between the two countries. In 1938 three separate agreements patched up the quarrel. The first settled the annuities question with the Irish paying a final lump sum of £10 million. The second stated that Anglo-Irish trade should be freer. The third was the most significant. The defence facilities retained by the United Kingdom under the 1921 Treaty were handed over to the Irish government. With this transfer de Valera asserted that Irish sovereignty in the 26 counties was finally established.

Despite his Republicanism, de Valera was not soft on militant extremists. After coming into power he was absolutely consistent in opposing the 'physical-force' tradition. In 1936 the government declared the IRA an illegal organisation, which it has remained ever since. Disgusted by de Valera's pragmatic, if conditional, acceptance of partition, in 1938 the IRA commenced a new campaign of violence. In November a series of arson attacks destroyed customs posts along the border. At the beginning of 1939 the IRA issued an ultimatum demanding the withdrawal of the British 'from every part of Ireland'. This was followed by direct action in

England – a strategy which had been tried to a limited extent in 1920–21 and which aimed literally to bring the struggle for Irish freedom home to the English nation. During 1939 there were over a hundred incidents in various parts of the country, including bombs planted in letter-boxes, public lavatories and railway stations. In July, one man was killed and 15 people injured in an explosion at King's Cross station in London. The worst single attack occurred in Coventry on 25 August when a bomb went off in a busy shopping street, killing five and injuring 60. This explosion marked the climax of the campaign. The authorities in both London and Dublin cracked down hard on the IRA and during the summer many IRA activists were arrested. In England two men were hanged for their part in the Coventry outrage and among others convicted was the young Brendan Behan, whose autobiography *Borstal Boy* describes his experience at that time. In Ireland de Valera rushed through additional legislation enabling the government to intern members of the IRA without trial.

The Second World War

Southern Ireland remained neutral from 1939 to 1945. It was scarcely possible that de Valera would bring his country in on England's side. Some, indeed, among the extreme Republicans actually favoured an alliance with Germany. But this was even more unlikely and would inevitably have provoked strong British countermeasures. Considering the deep divisions in Irish public opinion, the

only pragmatic option available to de Valera was a policy of neutrality. It was, in any case, a powerful demonstration of Irish sovereignty, a practical and substantial expression of independence. Ireland's neutrality, nevertheless, was not wholly evenhanded. It undoubtedly favoured the British, increasingly so as the tide of the war turned in the Allies' favour and the United States government pressed Dublin strongly to cooperate.

In a number of significant ways the Irish authorities tacitly supported the British war effort. Military aircraft based in Northern Ireland were allowed flying rights over parts of County Donegal in the northwest. This was particularly valuable to the anti-submarine seaplane units based on Lough Erne in County Fermanagh. Any German military personnel who landed in the 26 counties were interned for the duration. In contrast, by 1944 all such Allied personnel were allowed to return to the United Kingdom. Other assistance was afforded, including the use of wireless direction-finding stations in County Donegal and some intelligence cooperation with both British and American security services. Above all, the Dublin authorities placed no restriction on the estimated 50,000 volunteers from southern Ireland who enlisted in the British armed forces. Even for some of these, de Valera remained a hero. The story is told of a heated discussion about the Irish leader being conducted among the crew of a British bomber over Germany. 'I'll tell you one thing old Dev did for us,' remarked one of the RAF men, a Catholic from Cork, 'he kept us out of this blasted war.'

Despite the failure of their 1939 bombing campaign in England, after the war began the IRA believed that England's extremity might once again prove to be Ireland's opportunity. In December a unit raided the principal Irish munitions depot in Dublin and captured over a million rounds of smallarms ammunition. Most of this, however, was recovered, and the government responded by using draconian emergency powers against the IRA. Many members and sympathisers of the organisation were arrested and several hundred were interned at the Curragh Camp in County Kildare. Some internees adopted traditional methods in protesting against harsh prison conditions. Before the last internees had been released – after the end of the war – three IRA men had starved themselves to death on hunger strike. De Valera firmly resolved to resist the very tactic his own colleagues had employed against the British 20 years previously. Republican 'strip-strikes', when internees refused to wear prison clothes, cut no ice with the authorities either. Public sympathy for the IRA waned after incidents in which policemen were shot dead, and a number of Republicans were executed by firing squad after being convicted by military tribunals under the emergency laws.

The IRA campaign in the North

Although crippled by internal struggles, the IRA were also active in the North. In 1942 two RUC men and a B-Special were shot dead. Another Special died in a bomb attack in Belfast, and the following year a police constable was killed during a payroll raid. Two IRA men also died in shooting incidents, and the security forces, assisted by the fact that Northern Ireland was on a war footing, had considerable success in rounding up Republican activists; one of whom was hanged for the murder of a policeman. There were, however, notable prison escapes. In January 1943 four men, including Hugh McAteer who had been chief of staff of the IRA, broke out of Belfast's Crumlin Road gaol. The second exploit was more spectacular: in March the same year 21 prisoners escaped from the Londonderry gaol through a tunnel which had taken five months to dig. Fifteen of the men crossed the border on a commandeered lorry and were almost immediately arrested by the Irish Army and interned at the Curragh. By the end of the war the IRA had virtually become defunct. Their struggle seemed to have become largely irrelevant in the context of wartime preoccupations, sufferings and shortages in both parts of Ireland. Above all, the uncompromising opposition and stringent security measures applied by the authorities both North and South made it almost impossible

for the IRA to operate at all.

De Valera's wartime policy of neutrality was bitterly resented by Unionists in the North and by very many British people as well. The denial of Irish facilities undoubtedly hampered the British effort in the battle of the Atlantic in 1939–43 and there was a strong lobby in London which pressed for a forcible reoccupation of the Treaty Ports. In 1940 the British government offered de Valera a declaration 'accepting the principle of a United Ireland' and an assurance that practical steps would be taken to abolish partition in exchange for the use of Irish ports and other facilities. But the promise was too vague (no explanation of how the Northern Unionists were to be dealt with was given) and Irish feeling too strongly in favour of neutrality for de Valera to accept. After VE-Day Winston Churchill contrasted the 'loyalty and friendship' of Northern Ireland with the 'action of Mr de Valera', and noted the forbearance of Britain in leaving the Irish government unmolested 'to frolic with the Germans and later with the Japanese representatives to their hearts' content'.

The Treaty Ports, moreover, while important, were not absolutely vital because of the existence of facilities in Northern Ireland. A string of airfields was built in the northwest, and Londonderry became a major base for Allied (especially US, after December 1941) convoy protection units. During 1944 the province became an important training area for some 100,000 US troops for the invasion of western Europe. Northern Ireland, too, had its own blitz. In April 1941, 745 Belfast people were killed in the United Kingdom's single most costly bombing raid of the war outside London. In a second attack a fortnight later 150 died. Over 56,000 houses were damaged by the German bombers and more than 40,000 people left homeless. The suffering during the Belfast blitz provided a sacrifice to match and reinforce that of the Ulster Division at the Somme 25 years earlier. In 1943 Churchill remarked that 'the bonds of affection between Great Britain and the people of Northern Ireland have been tempered by fire' and were now, he believed, 'unbreakable'. The experience of the war certainly strengthened the Union and tended to confirm partition.

This was also true in the economic and social sphere. The development of Northern Ireland agriculture, industry and commerce to meet wartime needs brought employment and prosperity to the province. The unemployment rate, which had stood at over 25% in the mid-1930s, fell to less than 5% by the end of the war. Although sectarianism was by no means extinguished, the shared trials of the blitz, of rationing and of total civil mobilisation behind the war effort gave the whole

population of Northern Ireland more in common with each other than with southern compatriots. Along with their British neighbours, moreover, they looked forward to postwar reconstruction, with expectations raised by wartime promises of education, health and welfare reform.

The postwar years

Following the Second World War the principle became established that Northern Ireland, although the poorest distinct region in the United Kingdom, should enjoy more or less equal welfare benefits to those of Great Britain. This inevitably meant that the province required subsidies from the British Exchequer. By the end of the 1950s subventions from Britain were running at about £50 million annually. Other peripheral parts of the United Kingdom such as Cornwall or the Scottish Islands received similar levels of subsidy, but only Northern Ireland had a devolved local administration, which in order to maintain policy in step with the rest of the kingdom had to pass local legislation matching that of Westminster.

The Labour Party's landslide victory in the British general election of 1945 caused some concern in the Ulster Unionist Party, who feared that keeping in step with mainland

Above: Sean Lemass, appointed prime minister of the Republic of Ireland in 1959, on the retirement of de Valera from active politics. Right: Viscount Brookeborough, prime minister of Northern Ireland from 1943 to 1963, lays the foundation stone of a new factory, September 1955. His failure to cope with the growing crisis in the early 1960s led to his retirement.

policy might bring 'creeping socialism' to Northern Ireland. Traditionally allied with the British Conservative Party, the Ulster Unionists were led by a naturally conservative group of landowners and businessmen. During the war Craigavon had been succeeded briefly as prime minister by J.M. Andrews, a wealthy flax-spinner, and in 1943 by Sir Basil Brooke, who farmed substantial family estates in County Fermanagh. Brooke, created Viscount Brookeborough in 1952, remained prime minister for 20 years. But Brookeborough and his colleagues in the Unionist hierarchy depended on working-class Protestant votes for their political survival. Unlike the rest of the United Kingdom, Northern Ireland politics does not divide so much on social and economic lines, as sectarian. In times of economic or political adversity each group tends to close ranks but in a period of comparative prosperity and communal peace, such as the later war years and after, the loyalty of the rank and file becomes less automatic. Unionist leaders then have to take special care to retain grass-roots support. In the 1940s, therefore, the Northern Ireland Cabinet accepted the risk of creeping socialism and sponsored parallel measures to the London Labour government's reform legislation. In order perhaps to salve their consciences, the Unionist MPs at Westmin-

ster opposed the Labour proposals.

The introduction of increased welfare benefits such as unemployment assistance, family allowances and pensions, along with the implementation of the National Health Service, did much to remedy Northern Ireland's relative deprivation within the United Kingdom. The provision of free secondary schooling and grant-aided university places, following the British Butler Education Act of 1944, had a very considerable long-term effect. It gave able working-class Catholics the chance to break out of the vicious circle of poverty which they had borne during the miserable depression years between the wars. Over the two decades after the end of the war the number of Catholics working in health and welfare services, education, and the civil service, increased significantly. Many among this postwar generation were to espouse the cause of civil rights in the 1960s.

There was also economic development following the war. The government succeeded in attracting some new industries to the province with investment grants, rate relief schemes and new ready-built factories. An estimated 55,000 new jobs had been created by the mid-1960s. The domestic construction industry was stimulated by a large-scale house-building programme. In

the decade leading up to 1955 nearly 60,000 new dwellings were erected (though this figure should be set against a wartime estimate that 100,000 new houses were urgently needed). In agriculture, however, new developments actually increased unemployment. The rapid mechanisation of Ulster farming drove thousands off the land. The new postwar jobs, too, could not make up for the declining opportunities in the old staple industries. Unemployment rose after the end of the war and for 25 years varied between 5% and 10% – which was, however, considerably better than the situation before 1939.

Despite the economic and social advances of the 1940s and 1950s, in which the Catholic population of Northern Ireland undoubtedly shared, there was little or no political change. The Unionist government over which Lord Brookeborough somewhat complacently presided made no attempt to accommodate the minority community or to woo them away from their nationalist affiliations. This is in part because things did get better in material terms during these years and there was no apparent threat to the Stormont regime from nationalist political activity. An Anti-Partition League set up at the end of the war had little impact and faded away in the 1950s. Although Sinn Fein attracted 152,000 votes in the UK general election of 1955, in which two abstentionist MPs were returned (and later unseated since they were both serving prison sentences), this success was only temporary. In the 1959 election the same number of candidates won only 63,000 votes (11% of the total).

Unionist domination

Towards the end of the decade the chief challenge to the Unionists seemed to come from the Northern Ireland Labour Party (NILP) which gained support from Protestant workers worried about increasing unemployment. The NILP, however, was never able to capture the votes of Catholics and it went into a terminal decline in the 1960s. Government policy remained the same because for the most part the Unionist leaders had not the vision to see that the continuing discrimination against Catholics in council-house allocation, jobs and local government was merely storing up trouble for the future.

The establishment of the welfare state in Northern Ireland further distanced the province from the South of Ireland, where the standard of living lagged well below that of the North. The division between the two was also emphasised when the South became a republic. De Valera lost the 1948 general election in the South and a coalition government of Fine Gael, Labour and a radical Republican party, Clann na Poblachta

(Republican Family), took office under the Fine Gael leader, John Costello. Anxious, it seems, to prove his impeccable nationalist credentials, in 1948 Costello unexpectedly announced that Ireland would abandon the notion of 'external association' and finally leave the British Commonwealth. The decision was implemented by a statute which proclaimed that 'the description of the State shall be the Republic of Ireland'. It came into effect on Easter Monday 1949, the anniversary of the 1916 rising. The move was greeted with dismay in London where the government now had to make a definite decision regarding partition. So long as Dublin retained some residual allegiance to the British Crown (through the Commonwealth link) London was able to maintain a vague attitude towards the precise status of the Irish border. Now this was impossible and in the 1949 Ireland Act London unequivocally supported the continuance of partition and significantly guaranteed the Unionist position. Parliament, declared the Act, 'affirms that in no event will Northern Ireland or any part thereof cease to be a part of His Majesty's Dominion and of the United Kingdom without the consent of the Parliament of Northern Ireland'. Despite these constitutional changes citizens of the Irish Republic are not officially classed by Britain as 'foreign' and when in the UK they continue to enjoy the same benefits as ordinary British citizens.

Nationalists, both North and South, were shocked by the unambiguous guarantee given to the Unionists, but there was little the Dublin government could do beyond offering moral support to constitutional opposition in the North. By the 1950s partition had become institutionalised on both sides of the border and the gap between Northerners (both Protestant and Catholic) and their neighbours in the South was wider than ever. Even de Valera could not foresee unification – in 1963 he declared that 'Ireland is Ireland without the North.'

Resurgence of the IRA

But there were still irreconcilable Republicans committed to the physical-force tradition which de Valera had rejected. The establishment of the Republic and the confirmation of partition by the Ireland Act prompted them to consider a new campaign. In 1949 the IRA announced that its policy was 'to drive the invader from the Soil of Ireland' and 'prosecute a successful military campaign against the British forces of occupation in the Six Counties'. An important decision was taken not to use force in the Republic itself. The postwar years also saw the development of a twin Republican strategy with Sinn Fein pressing forward on the political side and the IRA preparing for action in the North. In the late 1940s the *United Irishman* was founded as a Republican propaganda newspaper.

The IRA, however, needed more than

Below: The scene outside a derelict shop in Caledonian Road, Islington, London, on 16 August 1955. Armed police and Special Branch officers broke into the shop to discover the hoard of ammunition seized earlier that month by the IRA from the Royal Electrical and Mechanical Engineers' depot at Arborfield in Berkshire; the photograph shows the arms cache being removed to safety. Despite the fact that the police were usually successful in tracking down the booty and arresting the culprits, raids like that at Arborfield did much to keep the physical-force tradition of Republicanism alive and in the public eye.
Right: A Sinn Fein rally in London, August 1955: Danny Ryan (standing on box) addresses a crowd, under the watchful eye of the police. In the aftermath of the Arborfield raid, this was a potentially provocative gathering, designed to inflame rather than quieten emotions.

Daily Mirror

MON FEB 17 1958

FORWARD WITH THE PEOPLE

No. 16,851

BIG LONDON POLICE SWOOP AFTER—

CALL-UP BOYS FIGHT I.R.A.

Recruit shot as six gunmen bind and gag the camp guard

DAILY MIRROR REPORTER

NINE soldiers were bound and gagged and a National Service man was shot in a raid by six Irish Republican Army gunmen on Blandford Army Camp, Dorset, yesterday.

Two of the soldiers who fought with the raiders were clubbed unconscious with pistol butts.

The condition of the shot sentry, who was hit in the stomach, was stated last night to be "not serious."

He is Private John Francis, 21, who had been in the Army only three weeks.

A VITAL CLUE

The object of the raiders, who struck at 1.30 a.m., was the camp armoury—but they got away with nothing. They are believed to have panicked because of the shooting.

The area was sealed off by the police after the raid but the raiders escaped in a car and a van. The car was later abandoned.

A vital clue the I.R.A. men left behind in the abandoned car is a slip of paper with a name and address on it.

A senior detective said: "I'm sure whoever left that bit of paper didn't mean to."

Last night Scotland Yard Special Branch officers swooped on a number of addresses in North London.

None of the sentries at the camp was armed.

Lieutenant-Colonel E. G. Hollis, C.O. of the raided REME unit which trains National Servicemen, said: "The lads were too inexperienced to have ammunition. They put up a good fight in the circumstances."

Lieutenant-Colonel Hollis—he said his men had no ammunition.

Clubbed

FULL STORY AND MORE PICTURES—SEE CENTRE PAGES

Left: Despite the failure of the Felsted and Arborfield raids, the IRA persisted. This headline tells of another – at Blandford, Dorset.

propaganda. During the early 1950s they mounted a series of arms raids. In 1951 a number of rifles and machine guns were taken from Ebrington Barracks in Londonderry. In 1953 the cadet force armoury at Felsted School in Essex was broken into, and 100 rifles and 20 machines guns were stolen. These were quickly recovered, together with the three raiders who each received eight-year prison sentences. Two of the three, Cathal Goulding and Sean MacStiofain (John Stephenson), later became IRA chiefs of staff. There was also a dramatically successful raid on Gough Barracks at Armagh in June 1954. Taking advantage of lax security – the sentry on the gate, for example, carried no magazine for his Sten gun – a party of IRA volunteers overpowered the handful of guards. In less than half an hour the barracks armoury was emptied of 12 Bren guns, 50 Sten guns and 340 rifles, which were safely spirited away across the border. In October the same year eight men were caught and imprisoned in an abortive night attack on the Royal Inniskilling Fusiliers' depot at Omagh. In August 1955 the Royal Electrical and Mechanical Engineers' depot at Arborfield in Berkshire was raided and 80,000 rounds of ammunition taken. Again, this was recaptured and a number of IRA men apprehended. Paradoxically, these operations, although mostly failures, boosted IRA morale. They gained valuable publicity by demonstrating the organisation's commitment.

Yet the absence of any full-scale campaign in the North frustrated many Republicans, and the movement as a whole was weakened by a number of splits. The most important splinter group was Saor Uladh (Free Ulster), a political party with a military wing known as Laochra Uladh or Fianna Uladh (Warriors or Soldiers of Ulster). Led by Tyrone-born Liam Kelly, this group attacked the RUC barracks at Roslea, County Fermanagh, in November 1955, but were driven off after one volunteer was shot dead. Impatient at the apparent inactivity of the IRA itself, on 11 November 1956 Laochra Uladh and another breakaway group led by a young Dublin law graduate, Joe Christle, mounted a coordinated series of bombings and burnings along the border, against customs posts and other targets such as telephone exchanges and road bridges. Prompted by this move, the IRA leadership, who had in fact been planning an offensive, launched a sustained campaign – Operation Harvest – on 12 December 1956 with a number of simultaneous attacks on military targets, a courthouse, three bridges and a BBC transmitter. 'Spearheaded by volunteers of the Irish Republican Army,' announced the Irish Republican Army Council, 'our people in the Six Counties have carried the fight to the enemy.'

The 1956–62 IRA campaign

During the 'Border Campaign' of 1956–62 the IRA leadership adopted three main tactics. First was the planting of bombs on fixed targets, including government buildings, the economic and communications infrastructure, police barracks and military installations. Second was the assassination of individual security-force personnel, especially those recruited locally. The third tactic involved larger-scale attacks on the security forces, either by ambush or against police barracks and the like. Each of these tactics had been employed in the 1919–21 Anglo-Irish War and the first two were to be used in the Republican campaign in Northern Ireland after 1970. They particularly lend themselves to classic guerrilla warfare and can be implemented by comparatively few people and with relatively simple equipment. The third tactic requires larger numbers, a more so-phisticated military organisation and, if it is to be sustained, a high level of community support with readily available training facilities.

Before the start of the 1956 campaign the IRA leadership believed that these factors would obtain and that a large-scale military effort could be directed against the security forces in Northern Ireland. In the mid-1950s the Irish police had turned a blind eye to IRA training activities throughout the Republic and it was assumed that this would continue after active operations began. But the Dublin government cracked down hard and obliged the Army Council to concentrate on more limited terror tactics. There was only one large-scale engagement during the campaign: the bungled raid at Brookeborough in County Fermanagh.

On New Year's Day 1957 a 12-man IRA flying column – including Daithi O Conaill (David O'Connell) who later helped to found the Provisional IRA – hijacked a lorry and drove to the centre of the village, stopping close to the Royal Ulster Constabulary barracks. Two home-made mines were planted, but failed to explode. At that moment a policeman emerged from the barracks and was fired on, but not hit. The IRA men had only three magazines for their single Bren gun, which quickly ran out of ammunition. Those on the back of the truck were sitting targets for the police who opened up from the first floor of the building. Several of the IRA men were wounded; one was injured when a grenade thrown at the barracks bounced back and rolled under the lorry. Eventually, the attackers drove away and all but two, who were fatally injured, escaped across the border. One of the dead, a 27-year-old Limerick man, was commemorated by a haunting and popular ballad, 'Sean South of Garryowen', and with that quixotic facility Irish Republicanism has of turning failure into victory, the raid became a symbol of noble sacrifice and steady adherence to the national cause.

In military terms the Brookeborough raid was a disaster; a waste of valuable men and material. Other large-scale operations were

THE FERMANAGH HERALD, SATURDAY, JANUARY 5, 1957

Two Men Die in Attack on Barracks
Machine-gun battle in Brookeboro' street
Body and Dying Man found by Police

Second Attack on Derrylin Police Barracks
Constable Sean Scally fatally wounded

contemplated but not carried out. One plan involved the seizure of the whole village of Clady, County Tyrone, at Easter in 1958, but it was abandoned for lack of men. For the most part, the IRA concentrated on tactics which again became familiar in the 1970s, such as the bombing of fixed targets. Obviously vulnerable points such as oil depots, telephone exchanges, barracks and other security installations were immediately given permanent guards, but it was impossible to protect everything. Road bridges and railway lines in remote areas became a favourite target. Using explosives, however, was risky. Five people died in November 1957 when an IRA bomb was being moved across the border from County Louth.

The other main tactic, assassination, was directed against the security forces themselves. Even so the numbers involved were comparatively small. Six policemen were killed and 19 wounded. Eleven members of the B-Specials and two members of the British armed forces were also wounded. Some of its attacks lost the IRA public

sympathy, such as that in August 1957 on Sergeant Arthur Ovens, who was lured to an unoccupied farmhouse and there killed by a booby-trap bomb. In January 1961 Constable Norman Anderson was murdered after having crossed the border to visit a girlfriend. The IRA left a note on his body denouncing him as a spy. The last killing of the campaign occurred in a more conventional attack when a police patrol was ambushed in County Armagh in November 1961. In response the new minister of justice in the Republic, Charles Haughey, announced further stringent security measures. This finally persuaded the IRA to cease operations.

Far left, top: Railway repair gangs work to reopen the Belfast–Dublin line, broken by an IRA bomb at the beginning of the 1956–62 campaign. Although obviously effective, such attacks were soon to be superseded by assaults on members of the RUC and B-Specials.
Far left, bottom: The abortive raid on Brookeborough Barracks, as reported in the Fermanagh Herald, 5 January 1957. Despite the almost farcical nature of the attack, a ballad commemorating one of the dead IRA men, 'Sean South of Garryowen', enjoyed widespread popularity in the Republic. The raid itself illustrates the Republican knack for turning failures into propaganda victories.

MURDER
£5,000 REWARD

A reward of £5,000 will be paid by the Government of Northern Ireland to any person who furnishes information leading to the arrest and conviction of one or more of the persons responsible for the murder of
SERGEANT ARTHUR JAMES OVENS,
Royal Ulster Constabulary,
near Coalisland, Co. Tyrone, on 17th August, 1957.

Information may be supplied in STRICT CONFIDENCE to The Inspector General, Royal Ulster Constabulary Headquarters, Belfast, Telephone No. Belfast 25421, any Police Station, or any member of the Force.

September, 1957.

Left: Brookeborough High Street in the aftermath of the IRA attack on 1 January 1957: the RUC post is by the telephone box. The sudden appearance of Sergeant Kenneth Cordner through the side door, just as the IRA truck was pulling up, disrupted the plan to reduce the building to rubble and led to a gun battle in which two IRA men died. Such operations, although militarily disastrous, kept the flame of Republican aspirations burning.
Above: A member of the RUC, armed with a Sten sub-machine gun, stands guard outside a police station in 1957. The reward poster is for information leading to the arrest of those responsible for the murder of Sergeant Arthur Ovens, blown up by an IRA booby-trap in County Tyrone on 17 August 1957. Such 'cold-blooded' killings, although more militarily expedient than pitched gun battles, lost the IRA a certain amount of public support, even in nationalist circles.

Although the so-called 'Border Campaign' was not formally called off until February 1962, it only seriously constituted an offensive for about seven months. After the campaign had finished the Northern Ireland authorities stated that there had been more than 600 incidents, but unlike the 1920s or the 1970s there was no large-scale civil strife. There were only 19 deaths over the five-year period. The impact of the campaign was mainly confined to a zone along the border, and it did not notably disrupt the everyday life of the province. The limited nature of Operation Harvest reflected, among other things, the weakness of the IRA. The Army Council deliberately decided not to take any action in Belfast since it did not believe that its army was strong enough to protect Catholics there against possible Protestant reprisals.

The 1956–62 campaign was crippled by the firm security measures taken by both the Belfast and the Dublin governments. In the North the Special Powers Act was invoked and over 180 IRA suspects were interned without trial. In the South de Valera, after being returned to power in a general election in March 1957, introduced internment on 8 July. Almost immediately 60 key IRA men were picked up. A total of over 200 men were held, again at the Curragh Camp, during the campaign. Internment seriously curtailed the

IRA effort. In Northern Ireland it was based on accurate intelligence. The RUC Special Branch were assisted by a senior MI5 officer who apparently got their IRA files into especially good order. In the South internment made life particularly difficult for the organisation, who had expected to be able to use the Republic as a safe haven. Another crucial constraint on the IRA was the lack of popular support among the nationalist population in the North, who, although still romantically attached to the abolition of partition, were not generally prepared to support violence to bring it about.

By the early 1960s people throughout Ireland were less concerned with partition than with more mundane bread-and-butter issues, such as jobs and living standards. The old order and the old issues of Irish politics seemed to be passing away. In 1959 de Valera retired from active politics and became president of the Republic. He was replaced as Taoiseach (prime minister) by Sean Lemass, a pragmatic, efficient politician who adopted a policy of modernisation and offered *de facto* recognition to Northern Ireland. In the North, Lord Brookeborough was coming under increasing criticism. At 74 years old, it seemed certain that his May 1962 general election victory would be his last. It was time Stormont had a new leader, one who might mirror the reformism of Lemass in the South.

Left: The border between North and South has always constituted a security problem: here armed RUC officers search a donkey cart for hidden arms as the owner nears a border crossing point.
Above: On 8 July 1957 Irish prime minister Eamon de Valera introduced internment of IRA suspects in the South. His policies alienated Sinn Fein, who organised this demonstration in London in March 1958.
Right: Anti-de Valera protest took many forms: here Liam O'Cealliag, on hunger strike outside the Irish Embassy in London, takes a drink, July 1958.

2. The Civil Rights Crisis 1962-1969

On 26 February 1962, the Irish Republican Publicity Bureau issued a 'Statement to the Irish People', in which the Irish Republican Army Council called an end to its six-year Border Campaign and ordered its volunteers to cease operations and dump their weapons. Without admitting that the IRA's strategy of achieving the reunification of Ireland by military means had failed, the statement bemoaned 'the attitude of the general public whose minds have been deliberately distracted from the supreme issue facing the Irish people – the Unity and Freedom of Ireland'.

Within the IRA, however, there were many who realised that the Border Campaign had been a total disaster which had left the cream of its volunteers and supporters either dead, imprisoned or interned. Not only had the campaign failed to mobilise anti-Unionist opinion in the North, but it had also led to the IRA becoming unpopular in the South.

Weakened, divided and isolated, the IRA seemed a spent and irrelevant force on both sides of the border it refused to recognise. Its loyal adherence to the Irish nationalist traditions of 'physical force', insurrection and terrorism, appeared to have brought it to the verge of extinction as a viable movement which could claim to be anything more than a tiny group of intransigent Republicans living on the intoxicating but sterile memories of glorious battles and courageous martyrs.

In the bitter aftermath of defeat, many Republican activists dropped out of the movement, and there were few young recruits to take their place. Critics of the old-style militarist leadership redoubled their efforts to swing the IRA away from a blind faith in the universal efficacy of the

Left: The grim reality of urban confrontation: a young Londonderry Catholic, petrol bombs concealed beneath the parapet, looks out over streets containing burnt-out houses and derelict factories. The dustbin lid is for banging on the concrete to warn others of approaching RUC or army patrols. Right: The continuing sectarian provocation: an Orange Lodge parade in Belfast, July 1971. Symbolic of the political, social and economic hold of Protestants on the life of Northern Ireland, such parades did little to ease the sectarian tension which was the root cause of the Troubles.

Thompson gun and the bomb towards a policy of greater political involvement and the mobilisation of support on both sides of the border through grass-roots organisations and the active pursuit of social and political reforms.

But it was only in 1964 that the IRA began to recover from the defeat of 1962. One of the most public manifestations of this partial recovery was the emergence of the Wolfe Tone Society, named after the Irish nationalist leader of the 18th century. This study and debating society began to spread Republican ideas and influence outside of the ranks of the committed traditionalist few. Cathal Goulding had meanwhile become chief of staff of the IRA, and though strongly influenced by the traditions of 'physical force' (he had served eight years in prison for his part in the Felsted School raid in 1953), he realised the need for a new approach to the problem of how to achieve a united Ireland. The Wolfe Tone Society was a sign of this new openness, and the most important figure behind it was Roy Johnston, a young computer scientist who returned to Dublin in 1963 after several years in London. Johnston had established strong links during his time in London with the pro-communist Connolly Association, which was active among Irishmen living in Britain and was heavily influenced by the British and Irish Communist Parties. He rapidly made contact with the new leadership of the IRA on his return to Ireland, and his ideas were backed by Goulding.

At the 1964 Sinn Feinn 'ard fheis' (annual conference), Johnston submitted a policy document which proposed that the Republican movement 'recognise realities' and abandon its line that the only legitimate authority in Ireland was the Second Dail, a body which had ceased to exist in 1921, but which had voted for the creation of a united Irish Republic. Johnston argued that Sinn Fein should put forward candidates for election to local councils and to the parliaments in Dublin, Stormont and Westminster, all of which had until then been branded as 'illegal assemblies' by the IRA, which had hitherto consistently abstained from taking up any seats won in elections North or South.

No decision was taken on this proposal in 1964, but at the 1965 ard fheis, Sinn Fein agreed in principle that it would take part in elections, but that it would only take up seats in the Dublin Dail or at Stormont if it won a majority in either of those assemblies. However far from the realities of Irish politics this optimistic view of the potential electoral support for Sinn Fein might appear, it was the only basis on which such an enormous break with tradition could be made. Even so, the new line was far from universally accepted, and there was still a strong element which continued to adhere to the militarism and right-wing ideas which were such a strong feature of the old-style IRA.

The main impact of the shift in policy was at first in the South, where Sinn Fein members became active in the countryside among agricultural workers, small farmers and fishermen, while in the towns Republican activists began to become prominent in tenants' associations and took an active part in trade-union organisations. Their aim was to create the mass base which their new socialist theories demanded as a precondition for the national revolution which they now saw as the means to achieve a united Ireland. The new strategy called for the gradual creation of unity between the Protestant and Catholic working class in order to overcome the sectarian divisions upon which they saw the border North – South as being based.

The industrial North

From the point of view of the new IRA leadership, the prospects for the success of this strategy in the North seemed excellent during the mid-1960s. Northern Ireland had traditionally been the region in which the bulk of Irish industry had been concentrated. The main industries were textiles, shipbuilding and engineering, though there was still an important agricultural sector, employing approximately 25% of all adult males. Protestant domination of Northern Irish society also extended to the field of employment, however, and the best industrial jobs were the almost exclusive preserve of Protestant workers. At the massive Harland and Wolff shipbuilding company in Belfast, for example, where some 10% of all manufacturing jobs in Northern Ireland were concentrated, only a handful of the 21,000 workers employed in the company's four yards were Catholics. In a region whose level of unemployment remained consistently four times higher than that of the rest of the United Kingdom throughout the 1950s, the overall statistics concealed the existence of a far higher level of unemployment in the Catholic ghettos of Belfast and Londonderry.

The end of the postwar economic boom in 1951 had hit Northern Ireland particularly severely, and there was a large decline in industrial production, especially in the linen industry, which faced heavy competition both from its Third World competitors and from the development of new synthetic fibres. Harland and Wolff also experienced strong foreign competition, and by the mid-1950s its European and Japanese rivals had recovered from the damage inflicted on their yards during the Second World War, and had re-equipped with the most advanced machinery, which left the Belfast company at a great disadvantage in a contracting market. Between 1961 and 1964, employment in the shipbuilding, ship-repair and marine-engineering industries in Northern Ireland declined by some 40%, and most of those made redundant were inevitably Protestants. The modernisation of agriculture, too, caused the loss of almost one-third of all jobs in that sector during the 1950s.

One of the most important foundations of the Unionist domination of Northern Ireland since the partition of 1921 had been the relative job security which sectarian employment practices had ensured the Protestant

working class at the expense of the Catholic minority. Not only did the Protestant workers vote Unionist and march in the Orange Lodge parades in order to defend Ulster from the constantly invoked threat of 'Papism' and 'Rome Rule' – they were also defending their families' bread and butter in a region of high unemployment.

Recession and unemployment

In early 1961, Harland and Wolff announced that some 8000 of its 21,000 workforce would be made redundant by the summer of that year, and there were rumours of 8000 redundancies at the Short Brothers' aircraft factory. The Confederation of Shipbuilding and Engineering Unions organised a one-day strike and a mass demonstration (in which over 20,000 took part) to demand government action to reduce unemployment and avert the threatened redundancies. By July, however, the 8000 jobs at Harland and Wolff had gone, and the unemployment rate in Northern Ireland stood at 7%, compared to 1.2% for the United Kingdom as a whole.

The situation was even worse in 1962, when a further 2000 workers were made redundant at Harland and Wolff, and Short Brothers was threatened with closure if no new orders were received. In the Stormont elections that year, the Northern Ireland Labour Party (NILP) increased its vote by 15%, and the erosion of working-class support for the Unionist Party led to pressure from within the party for change.

Criticism was levelled especially at the leadership of Lord Brookeborough, prime minister of Northern Ireland since 1943. Unionist MPs who saw their previously rock-solid majorities coming under threat from the NILP pressed him to demand increased economic assistance from the Conservative government in London. Although Brookeborough won a number of concessions from Whitehall, their effect was limited and his position was rapidly undermined, particularly by Terence O'Neill, who as Northern Ireland minister of finance seemed to represent a more modern approach to the economic problems of the province.

The publication of the Hall Report in

November 1962 was a fatal blow to Brookeborough, who had staked his future on its providing an answer to the crisis. The report was pessimistic about the economic future of Northern Ireland, and seemed to suggest that emigration might be the only solution to the region's rising unemployment statistics. In fact, the essence of the Hall proposals was that economic incentives should be concentrated on encouraging new, modern industries, and that the older, more labour-intensive industries traditionally associated with the province should be allowed to go to the wall. Either way, there was little to encourage the Unionist Party's working-class supporters.

In March 1963, Lord Brookeborough retired, at the age of 75, and Captain Terence O'Neill became the fourth prime minister of Northern Ireland. O'Neill came from the same land-owning Protestant Ulster elite as his predecessor, but he appeared to be a

Below: An arch commemorating Protestant King Billy in Belfast's Sandy Row area. The anniversary of the defeat of the Catholics at the battle of the Boyne in 1690 by William of Orange is still celebrated by Loyalists.
Right: Captain Terence O'Neill, the fourth prime minister of Northern Ireland. He came to power on the resignation of Viscount Brookeborough in 1963.

moderate who was prepared to accept the necessity for change. In particular, O'Neill favoured the then fashionable ideas of regional economic planning, and aimed to modernise and rebuild the economy of the North by attracting investment from abroad.

One of O'Neill's first acts as prime minister was to announce a £450 million programme to revitalise Ulster industry and combat unemployment, which had by then risen to 11.2%. O'Neill's strategy of economic modernisation also demanded an overhaul of the administrative and economic infrastructure, and he appointed William Craig, first as minister of home affairs, and then in July 1964 as minister of health and local government, a post he occupied until 1965 when he took over the new ministry of development.

Modernisation and reform

Craig, a firm believer in maintaining the Protestant domination of Northern Ireland, and as Unionist Party Chief Whip a key figure in the selection of O'Neill as the successor to Brookeborough, was responsible for the implementation of O'Neill's programme of modernising transport, housing and local government. In this role he came up against stiff resistance from the most conservative elements of the Unionist Party, particularly when they feared that he might weaken their monopoly of power in local government. The success of his reforms, however, helped to secure a 7% swing to the Unionist Party in the general elections to the Stormont parliament in November 1965 – a victory which was achieved at the expense of the NILP, which lost two seats in Protestant working-class areas of Belfast. Despite the apparent success of the O'Neill government, however, modernisation and the consolidation of Unionist opinion were not enough to satisfy the various demands which were being made for change in Northern Ireland.

A crucial factor in the development of the crisis which was later to beset the O'Neill government was the election of a Labour government in Britain in 1964. The new Labour prime minister, Harold Wilson, was on record as being in favour of a united Ireland, and he had little sympathy for the Unionist administration in Ulster, which had enjoyed a close relationship with previous Conservative governments. O'Neill therefore felt pressure to introduce a sufficient degree of reform to avert direct Whitehall interference, without fundamentally altering the balance of power in Northern Ireland, which ever since partition in 1921 had been firmly in the hands of the Protestant majority.

The need to placate London, as well as O'Neill's own conviction that the economic future of Ulster depended upon the develop-

ment of closer links with the South, was behind the meeting which took place at Stormont on 14 January 1965 between O'Neill and the Taoiseach (prime minister) of the Irish Republic, Sean Lemass. This was the first such meeting between the heads of the two Irish governments since partition. Coming after the defeat of the IRA's Border Campaign, the O'Neill–Lemass summit suggested that the paralysing effect that the border issue had hitherto had upon Irish politics, particularly in the North, might at last be coming to an end. With both Britain and the Republic of Ireland eager to enter the European Economic Community, the normalisation of relations between Dublin and Stormont seemed a logical step.

But the possibility of improved relations between North and South leading to a new political situation in the North, where Unionist domination of the government had resulted in what was virtually a one-party state, with normal political discussion and activity being stifled by the conflict between Protestant Unionist and Catholic nationalist, provoked an angry reaction from the more extreme sections of Protestant opinion. The Reverend Ian Paisley, for example, founder and leader of the Free Presbyterian Church, and a loud, vigorous exponent of militant Protestantism, attacked O'Neill for selling out to Catholicism and the South. He launched a campaign around the slogan 'O'Neill must go', and during 1966 pursued a 'strategy of tension', which was designed to undermine the O'Neill government and prevent any *rapprochement* with Ulster's Catholic minority or with the Republic.

The civil rights movement

Another serious challenge to O'Neill came from the rapidly emerging and largely Catholic civil rights movement which was demanding fundamental social and political reforms. O'Neill's modernisation plans had been limited to increasing efficiency, and had left the political status quo largely untouched. Indeed, he had gone so far as to deny that any such change was necessary, and had rejected accusations that a form of religious apartheid existed in Northern Ireland.

One of the first steps in the creation of the civil rights movement was the establishment of the Campaign for Social Justice (CSJ) in January 1964. Based in Dungannon, and led by Dr Con McCluskey and his wife, local councillor Patricia McCluskey, the CSJ aimed to collect information on cases of discrimination and injustice in Northern Ireland, and to fight for an end to sectarian discrimination in the areas of housing, employment, public appointments and electoral practice. The CSJ developed strong links with

the British Labour Party, particularly with the Campaign for Democracy in Ulster, an organisation set up by a group of 60 Labour MPs in June 1965, which pressed for reform of the situation in Northern Ireland.

The civil rights movement emerged at a time when the established parties which had traditionally represented Catholic opinion in Ulster were weakened and in decline, leaving a vacuum which the civil rights activists were quick to fill. Rural Catholic voters had been largely represented by the Nationalist Party, dominated by the clergy and rural Catholic middle class. Strictly constitutionalist and conservative, it became increasingly moderate and conciliatory on the question of civil rights and community relations after O'Neill came to power, and willingly adopted the role of an official parliamentary opposition, first suggested by Sean Lemass, in 1965. The Nationalist Party had never possessed any strong organisational structure, and though it attempted to develop a modern political machine after it took on the opposition role, it was largely unsuccessful, and remained basically an association of local councillors and MPs, without any solid mass base and increasingly isolated and irrelevant. Urban Catholic opinion had been expressed mainly through the NILP until the 1940s, but its willingness to compromise on the constitutional issue (i.e. recognition of the border and the division of

The Reverend Ian Paisley, hard-line Protestant and Unionist leader, notorious for his fierce religious views and fiery speeches.

Ireland) led to the formation of a number of more radical small breakaway groups more clearly committed to a united Ireland. Although the NILP had achieved a degree of success in the Northern Ireland elections of 1958 and 1962, by 1965 its support had begun to decline dramatically.

The growth of the civil rights movement was also assisted by the gradual demilitaris-ation of the IRA and the shift in its strategy which tended to remove the border issue from the centre of the political stage. Mem-bers of the Republican Clubs, which had been formed in order to overcome the ban on Sinn Fein in Northern Ireland, were active sup-porters of the campaign for reform, but there remained a strong opposition element within the IRA which persisted in its belief in the necessity for a military solution to the division of Ireland. Although Sinn Fein president Tomas MacGoilla promised at the 1966 ard fheis that his party would make every effort to win a majority in the Dublin Dail within

five years, there were fresh outbreaks of Republican-inspired violence in a year which marked the 50th anniversary of the 1916 Easter Rising. Among these, the most spec-tacular was the bomb explosion which de-stroyed Nelson's Pillar in the centre of Dublin, while a breakaway Republican group known as the Saor Eire Action Group was responsible for a series of bank robberies in the Republic during 1966 and 1967.

Also in 1966 came the resurgence of Prot-estant terrorism in the North, where an extremist group calling itself the Ulster Volunteer Force (UVF) – named after the paramilitary organisation created by Edward Carson in 1913 to resist the introduction of Irish Home Rule – issued a statement in May threatening the IRA with war and the murder of its members. Six days later, a UVF squad toured the Clonard area of Belfast in search of a prominent Republican activist, Leo Martin. Failing to find Martin, they shot and fatally wounded 28-year-old John Patrick Scullion,

an innocent Catholic who was on his way home at the time. On 26 June, two UVF gunmen shot and killed Peter Ward, an 18-year-old Catholic barman, as he left a bar in Malvern Street, in the Protestant Shankill area of Belfast. Augustus ('Gusty') Spence, a well-known UVF leader, was later sentenced to life imprisonment for the murder.

Although O'Neill had previously refused to ban the UVF or any other Protestant extremist organisations, the Ward killing forced his hand, and the UVF was proscribed. O'Neill used the occasion to attack Ian Pais-ley, whom he accused of maintaining links with the UVF, and drew a parallel between Paisley's demagogic style and the rise of the Nazis in 1930s Germany.

Despite the criticism of the Protestant right, however, O'Neill had done little to satisfy the demand for reform voiced by the Catholic opposition, and on 29 January 1967 the Northern Ireland Civil Rights Association (NICRA) was formed at a meeting at Belfast's

International Hotel. It was headed by a 13-strong committee, which included a number of prominent Northern Ireland trade unionists such as its chairman, Noel Harris of the draughtsmen's union DATA, Republicans such as Fred Heatley and Jack Bennet of the Wolfe Tone Society, Betty Sinclair, a member of the Communist Party who represented Belfast Trades Council, Paddy Devlin of the NILP, John Quinn of the Ulster Liberal Party, Joe Sherry of the Republican Labour Party, and Michael Dolley and Robin Cole, both of Queen's University Belfast, where Cole was chairman of the Young Unionist Group. Con McCluskey of the CSJ was NICRA vice-chairman, and CSJ members were an important element among the new movement's early supporters.

Non-violent protest

The aims of NICRA were: abolition of the ratepayer's franchise, which allowed prosperous businessmen (almost always Protestants) more than one vote in local council elections; an end to the gerrymandering of electoral boundaries; the creation of machinery to prevent sectarian discrimination by public authorities, and to deal with any complaints; the fair allocation of housing; the repeal of the draconian and highly controversial Special Powers Act; and the disbandment of the B-Specials. There was no mention of the border issue, and though the strategy of NICRA was to achieve reform through non-violent political action, it was immediately branded as a front for the IRA by Paisley and other Protestant extremists. IRA members were indeed involved in the activities of the new organisation, but they maintained a very low

profile, and there was no evidence that they controlled it or exercised any dominant influence over its policies. Most of NICRA's supporters were in fact middle-class Catholic liberals, for whom a united Ireland held little attraction. Their aim was to establish the same political and social freedoms in Northern Ireland that existed in the rest of the United Kingdom, by means of petitions, sit-ins and demonstrations.

One of the most blatant features of Protestant domination was in the area of housing, where Unionist-controlled local authorities discriminated against Catholics and gave preference to Protestants in the allocation of accommodation. In Caledon, County Tyrone, a group of squatters occupied some newly completed council houses in late 1967 to protest against this practice, and NICRA became involved in supporting them. NICRA had worked with Nationalist MP Austin Currie in compiling a survey of the housing situation in the Dungannon area, which established that although the district had a 53% Catholic majority, from 1945 to 1968 71% of publicly built homes had been allocated to Protestants. Currie raised the issue in the Stormont parliament, but its Unionist majority merely ignored him. Outraged, Currie himself went to occupy a house in Caledon whose Catholic squatters had been evicted by the authorities. He too was evicted, and he exploited the event to win publicity for his case.

Heartened by Currie's success, NICRA went on to organise the province's first civil rights demonstration at Dungannon on 24 August 1968. An estimated 2500 people marched from Coalisland to Dungannon, where they were joined by 1500 more. The

marchers sang 'We Shall Overcome' in imitation of the black civil rights campaigners in the United States, upon whom they had modelled their own fight. Although the demonstration passed quite peacefully, the marchers were heckled by members of Ian Paisley's Ulster Protestant Volunteers (UPV) in Dungannon market square. The UPV, a working-class paramilitary organisation set up by a colleague of Paisley's, Noel Doherty, in 1964, was dedicated to maintaining the Union 'as long as the United Kingdom maintains a Protestant Monarchy'. Together with Paisley's Ulster Constitution Defence Committee (UCDC), it was to play a crucial role in the events that were to follow.

After the success of the Dungannon march, NICRA turned its attention to the organisation of a demonstration in Londonderry, Ulster's second city and scene of some of the clearest examples of sectarian discrimination

Above left: Nelson's Pillar, in O'Connell Street, Dublin, decapitated by a bomb in March 1966. As a publicity stunt, the target was well chosen: to the left of the symbol of British imperialism is the GPO building, evoking memories of the 1916 Easter Rising.
Above right: 12 July 1966: the RUC takes a passive role as Belfast Protestants light bonfires in the streets to celebrate the anniversary of the battle of the Boyne.
Right: Civil rights protesters take to the streets in August 1968, marching from Coalisland to Dungannon in peaceful protest against the glaring inequalities of life in the North.

by the Unionist-controlled administration. The city had a Catholic majority, and it was only by dividing it into three unequal wards, into one of which the bulk of the Catholic electorate was concentrated, that Unionist control of the city council was preserved. In 1967, for example, there were 14,429 Catholic voters in Londonderry, and only 8781 from other denominations, yet there were 12 Unionist and only eight non-Unionist councillors. This gerrymandering of electoral boundaries had originally been carried out in 1936, but by the mid-1960s the growth of the Catholic population and lack of building land in the South ward had reached a level where it was becoming necessary to rehouse Catholics in the hitherto predominantly Protestant North and Waterside wards. This posed a direct threat to the maintenance of the Protestant grip on the city council, however, and the Unionist authorities' solution was simple – they ceased to build any more council houses in the city, thereby condemning its Catholic population not only to political under-representation, but also to increasingly intolerable housing conditions. Londonderry, which also had an unemployment rate some eight times the national average, was a city which represented everything which the civil rights movement was out to change.

March and counter-march

A few days before the planned NICRA march was due to take place, however, William Craig (now once more minister of home affairs) banned it on the grounds that its proposed route went through what he claimed were traditionally Protestant areas of Londonderry, and that it would take place on the same day as a parade by the city's Protestant Apprentice Boys, both factors which might lead to confrontation and violence. In fact, the Apprentice Boys' parade (celebrating the city's resistance to the Catholic King James II in 1689) had been organised at short notice as a counter-demonstration to the NICRA protest march, a tactic often employed to intimidate Ulster's Catholic minority.

Nevertheless, the NICRA march went ahead, on 5 October 1968, and some 2000 civil rights supporters assembled to take part. Their way was blocked by a cordon of about 130 men of the Royal Ulster Constabulary (RUC), who also cut off their retreat, so preventing them from dispersing peacefully. Caught between two lines of police in a narrow street, the marchers were subjected to baton charges and battered by the powerful jets of police water-cannon. Thirty-six arrests were made, and 88 people were injured, including Belfast MP Gerry Fitt, who re-

ceived a severe cut to his head from a police baton. The violence escalated into full-scale riots in the city's Catholic Bogside area which went on all through that night and lasted into the following day.

The events of 5 October were a shock to the moderate middle-class supporters of the civil rights campaign, who had no previous experience of the brutality for which the RUC and its B-Special auxiliaries were noted in Ulster's working-class Catholic districts. In particular, it gave impetus to the radicalisation of large number of students at Queen's University Belfast (QUB), many of whom had taken part in the Londonderry demonstration. On 6 October, QUB students – both Protestant and Catholic – picketed the Belfast home of William Craig, and they staged a sit-down protest in the centre of the city on the following day. A number of the most committed QUB student activists met on 9 October inside the university to found an organisation known as the People's Democracy (PD), which was heavily influenced by the wave of left-wing student protest which was sweeping the world during 1968. PD echoed many of the demands already put forward by NICRA, but its methods were more radical, which was in line with its vague mixture of Marxist and anarchist ideas. PD agreed with NICRA, however, that the issue of civil rights in the North was far more important than the question of the reunification of Ireland, and though several of the most prominent PD leaders regarded a united Ireland as a desirable long-term aim, they had

little sympathy for the highly conservative society which existed in the South.

O'Neill, meanwhile, had come under heavy pressure from the Labour government in London for immediate action to introduce reforms – there was a strongly implied threat that otherwise Westminster might be forced to intervene more directly, a situation which O'Neill wished to avoid at all costs. Craig, on the other hand, counselled O'Neill to resist the demand for reform and led the opposition to the proposals which the Ulster prime minister introduced on 22 November for a five-point programme of legislative measures to meet the main criticisms of the civil rights movement. These included the appointment of an Ombudsman to deal with complaints; a points system in the allocation of housing; the abolition of plural voting in council elections, thereby meeting the demand for one man, one vote; a review of the Special Powers Act; and the creation of a Londonderry Development Corporation to alleviate the economic and social depression which had contributed to the bitterness of Catholic feeling in that city, and to replace the Unionist-controlled Londonderry County Borough Council.

O'Neill had to react firmly in order to crush a revolt within the Unionist Party by those who opposed the introduction of the reforms. Three of his ministers resigned, and in December 1968 he sacked Craig from his position as minister of home affairs, accusing him of advocating a form of UDI along the lines of the Ian Smith regime in Rhodesia. On 9 December O'Neill made a televised speech

Right: Bernadette Devlin, photographed in August 1969 in the Bogside, Londonderry. A committed civil rights activist, she helped to organise the protection of Catholic areas and was prominent throughout the early years of the crisis, serving as an MP at Westminster and helping to found the IRSP. She is seen here during a lull in the sectarian riots of 1969: the goggles are protection against CS gas.

in which he gave the warning: 'Ulster stands at the crossroads.' The choice he posed was between limited change and violent conflict, which might lead to the destruction of Ulster society. Protestant opinion rallied temporarily around O'Neill, and he was able to win an overwhelming vote of confidence from his Unionist parliamentary party.

Events in the New Year rapidly eroded the strength of O'Neill's position, however, leading to his total isolation within a matter of months. PD decided to continue their campaign and to consolidate the successes of the civil rights movement by organising a march from Belfast to Londonderry (a distance of 120 kilometres), which began on 1 January 1969. The march was modelled on that led by American civil rights leader Martin Luther King in 1965 from Selma to Montgomery in the southern state of Alabama. The PD march began inauspiciously, however, with only about a hundred setting out from Belfast City Hall amid heckling and abuse from Loyalist Protestant bystanders. The marchers were accompanied every step of the way by a contingent of up to 80 RUC men, who diverted them whenever they approached towns with large Unionist populations.

On 4 January, the cold, exhausted marchers were approaching Burntollet Bridge, which spans the River Faughan 13 kilometres from Londonderry, when they were viciously attacked by a mob of at least 200 club-wielding Protestants, including a number of off-duty B-Specials. The RUC escort provided little protection as the attackers inflicted severe

Right: Violence flares at Burntollet Bridge, 4 January 1969. The PD-organised civil rights march from Belfast was attacked just outside Londonderry by a mob of about 200 Protestants armed with clubs. Several marchers were injured in the attack, news of which provoked worldwide criticism and led to the erection of barricades in Londonderry's Catholic Bogside district.

injuries on a number of marchers and drove others into the river. The incident led to worldwide criticism of the Ulster regime and to charges of RUC complicity in what was clearly a well-planned and totally unprovoked attack.

Barricades in the Bogside

When news of the events at Burntollet reached Londonderry that evening, the people of the Catholic Bogside district erected barricades to defend themselves from attack by Protestant extremists. There were further scenes of violence, however, as members of the police engaged in what a later government-appointed inquiry described as 'assault and battery', 'malicious damage to property', and 'the use of provocative sectarian and political slogans'.

The commission of inquiry, chaired by Lord Cameron, was set up by O'Neill in March 1969 to investigate the causes of the violence in Northern Ireland since 5 October 1968, as well as into the organisations which might be involved. The decision to set up the

Right: Despite the evidence of this photograph, the contingent of RUC men accompanying the civil rights marchers did little to protect them from the Protestant mob – which was itself partly made up of off-duty B-Specials.

commission led to the resignation of the minister of finance, Brian Faulkner, who had been a consistent critic of any moves to accommodate opposition Catholic opinion. The results of the commission's investigations were published in September 1969, and pinpointed as causes of the violence a growing Catholic sense of injustice set against Protestant fears that Catholic protest might lead to an end of Unionist domination in the province. This situation had been made worse by the activities of Paisley's followers, the UPV and UCDC, who had provoked a hostile, violent reaction to the moderate proposals of the civil rights campaigners. The commission also went on to criticise the RUC for its handling of the situation, and reported that 'subversive elements' had sought to use the civil rights campaign to provoke violence.

O'Neill, meanwhile, came under renewed pressure from within the ranks of his own party, and a group of 12 Unionist MPs, including Craig, demanded a change in the party leadership in early February 1969. O'Neill responded to the new challenge by calling a general election for 24 February.

On the surface, the results of the February 1969 election did nothing to alter the balance of power in Northern Ireland, and the Unionist Party retained its overwhelming majority in the Stormont parliament. But the split in Loyalist Protestant opinion was reflected by reduced majorities for many pro-O'Neill politicians, while O'Neill himself lost many votes to Ian Paisley in his own Bannside constituency. In addition, of the 36 official Unionist MPs returned to Stormont, 12 belonged to the anti-O'Neill faction. Unable to reassert his control over the Unionist Party despite the election success, O'Neill resigned as prime minister on 28 April 1969, and was succeeded on 1 May by James Chichester-Clark, who had himself resigned as agriculture minister on 23 April.

One of Chichester-Clark's first measures was to order an amnesty for all those charged with or convicted of political offences since the beginning of the violence in October the previous year. Though designed to promote conciliation and defuse the tense situation, the amnesty included Paisley, who had been serving a six-week prison sentence for unlawful assembly. Paisley, for one, had no intention of responding to Chichester-Clark's gesture, and continued to demand the suppression of the civil rights campaign and the removal of the new prime minister.

The February 1969 general election also showed the extent to which Catholic politics in Northern Ireland had changed under the impact of the civil rights agitation. Three independents linked to NICRA took seats from Nationalist Party MPs; one of these was John Hume, a former teacher from Londonderry who had been vice-chairman of the Derry Citizens' Action Committee, a civil rights group formed in the wake of the events of 5 October. People's Democracy candidates also took part in the election. One such was Bernadette Devlin, a young final-year psychology student at QUB, who stood against Chichester-Clark in South Derry. Although none of the PD candidates was elected, their relatively high vote enhanced their prestige within NICRA, where PD activists won a number of seats in elections to the executive committee held in March 1969.

The radicalisation of NICRA and the continued intransigence of the Protestant diehards seemed to make further clashes inevitable. Tension was increased by a number of bomb attacks during March and April on electricity pylons and reservoir pipelines. Although at first it seemed that the IRA had returned to its previous military tactics, the attacks were later revealed to be the work of UVF and UCDC members seeking to remove O'Neill from power.

In fact, far from embarking upon new military adventures, in May 1969 the Irish Republican Army Council refused a request from a group of Belfast IRA leaders for a supply of weapons from the South with which to protect the Catholic ghettos from Protestant attack. The reasons given for the refusal were, first, that it would be politically dangerous to be found moving arms into the North at a time when Protestant extremists were looking for any reason to brand the non-violent civil rights campaigners as dupes of the IRA; and secondly, that the weapons just were not available. The IRA leadership's concentration upon the development of political activity had left its arsenal depleted, and it was unable to offer the assistance which the Belfast IRA activists thought vitally necessary in view of the possibility of a violent Protestant backlash. This dispute marked the beginning of a split within the IRA which was later to surface with the creation of the breakaway Provisional IRA.

Bernadette at Westminster

Meanwhile, PD achieved a significant breakthrough in April 1969 with the election of 21-year-old Bernadette Devlin as Westminster MP for Mid-Ulster. Her arrival in parliament served to increase the sympathy which many Labour MPs felt for the Northern Irish civil rights movement, and her passionate attacks on injustice in Northern Ireland helped fuel the demands for more fundamental reform which were being voiced in Great Britain.

This period was perhaps the high point for the civil rights movement and its strategy of non-violent protest. Without a serious confrontation with the entrenched power of the Protestant majority there was a limit to the extent to which reform could be achieved in Ulster and by the summer of 1969 the ability of both NICRA and PD to influence events was coming to an end. As tension mounted and turned into violence, the sectarian barriers between the Protestant and Catholic communities in Northern Ireland hardened, and their deep-seated mutual fears began to feed an escalating chain of violence which finally placed the initiative in the hands of those who had all along been opposed to a peaceful solution to the province's problems.

Protestant fears were provoked by the new Catholic assertiveness, and led to the formation of a number of local Loyalist paramilitary groups, such as the Shankill Defence Association in Belfast (some of whose members later became notorious as the 'Shankill Butchers'). The populations of the Catholic ghettos were in their turn alarmed that Protestant extremists might go over to the offensive and carry out the kind of violent anti-Catholic attacks which had been a feature of life in Ulster during the 1920s and

Below: The response of the RUC to the rioting of 12 August 1969 in Londonderry: an officer in gas mask and helmet fires CS gas at a hostile crowd during the disturbances that followed the Apprentice Boys' march. The riots led to the establishment of 'Free Derry', the first of the 'No-Go' areas.

1930s. Nor did they have any confidence in the protection that might be offered by either the RUC or the B-Specials, both of which were regarded as enemy occupation forces.

Tension came to a violent head during the Apprentice Boys' parade in Londonderry on 12 August 1969, the 280th anniversary of the city's defiance of the Catholic James II. Despite warnings that it might provoke bloodshed, the march was allowed to proceed. The trouble began when Loyalists assembling on the old city walls, overlooking the Catholic Bogside district, began to throw pennies down at the people below in a provocative gesture of contempt. After the parade had started, nails and stones were flung by the Bogside crowd at the Protestant marchers and at the RUC. The police at first adopted a strategy of static defence, and endured a hail of missiles for over two hours,

Right: The rule of the mob: RUC officers look on helplessly as rioters move freely through the streets of Londonderry, 12 August 1969. The inability of the police to cope with the riots left the authorities with no choice but to deploy the British Army on the streets of Northern Ireland. Below: Against a background of burning property and vehicles, a Catholic crowd in Londonderry is addressed by British Labour MP Stan Orme during the riots of August 1969.

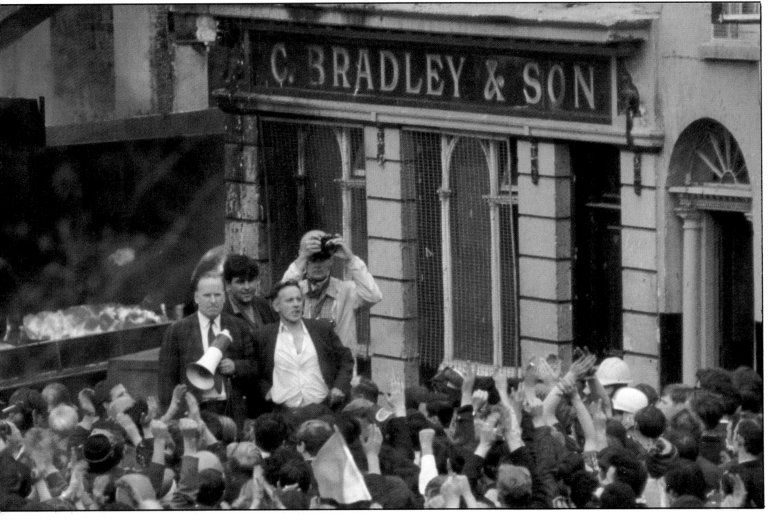

The B-Specials and the Special Powers Act

One demand common to all sections of the civil rights and Republican opposition to the Unionist regime in Northern Ireland was the disbandment of the B-Specials, a part-time armed police force which had an unenviable reputation for violence and sectarian prejudice. They had been formed as part of the new Ulster Special Constabulary (USC) in November 1920, at the height of the Anglo-Irish War, to combat the growing threat of the IRA. In theory the USC was to be one-third Catholic, but in practice it was entirely Protestant, most of its recruits being former members of the Protestant paramilitary Ulster Volunteer Force.

Recruitment to the USC was originally in three separate classes: Class A comprised full-time members who were prepared to serve anywhere in Ulster; Class B was for part-time volunteers who were only called upon to serve in their own localities; while Class C was a reserve, only mobilised in emergencies. With the division of Ireland and the establishment of the full-time Royal Ulster Constabulary (RUC) in the North in 1922, Classes A and C were disbanded, but Class B remained, giving the USC the name by which it was most commonly known – the B-Specials.

The B-Specials were active in all the campaigns the IRA has embarked upon since the First World War, and their existence was a major factor in keeping it on the defensive in the North, unable to make any progress in its aim of overthrowing the Unionist government and reuniting Ireland. During the IRA's 1956–62 Border Campaign, some Protestants living in the South even crossed the border in order to serve with the B-Specials. Apart from any other motives, the pay was always useful. During 1968–9, the B-Specials were often accused of brutality towards civil rights demonstrators, and it was also alleged that off-duty members of the B-Specials had taken part in unprovoked attacks on civil rights

marchers, such as that at Burntollet Bridge in January 1969.

The clearly sectarian nature of the B-Specials was revealed by the fact that on 1 August 1969, shortly before the violence which was to lead to the introduction of British troops, of the 425 full-time and 8481 part-time members of the force, not a single one was a Catholic. By contrast, the RUC was 11% Catholic.

Following the August 1969 disturbances, the Westminster government responded to criticisms of the police by appointing a commission of inquiry under Lord Hunt, whose report (published on 10 October 1969) called for drastic reforms of the security forces in Northern Ireland. Hunt recommended that the RUC be disarmed and that the B-Specials be disbanded, to be replaced by a part-time military force responsible to the army. On 30 April 1970, the notorious B-Specials were finally stood down, but many were able to join the Ulster Defence Regiment which had been formed on 1 January that year.

Another key demand of the civil rights movement was for the abolition of the Special Powers Act. Many of the most common abuses of power, particularly by the security forces, were carried out under the authority of its provisions, which were so draconian that they had reportedly prompted the envious admiration of the South African government. Emergency powers had first been introduced in Northern Ireland with the Civil Authorities (Special Powers) Act of 1922, which had provided the minister of home affairs with the authority 'to take all such steps and issue all such orders as may be necessary for preserving the peace'.

Under this Act, the RUC and B-Specials were empowered to arrest without warrant anyone 'on suspicion of acting, having acted, or being about to act' in a manner contrary to

the peace. Prisoners could be held indefinitely without charge, and the police were given authority to carry out searches without warrant and to seize property. Although originally passed to combat the IRA during the height of its activities in the North, the Act was renewed annually until 1933, when it was superseded by a permanent Act with similar provisions. The existence of the Special Powers Act brought into question the democratic credentials and even the permanency of the Northern Ireland state. The institutionalisation of extraordinary powers akin to martial law indicated how seriously the Unionist authorities took the threat of nationalist subversion. It implied an almost permanent state of civil war, in which the Catholic minority was seen as the internal enemy without guaranteed constitutional rights.

The Act survived the arrival of British troops on the streets of Northern Ireland by several years, but was finally replaced by an Order in Council in November 1972, which limited the period for which the security forces could detain suspects to 48 hours, though this could be extended to 28 days upon application for an interim custody order. In 1973 the Northern Ireland (Emergency Provisions) Act extended the time for which suspects could be initially held to 72 hours. The following year the Prevention of Terrorism (Temporary Provisions) Act applied similar emergency powers in Great Britain. Under the Act, the police are empowered to detain suspects pending investigation for two days, and for a further five days with the home secretary's authority. The Act was introduced after bombs planted by the IRA in Birmingham city centre killed and injured over 200 people, and it marked the extent to which the fight against terrorism had ceased to be a problem confined solely to Northern Ireland.

---

before mounting a series of baton charges against the Catholic crowd.

Rioting broke out, and soon the whole of the Bogside was a raging battlefield, with barricades being erected to prevent the entry of the RUC, who were bombarded with stones and petrol bombs by Catholic youths. By the next day, over 200 people had been injured, and the defiant Bogsiders had proclaimed the establishment of 'Free Derry', the first of Northern Ireland's 'No-Go' areas, where the writ of the RUC and Stormont no longer ran. During the night of 12/13 August the police, using armoured cars and CS gas (over 1000 canisters were used in three days), and accompanied by Protestant rioters, again

attempted to subdue Free Derry. But they were unable to breach the barricades, and the 'battle of the Bogside' continued for two more days. Meanwhile the fighting spread to several other towns in Northern Ireland, and in Armagh city on 14 August, B-Specials fired on a crowd, killing a 31-year-old Catholic, John Gallagher.

The troops move in

The crisis was rapidly moving beyond the control of the Stormont authorities, and Chichester-Clark was reluctantly forced to agree to the deployment of British troops in order to maintain order. On 14 August 1969,

400 men of the Prince of Wales's Own Regiment of Yorkshire entered Londonderry to take up internal security duties and end the rioting. The most bitter violence was yet to come, however, and on the evening of the 14th, Protestant extremists from Belfast's Shankill area responded to a demonstration in the Catholic Falls Road district with a full-scale invasion. During that night and well into the next day, the Protestant mob rampaged through the Falls, burning houses and attacking the inhabitants.

The RUC did nothing to curb the Protestant attack, and instead raced through the area in Shorland armoured cars mounted with machine guns, firing indiscriminately.

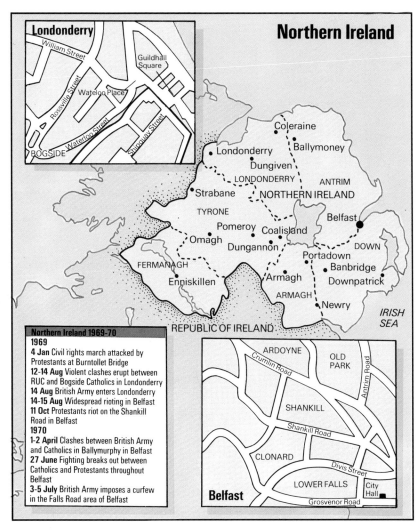

Londonderry

William Street
Rossville Street
Waterloo Place
Waterloo Street
Guildhall Square
BOGSIDE
Shipquay Street

Northern Ireland

Coleraine
Ballymoney
Londonderry
Dungiven
LONDONDERRY
ANTRIM
Strabane
NORTHERN IRELAND
TYRONE
Belfast
Pomeroy
Coalisland
Omagh
Dungannon
DOWN
Portadown
Banbridge
FERMANAGH
Armagh
Downpatrick
Enniskillen
ARMAGH
Newry
REPUBLIC OF IRELAND
IRISH SEA

Northern Ireland 1969-70
1969
4 Jan Civil rights march attacked by Protestants at Burntollet Bridge
12-14 Aug Violent clashes erupt between RUC and Bogside Catholics in Londonderry
14 Aug British Army enters Londonderry
14-15 Aug Widespread rioting in Belfast
11 Oct Protestants riot on the Shankill Road in Belfast
1970
1-2 April Clashes between British Army and Catholics in Ballymurphy in Belfast
27 June Fighting breaks out between Catholics and Protestants throughout Belfast
3-5 July British Army imposes a curfew in the Falls Road area of Belfast

ARDOYNE
OLD PARK
Crumlin Road
Antrim Road
SHANKILL
Shankill Road
CLONARD
Divis Street
LOWER FALLS
City Hall
Belfast
Grosvenor Road

Above: The horror of 1969: an RUC man discovers that his riot shield is no defence against petrol bombs.

Below: A snatch-squad of Royal Anglians rushes into action, intent on seizing riot ringleaders.

Above: Map of Northern Ireland with insets of Londonderry and Belfast. The chronology charts the events of 1969 and early 1970, the period of growing crisis and sectarian confrontation.

Among those killed was a British soldier on leave who was shot dead on the balcony of his home in the Divis Flats. He had been making petrol bombs for self-defence against the Protestant rioters, and died as he pushed two women with him out of the line of fire. Nine-year-old Patrick Rooney was also killed as he sheltered with his family in a back room in the same block of flats. During the fighting in Belfast, eight people were killed and over 400 injured, while around 200 Catholic homes were either seriously damaged or destroyed by fire. The violence ended on the afternoon of 15 August, when British troops arrived to impose an uneasy ceasefire.

The Wilson government acted quickly to assert control of the situation in Northern Ireland, and called Chichester-Clark to a meeting in London on 19 August. It was decided that overall responsibility for internal security in Ulster would now be in the hands of the Westminster government and the

British Army General Officer Commanding Northern Ireland, Lieutenant-General Sir Ian Freeland. After their meeting, Wilson and Chichester-Clark issued what came to be known as the Downing Street Declaration, which sought to pacify Protestant fears by reaffirming that Ulster would remain a part of the United Kingdom for as long as its Protestant majority wished.

The events of August 1969 in Belfast not only drastically changed the relationship between Stormont and Westminster, paving the way for the introduction of direct rule in 1972, but also provoked a serious crisis in the Irish Republic, where many Catholic victims of the Falls Road rioting had sought refuge. The Fianna Fail government of prime minister Jack Lynch ordered the Irish Army to move up to positions along the border with the North, and field hospitals were set up to provide medical attention for the wounded, while refugee centres were established at military bases. The Dublin government also sought to secure the creation of a United Nations peacekeeping force to be stationed in Northern Ireland, but this move was blocked by Britain, which insisted that the problem was purely a matter of internal UK security. There were some members of the Irish government who pressed for more vigorous measures, including the supply of arms to the IRA in order to defend Catholic areas in the North, but Lynch was eager to avoid a direct confrontation with Britain, and he resisted their demands.

Split in the IRA

A small number of Irish Army officers did allegedly visit the North to coordinate the activities of the Central Citizens' Defence Committee, which had been formed in Belfast to protect Catholic areas from Protestant attack. This role had traditionally been played by the IRA, but during the fighting of August 1969, IRA activity had been limited to a handful of volunteers, armed with old shotguns and pistols, who had disobeyed the orders of the Army Council and gone out to fight off the Protestant mobs terrorising the Catholic population of the Falls. The apparent failure of the left-wing IRA leadership's strategy of concentrating on political activity to the exclusion of all military preparation, and its total failure to respond to calls from IRA members in the North for weapons with which to defend the Catholic ghettos from Protestant attack widened the split between

Left: Protesters hurl bricks at the RUC from behind the shelter of a wall, Londonderry, 12 August 1969. Scenes such as this, showing familiar advertising slogans and street signs, shocked public opinion in Britain.

militarists, largely based in the North, and the left-wing gradualists who dominated the leadership of the IRA and its organisation in the South.

The summer of 1969, then, ended with the efforts at peaceful agitation for limited political reform by the predominantly Catholic middle-class civil rights movement being overtaken by the violence of the Protestant backlash, which itself led to the direct involvement of Westminster – something that Unionist leaders had tried in vain to avoid. While taking a more prominent role in the situation in Northern Ireland, Westminster also guaranteed the maintenance of a Loyalist veto over any fundamental constitutional change. Within months the British troops who had been welcomed in August by the Catholic population of Ulster as impartial protectors became in their turn objects of suspicion as they became increasingly identified with the province's Protestant majority and the preservation of the status quo.

August 1969 was not so much the end of a crisis as the beginning of a long war.

Above: The RUC charge a Catholic demonstration in Londonderry, August 1969. RUC tactics were not always as successful as this.

Below: British soldiers of the Royal Regiment of Fusiliers drink tea with Catholic families, Belfast, 1969. Friendly relations did not last.

3. Escalating Violence 1969-1972

The arrival of British troops on the streets of Londonderry and Belfast opened a new phase in the Northern Ireland crisis. The fact that the Stormont government had been forced to call on the British Army to control the situation fundamentally weakened its position in relation to the British government. The prime minister, Harold Wilson, was not prepared to carry out his earlier threat to abolish Stormont if the troops were used, but was determined that the Belfast government would pay a price for the British Army's involvement.

On 19 August 1969 the prime minister of Northern Ireland, Major Chichester-Clark, met Wilson and his home secretary, James Callaghan, in London. He was told that reforms must be carried out to remove the causes of Catholic discontent. Stormont would be allowed to govern, but only under the watchful eye of two senior British civil servants posted to Belfast to monitor the administration of the province. There would also be joint working parties of the Westminster and Stormont governments set up to see that the pace of reform was maintained. The Royal Ulster Constabulary and the B-Specials – whose behaviour over the previous year had especially attracted Wilson's disapproval – were to be the subject of an immediate inquiry headed by Lord Hunt.

There could be no question of the British government's genuine commitment to reform. Callaghan, in particular, associated himself publicly with that cause. Towards the end of August he visited Ulster and received a rapturous welcome from the Catholic population. In private, his attitude to Ulster's Protestant leaders was blunt and uncompromising. Yet the basic decision to leave Stormont intact – motivated by the British government's desire at all costs to keep the Northern Ireland situation at arm's length – blocked the path towards reform and reconciliation.

Keeping the peace

On the streets, meanwhile, the keynote of the British Army approach was conciliation. Viewing itself as essentially a peacekeeping force, the army set out to defuse the confrontation between Protestant and Catholic by creating a climate of security, with the eventual aim of handing back responsibility for order to a reformed RUC. The army presence was generally expected to last a matter of months, rather than years.

The first objective was to 'talk down' the barricades that had been thrown up in the heat of the August rioting. Local army commanders were instructed to establish contact with people who could be regarded as exercising some authority or commanding respect in a

given district, and to cooperate with them in restoring normality. By this means agreement to dismantle the barricades was achieved, although at the expense of scandalising the Loyalist population, since many of the community leaders in Catholic areas were well-known nationalists or longstanding members of the IRA. In Republican circles there were also many who felt a sense of outrage or irony at the turn events had taken – the British Army was, after all, the ultimate traditional enemy for the Republican movement. The sight of IRA leaders cooperating with the 'Brits' was to play an important part in motivating the split within the IRA that led to the formation of the Provisionals some months later.

However, in these early months the army was undoubtedly popular with the Catholics, and its first serious clash with the local population was a confrontation with Union-Flag-waving Protestants. This confrontation was occasioned by the publication of the conclusions of Lord Hunt's inquiry into the RUC and B-Specials on Friday 10 October. The Hunt Report's recommendations, immediately endorsed by the British government, called for the disbandment of the B-Specials and the disarming of the RUC. On the Saturday night of 11/12 October Protestant rioters confronted the police (including a contingent of B-Specials) and the army on the Shankill Road; among them were armed Protestant paramilitaries. According to the

Left: A British soldier, alert to danger, prepares to move against rioters. His weapon is used to fire rubber bullets, two of which are in his hand. Above: A scene familiar in the early 1970s: British soldiers face a hostile crowd.

army, the gunmen opened fire, and by a bitter irony killed Constable Victor Arbuckle, the first RUC man to die in the Troubles. After 90 minutes of restraint, the army returned fire and sent in snatch squads against the rioters; two Protestants were killed and many injured. The events of that night confirmed the general impression that the British Army was siding with the Catholics – it was Ian Paisley, rather than the IRA, who first described the army as 'like the SS'. It also seemed to show that strong military action could work to contain disorder: for almost nine months after this army display of force, no guns were used on the streets of Ulster.

Yet during that period, the initial Catholic support for the British Army presence and British government policies was lost. There were several reasons for this. First, the pace of reform was slow and did not satisfy the expectations aroused in August 1969. British policy was to avoid over-hasty measures which could alienate the Protestant majority, while attempting to satisfy minority aspirations – under the circumstances, an impossible compromise. But in any case, the most important Catholic needs – an end to high unemployment and poor housing – had no

short-term solutions. Throughout early 1970 many in the minority community grew sceptical of the promises of change. In January 1970 the Ulster Defence Regiment (UDR) was formed as part of the British Army. Despite efforts to attract Catholics to the new force, however, only 18% of its early intake was from the minority population, while it was noted that large numbers of former B-Specials were enrolled. Suspicions were inevitably aroused that the Specials were effectively back in a new guise.

As reform marked time, the British Army became inexorably identified with the Protestant authorities. The army had been deployed 'in support of the civil power', and the civil power in Ulster was still the Protestant establishment. In their everyday duties, British soldiers inevitably cooperated closely with the Protestant-dominated police and law courts; at a higher level, the British commander, Lieutenant-General Sir Ian Freeland, was in close contact with the Protestant political leaders. This British–Protestant cooperation was observed by the Catholics both at street level and through the media.

The discontent at the pace of reform and apparent British support for continuing Protestant domination only turned to a sense of open hostility, however, through the abrasive experience of military action on the streets. Standing between the two sides in Ulster, the army was bound to find itself eventually engaged in some serious confrontation with Catholic rioters. After a smattering of incidents involving stone-throwing youths – with the occasional nail- or petrol-bomb attack as well – on 1 April 1970 the situation seriously threatened to get out of hand. Near the Ballymurphy estate in Belfast, a group of

Junior Orangemen was attacked by a Catholic crowd. The intervention of soldiers of the Royal Scots to protect the Protestants only escalated the fighting, soon aimed chiefly at the soldiers themselves. The following day it took 600 troops, five armoured cars and 100 CS-gas canisters to quell the riots. Freeland announced that youths throwing petrol bombs or nail bombs were liable to be shot, and more troops were sent to Ulster. It was the top of a slippery slope; the army had now found itself in the same position as the RUC the previous summer, defending Orangemen against Catholics. There was little Catholic goodwill left.

Organised force

Meanwhile the force that was to exploit the new crisis gathering in Ulster had begun to organise itself: it was, of course, the Provisional IRA. The events of the summer of 1969 had caught the IRA in Northern Ireland completely unprepared to fulfil its traditional role of defender of the Catholic enclaves. The slogan 'IRA – I Ran Away' appeared daubed on the walls of west Belfast and Londonderry. Dissension was rife within the IRA, which since 1963 had been under the leadership of Cathal Goulding in Dublin. Opposition to Goulding's long-term policy of non-military action in pursuit of socialist goals flared up afresh, while the local leadership in Northern Ireland faced hostility from those who rejected cooperation with the British Army. In December 1969 Goulding's Irish Republican Army Council finally provoked a split in the

movement by announcing recognition of the Dublin, Stormont and Westminster governments, effectively accepting the division of Ireland at least as a *fait accompli*. A group of dissenters, led by Sean MacStiofain (John Stephenson), a member of the Dublin IRA leadership, set up a 'Provisional Army Council'. The IRA's political wing, Sinn Fein, was soon to follow suit. From then onwards, Goulding's movement was known as the Official IRA (OIRA), and the breakaway organisation as the Provisional IRA (PIRA). In the North the IRA split in the same way.

The leaders of the Provisionals were IRA activists of long standing, even if some had been alienated from the movement for some years. The impulse behind their breakaway was a return to the IRA's roots – they wanted armed action to achieve the famous 'full national demand' of British withdrawal from Ulster. As well as the English-born MacStiofain – a deeply religious Catholic who had served in the Royal Air Force and had also spent a spell in a British gaol for his part in the Felsted School arms raid in 1953 – the Provisional leaders in the South were Ruairi O Bradaigh (Rory Brady) and Daithi O Conaill (David O'Connell). In the North, the prominent figures were Seamus Twomey, Joe Cahill and Billy McKee. It was McKee who became the first chief of staff of the Belfast Brigade; two other brigades were set up in the North, for Londonderry and the border area.

Despite this pretentious organisation, in the first half of 1970 the Provisionals were extremely weak: they probably numbered no

Above left: Sean MacStiofain, the first chief of staff of the Provisional IRA. An English-born Irish nationalist, MacStiofain was the man responsible for organising armed opposition to the RUC and army in 1970–71, and is credited with initiating the use of 'one-shot' snipers on the streets of Northern Ireland. On the right in the photograph is Seamus Twomey, one of the more extreme Provisional leaders: he organised the car-bomb offensive in Belfast in 1972 which did much to escalate the violence.
Right: Joe Cahill, chief of staff of the Belfast Brigade of the Provisional IRA in the early 1970s. He was one of the IRA's 'old guard', linking the Troubles with the 1956–62 campaign.

more than 30 or 40 members in Belfast, for example, where the OIRA could certainly muster well over 100 men. Money and arms were in very short supply. But the events of the summer of 1970 allowed the Provisionals to emerge as a major force in the North.

By June 1970, the situation in the province had once more reached breaking point. In the absence of any serious political initiative, it was to be expected – and was expected by the security forces – that serious trouble would once more erupt. The authorities anticipated that the 12 July Orange parade would be the signal for an outburst of rioting, and three battalions of reinforcements were earmarked to strengthen the British Army presence in the first week of July. By mischance, the calculations were wrong: trouble broke out in the last week of June.

Gunmen on the streets

The starting point for rioting was by now familiar. On 27 June an Orange march in the Springfield Road area of Belfast provided an opportunity for Catholics and Protestants from neighbouring communities to engage in mutual taunting and abuse, soon escalating through the throwing of missiles into running battles on the street, with the security forces attempting to separate the two sides and themselves becoming the object of attacks. But the scale of fighting on the night of 27/28 June was beyond anything seen since the previous August. As rioting spread to many areas of Belfast, the army was overstretched and lost control. In the Ardoyne and Short Strand districts Protestant and Catholic gunmen exchanged fire; by dawn five civilians were dead, and two more were later to die of wounds sustained that night.

The fighting in the Short Strand was the Provisionals' first armed action. The Short Strand district is a peculiarly isolated Catholic

enclave, and in the desperate effort to cope with widespread disturbances the security forces had left it unprotected. A Protestant crowd led by gunmen attacked a Catholic church in the district – St Matthew's – and it was defended by the Provisionals. A prolonged gunfight left Belfast chief of staff McKee badly wounded, but the Protestant attack was repulsed. This action permitted the Provisionals to claim that they had defended the Catholic community when the security forces had not.

Above left: The innocents begin to suffer: a small boy, hit by an army rubber bullet, is rushed to a first-aid post. Although designed to control rioters by administering a sharp blow, the rubber bullet could do more permanent damage to the very young, frail or old. Its replacement, the plastic round, has also been proved dangerous if fired from close range.
Above: As a rioter is dragged away, a snatch-squad of Royal Anglians keeps the crowd at bay. The inadequate nature of early pattern shields is well illustrated.
Left: A shocked soldier of the Royal Green Jackets, wounded by a nail bomb, is helped into an army vehicle.

The events of 27 June could not be ignored: not only had there been shooting and deaths, but also incendiary attacks on shops in central Belfast, looting on the Crumlin Road, and the occupation of a police station in Ballymurphy by rioters. Although the army knew that lack of the reinforcements due to arrive the following week had been crucial to its failure to control events, it was inevitable that the whole style of security operation so far adopted should come in for criticism. The Stormont government and its Unionist supporters had long argued that the army should take a tougher line, rather than follow the policy of containment and conciliation. They now felt their arguments had received powerful confirmation. By chance, a new Conservative government had just come to power in Westminster which was more inclined to support tough security policies.

Despite having a close relationship of long standing with the Ulster Unionists, the Conservatives had largely supported the policies of Wilson's Labour government with regard to Northern Ireland. After the Tories' election victory in June 1970, however, they suddenly faced the renewal of large-scale violence in Belfast. The new home secretary, Reginald Maudling, backed an agreement between the Ulster leaders and General Freeland on 1 July that a display of force would help to prevent further rioting.

On 3 July the army received a tip-off that arms were to be found in a certain house in Balkan Street, in the Catholic Lower Falls area of Belfast. That afternoon·a unit of the Royal Scots moved in, sealed off the street and searched the house. Their information turned out to be correct: they discovered 12 pistols, a World War II Schmeisser sub-machine gun, explosives and ammunition – all belonging, as it turned out, to the OIRA, who were strongly represented in the Lower Falls.

The Falls Road curfew

It was as the soldiers tried to move off with their booty that the trouble started. They were surrounded by an angry crowd and as they sought to force their way out of the street, a man was crushed by an armoured car. Within minutes, rioters had gathered from throughout the district, and the Royal Scots were forced to radio for help as missile-throwing youths pinned them down in defensive positions. More army units quickly went in to their aid, firing large quantities of CS gas. Confusion reigned as the gas blanketed the area; many residents as yet uninvolved in the fighting were outraged to find themselves victims of the drifting gas, and rushed to join in. All around the Lower Falls barricades went up – passing buses or other vehicles were commandeered for the purpose. Nail bombs and petrol bombs rained on the army. By 8pm the troops had withdrawn to form a cordon around the Lower Falls. They had already suffered serious casualties – a hand grenade had injured five men of the 1st Battalion, Royal Regiment of Fusiliers standing unwisely close together.

Under the newly agreed policy of tougher action to enforce order, the army was not, as it might have been in earlier months, ordered to contain the situation while efforts were made to defuse the confrontation; instead,

Above: Catholic women and children march towards a British Army barricade on the Falls Road during the curfew of 3/4 July 1970. Militarily the curfew may have been justified but politically it was a poor move, alienating the Catholics and driving a wedge between the army and the people they had been brought in to protect.
Right: The face of modern terrorism: a member of the Provisional IRA, in balaclava hood and combat jacket, poses for the camera. The only link with the past is the Thompson sub-machine gun, traditional weapon of the IRA since the Troubles in the 1920s.

they were instructed to restore control of the Lower Falls immediately. As units were sent in to dismantle the barricades, a night of confused fighting began. The OIRA organised snipers while youths attacked advancing troops with petrol and gelignite bombs. At 10pm the army announced a curfew, but the skirmishes continued. Sniping was heavy at times – 13 soldiers received bullet wounds during the course of the night. It was later alleged, however, that the army had been far too free with their firearms, firing possibly over 1500 rounds during the fighting. Some of the units thrown into the conflict had just arrived from England and were quite unprepared for conditions in Belfast. By the morning, five civilians had been killed, four shot and one run over by a military vehicle. The

Armalite Assault Rifle

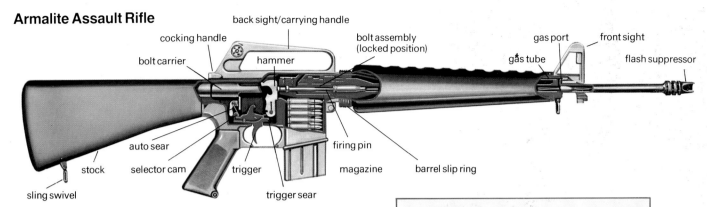

cocking handle · back sight/carrying handle · bolt assembly (locked position) · gas port · front sight

bolt carrier · hammer · gas tube · flash suppressor

auto sear · firing pin

stock · selector cam · trigger · magazine · barrel slip ring

sling swivel · trigger sear

army claimed only to have fired at bomb-throwers and snipers, but it seems probable that all the dead were innocent observers – one, for example, was a Polish photographer.

The curfew in the Lower Falls was not lifted when morning came. It was maintained for 36 hours (with a two-hour break for shopping after protests that the population was being starved), during which time the army carried out a house-to-house search of the entire area. Substantial quantities of arms, ammunition and explosives were uncovered, vindicating the operation in purely military terms. But the effect of the curfew on Catholic opinion was disastrous. The damage to property involved in searching a house for arms was a minor factor compared with the moral humiliation felt by innocent Catholics in having their homes turned upside down by troops. The house-to-house search was an indiscriminate measure which, like CS gas, affected all residents of whatever shade of political opinion. When the curfew was finally lifted, two Unionist ministers were driven around the Lower Falls by the army; this confirmed the Catholics in their view that the British Army was the agent of their Protestant enemies.

The chief beneficiary of the Lower Falls curfew was the PIRA. Clearly identified with the policy of armed action to drive the British out of Ulster, and credited with the successful defence of the Short Strand against the Protestants in June, the Provisionals received a flood of recruits. The disaffected youth of the Catholic areas, their lives circumscribed by poverty and unemployment, joined in such numbers that by the beginning of 1971 the Provisionals could count on over 1000 volunteers in Belfast alone. As many as possible of these were given about ten days' basic training in some remote location in the Irish Republic or in the rural border areas of Ulster. Simultaneously, the Provisionals undertook a major effort to obtain arms and explosives for their expanding army. Despite flirtation with various possible backers, including east European countries and Colonel Gaddafi's Libya, the main source of arms was

Above: Cutaway drawing of the 5.56mm calibre Armalite, a commercially available version of the US Army's M16 assault rifle. When the Provisional IRA began to rearm in 1970–71, they turned for help to the Irish nationalists in the United States, who supplied significant numbers of Armalites, increasing the hitting power of the gunmen and enabling them to mount devastating sniper attacks on the security forces.
Right, centre: The Armalite was not the only new weapon acquired by the Provisionals in the early 1970s; here an IRA gunman aims a 7.62mm calibre FN FAL, of the type known to the British Army as the Self Loading Rifle (SLR).
Right, bottom: A British soldier advances warily down a street in Nothern Ireland, his 7.62mm SLR at the ready. The lack of anti-riot protection dates this photograph in the early months of the Troubles, before the issue of appropriate equipment.

Armalite Assault Rifle

Calibre 5.56mm
Length 99cm (39in)
Weight (loaded with 30-round magazine) 3.82kg (8.42lb)
Rate of fire Cyclical 700-900rpm; practical automatic 150-200rpm; practical semi-automatic 45-65rpm
Maximum effective range 460m (500yds)
Magazine 20 or 30-round box
Cartridge M193 5.56×45mm round
Muzzle velocity 1000mps (3280 fps)

from the outset, as it has remained, the Irish population of the United States. The Irish Northern Aid Committee (Noraid) was founded in the United States in 1970 by Michael Flannery, a veteran of the Troubles of the 1920s, and other like-minded people, to raise funds (ostensibly for humanitarian aid) for Northern Ireland. It was from America that the Provisionals were to obtain their most characteristic weapon, the Armalite rifle, a commercially available equivalent of

the US Army's M16. However, in these early days the supply of arms was a mere trickle and many of the weapons available to the Provisionals were elderly bolt-action rifles or Thompson sub-machine guns.

PIRA strategy

The Provisionals were not keen to take on the security forces as they attempted to train and organise their young recruits. In any case, attitudes within the Provisionals remained ambiguous, with a defensive mentality concentrating on the protection of the Catholic enclaves tending to prevail over wider long-term ambitions to reunify Ireland by an aggressive campaign. Thus the second half of 1970 was relatively quiet. Incidents which alienated the Catholic population continued to accumulate as the British Army coped forcefully with the sporadic rioting which was now becoming a more or less standard response to their presence on the streets of some Catholic enclaves. It was widely felt that the courts were biased in the treatment of those arrested by the army, sending Catholics to prison for relatively trivial offences while Protestants received suspended sentences for more serious crimes.

Whatever the truth of allegations of unjust punishments and the use of excessive force by the security forces – many Protestants felt that, on the contrary, the army and the courts were too soft on rioters – this Catholic

perception of events continued to breed discontent. Responding to the changing mood among Catholics, on 21 August 1970 six anti-Unionist Stormont MPs, including Gerry Fitt and John Hume, formed the Social Democratic and Labour Party (SDLP). They were against violence, but committed to achieving reform in Ulster and the eventual reunification of Ireland. They wished to wrest back the leadership of the minority community from the 'men of violence' and achieve some real political progress which, they thought, might prevent the situation deteriorating any further.

The programme of reforms forced on the Stormont government by the British government in 1969 was beginning to reach the statute books. Two Electoral Law Acts had by the spring of 1971 brought Northern Ireland's franchise into line with Britain's, ending the anomalies which the civil rights movement had exposed. Another civil rights demand, for the allocation of council housing on a fair points system, had also in principle been met. Achieving an end to the discrimination deeply entrenched in Ulster's political and economic system was not an easy matter, however, despite the establishment of complaints procedures and a Community Relations Commission. Many Protestants at all levels of government were, to say the least, unenthusiastic about reform. Pushing through the reform legislation damaged prime minister Chichester-Clark's standing

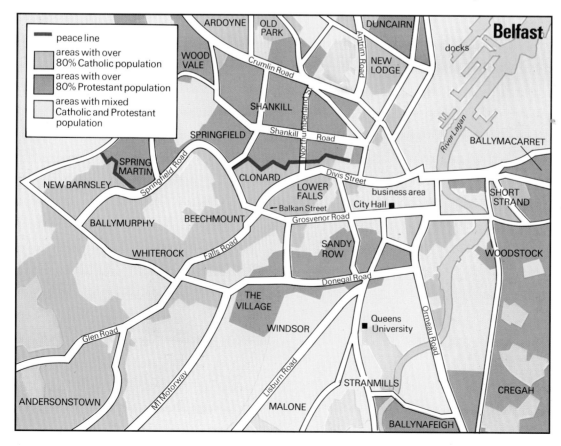

Above left: Gerry Fitt, leader of the Catholic-supported Social Democratic and Labour Party in Northern Ireland, photographed outside his heavily protected home in west Belfast in 1979. A civil rights activist in the late 1960s, Fitt helped to found the SDLP as a moderate, constitutional party, but this policy attracted violence from extremists on both sides of the sectarian divide.
Left: Map of Belfast, showing the 'tribal' divisions.
Above right: Rescuers, including soldiers and firemen, pull survivors from the wreckage of a building in Belfast bombed by the IRA in 1972.
Right: Catholics prepare to defend their homes, early 1970s. Empty bottles, part filled with petrol and fitted with a wick, make potentially lethal weapons.

with his less flexible backbenchers and constituents. On the other hand, it won little support or gratitude from the Catholic community. Events had got beyond the point at which legislative changes alone could repair the damage.

It was during the early months of 1971 that the situation in Northern Ireland began to slip from communal disorder towards urban guerrilla warfare. The process may be said to have begun with events in the Ballymurphy area of west Belfast during January. Security in Ballymurphy was the responsibility of the 2nd Battalion, Royal Anglian Regiment, whose local commander was making a good job of the well-established policy of using contacts with local leaders of the community

to defuse conflict. By 1971, the local people the soldiers were talking to were members of the PIRA. The Provisionals were keen to obtain the degree of legitimacy of their authority in the area that the army seemed to confer – it seems clear that, in the absence of normal police patrols, the PIRA was expected to play a role in maintaining order – and did

not want any confrontation with the British at this premature stage. On 10 January, however, stone-throwing by local youths began, developing the following day into rioting on a considerable scale. In response, on 14 January, the army penetrated the enclave in force – 700 troops carried out house-to-house searches in the face of petrol bombs,

bottles of sulphuric acid and some gunfire. By 16 January the riots had subsided, but by then they had precipitated a slow-motion political crisis.

Major Chichester-Clark's position had been weakening over the previous six months; to stay in power he needed to convince the Protestant rank-and-file that he could see to it that order was upheld. On 16 January he informed the British government that he would resign if they refused to take a stronger line, including the introduction of internment without trial – allowed for under the Special Powers Act – and the dispatch of more troops to Ulster. All he obtained from home secretary Maudling was a statement that the army was permitted to take the offensive against the IRA. Chichester-Clark did not resign, but his hold on power was precarious. At the end of January, the hardline Unionist William Craig caused a political storm by revealing the army's policy on the Catholic areas to the general public – he alleged, quite accurately, that the army was effectively allowing the Provisionals to control parts of Ulster's cities. The army had to respond by asserting its authority.

On 3 February 1971 the 2nd Battalion, Royal Anglians cordoned and searched the Catholic Clonard and Ardoyne areas of Belfast. On the following two nights, the army faced bitter rioting in which eight soldiers were injured, five of them in one burst of Thompson machine-gun fire on the New Lodge Road. Worse was to come: on 6 February, 20-year-old Gunner Robert Curtis became the first British soldier to be killed in the present Ulster crisis, shot dead by a

Provisional sniper in the New Lodge Road. That same night, two Catholics were killed, one a member of the Provisionals. Seven soldiers were wounded. The next day, Chichester-Clark declared that 'Northern Ireland is at war with the IRA Provisionals.'

The British government still ignored Chichester-Clark's increasingly frantic requests for tougher measures to satisfy his party. On 10 March 1971, three young Scottish soldiers were shot in the back of the head after being lured out of a country pub near Belfast; these murders outraged Protestant opinion against the Provisionals, and indirectly sealed Chichester-Clark's fate. Once again he requested more troops and a more aggressive approach, but only a small increase in army numbers was granted by the British government. This time Chichester-Clark did resign, to be replaced by Brian Faulkner.

Faulkner was an astute and able politician, but by the time he was installed in office the security situation in the province was rapidly deteriorating as the PIRA moved increasingly onto the offensive. Sniper-fire was becoming a daily hazard for the army and the police, but the main thrust of the Provisionals' campaign was an ever-growing number of bombings, aimed chiefly at commercial premises. There had been sporadic bomb attacks during 1970, but this was now a concerted campaign on an unprecedented scale. There were 37 bombings in April 1971, 47 in May, 50 in June, and 91 in July. According to the Provisionals, the aim was twofold: to put the army at full stretch, thus distracting it from operations in the Catholic areas, and to ruin the Ulster economy, inflicting highly expensive damage for which the British would have to pay. The bombing campaign was also an effective way of hitting at Protestants, since the business life of Ulster was largely in their hands. The choice of the bomb as a weapon was clearly dictated by practical considerations – the Provisionals were not sufficiently numerous, well equipped or trained to take on the security forces directly. But a bombing campaign was very difficult for the authorities to stop.

Bombs and bombers

At first the bombers depended on stolen gelignite from both north and south of the border. When controls on gelignite were tightened up, they turned to mixes of readily available chemicals to make their explosives. Fertilisers were an especially fruitful base for bombs, along with such everyday items as sugar, washing soda and Epsom salts. Many of the resultant blends were highly unstable, taking their toll of bomb-makers and would-be bomb-planters. The primitive timing de-

vices used – such as a fuse attached to an alarm-clock – also led to some premature explosions. But the high level of recruitment to the Provisionals made such losses of personnel – known to the security forces as 'own goals' – relatively acceptable.

The early bombs were generally small – typically about 5 kilograms of explosives in a duffel-bag or holdall. With increasing technical skill and better-organised supplies of explosives, however, the Provisionals began to use larger bombs against bigger targets. Some care was taken to avoid civilian casualties, but about 100 people were injured in bombings during the first half of 1971.

Against this background of sniping, bombing and rioting, Brian Faulkner launched a striking political initiative. Faulkner was a strong believer in tough measures against the IRA, and from the moment he became Stormont prime minister in March he began pushing the British towards acceptance of internment as a necessary security measure. But at the same time, he recognised the need to detach the Catholic community from support for violence and to win their allegiance to Stormont. Accordingly, in June he proposed that the chairmanship of two new committees examining crucial areas of government policy should be handed to the non-Unionists. By Ulster standards, this was a remarkable gesture towards sharing power with the minority community. It was favourably received by the opposition representatives at Stormont, and preliminary discussions

started with a view to implementing the arrangement.

But it was not to be. Events at street level overtook the political discussions. In early July the Bogside district of Londonderry was the scene of prolonged riots, met by the army with rubber bullets, CS gas and other crowd-control gear. On 7–8 July, however, the army twice used live ammunition to deadly effect, killing two local men, Seamus Cusack and Desmond Beattie. The army asserted that both men had been carrying firearms (in Beattie's case this assertion quickly changed to the version that he was throwing a bomb), but Bogsiders were adamant that neither man had been involved in violence of any kind. The deaths caused a political storm: the Social Democratic and Labour Party (SDLP) leaders demanded that the British government set up a public inquiry into the events. The request was refused, and on 15 July the SDLP members withdrew from the Stormont parliament. The Faulkner initiative was aborted.

Internment

There still remained the other half of Faulkner's policy, however – the introduction of internment. The British government had effectively been no more favourably disposed to Faulkner's first approach on the subject than they had to that of his predecessor. But in April a working party of British military intelligence officers and RUC Special Branch men was established to draw up a list

of possible internees, in case the need should arise. Their level of intelligence about the PIRA was very poor: it is reported that after Billy McKee was arrested in March 1971 it took the intelligence services five months to find out the name of his successor as Belfast Brigade commander – Joe Cahill. About the lower ranks of the Provisionals, the mass of young recruits who had joined since mid-1970, the police and army knew nothing. Thus the list of possible internees they drew up – numbering about 500 – was predominantly composed of old-style Republicans and OIRA men, on whom they were much better informed, along with a few civil rights activists from the pre-1969 movement.

The working party was still considering who to put on their list when the security situation in Northern Ireland took another turn for the worse. First, on 16 July a PIRA prisoner who was receiving medical treat-ment in the Royal Victoria Hospital, Belfast, was seized from under the noses of his guards by four men armed with sub-machine guns.

Immediately after this humiliation for the security forces, on 17 July, the Provisionals carried out their largest-scale bombing yet, destroying a new £2 million *Daily Mirror* printing plant at Dunmurry. Two days later, Faulkner telephoned British prime minister Edward Heath and told him that, in his opinion, the time for internment had come.

The British General Officer Commanding in Northern Ireland, General Sir Harry Tuzo (who had replaced Freeland the previous February), was known to be against internment, but when pressed by the British government he could offer no alternative means of bringing the situation under control. The British government, for its part, continued to be sceptical about the effectiveness of internment, yet recognised that at the very least a gesture was needed to prop up the Stormont government and if possible restore some confidence in Ulster. The only serious alternative was direct rule, a measure to which the Conservative government was even more averse than the previous Labour government had been. There were long-established links between the Conservative Party and the Unionists; it would have gone very much against the grain for the Tories to deprive the Unionist Party of its power. Besides, for 50 years Westminster had avoided any direct involvement in Irish affairs, and many in London still believed that the British government could confine its role to influencing policy behind the scenes. On 5 August 1971, Brian Faulkner visited London to meet the British government leaders. Lacking an alternative, they agreed to introduce internment.

Far left: British troops, on the alert for a possible sniper attack, stand guard as a building burns in Belfast. Left: Catholic women warn of an approaching security-force patrol, banging dustbin lids on the road and blowing whistles. The Catholics had welcomed the soldiers as protectors in August 1969 – but by 1972 the alienation was complete. Above: Using the shelter of a street corner, an army squad fires rubber bullets and CS gas into a rioting mob. Below: A blood-spattered rioter is seized by an army snatch-squad.

Operation Demetrius

It is now generally accepted that internment was a disaster. Even judged in technical terms as a security operation, it was clumsy and inefficient. Preliminary efforts by the army to improve intelligence while awaiting a decision during the last weeks of July involved a lot of untoward activity which alerted the IRA to what was to come. Then, at the last minute, the internment sweep had to be carried out ahead of schedule. Originally, Operation Demetrius, as it was known to the army, was scheduled for 10 August. But on 7 August an innocent Catholic, Harry Thornton, was driving down the Springfield Road in Belfast when his van backfired opposite an RUC post; believing he had heard a gunshot, a soldier outside the police post fired on the van and Thornton was killed. The subsequent rioting was so fierce that the internment sweep was brought forward by 24 hours.

At 4.15am on 9 August the army moved into Catholic areas throughout Northern Ireland with orders to pick up some 450 individuals. The Catholic response surpassed

The special interrogations

There was nothing new about most of the techniques employed by interrogators to get information out of suspects picked up for internment: mental stress, physical fear and exhaustion were induced by forms of rough treatment that were no more than a systematic extension of procedures already common in security-force operations. These included wall-standing and occasional blows to sensitive parts of the body. Wall-standing was an accepted procedure for searching subjects in the street, but the position involved – legs apart, arms raised above head height against the wall, feet one metre from the base of the wall, pulling the weight of the body onto the toes and fingers – could produce oxygen fatigue, cramp, and eventual loss of consciousness if sustained for long periods. Hooding was another technique widely employed in interrogation, although officially intended only to prevent visual contact between suspects and make them easier to control.

In the case of 14 suspects, however, an experimental form of interrogation in depth was applied, involving elements of the standard techniques combined with original methods of breaking down mental resistance. Nato intelligence services had been interested in 'sensory deprivation' or 'disorientation' techniques since the 1960s, initially because of their potential effect on their own men if used by the Russians. But the possible usefulness of sensory deprivation in counter-insurgency operations was not lost on them. In April 1971

Left: The RUC interrogation centre at Castlereagh, location for numerous allegations of police brutality and torture.

members of the RUC Special Branch received training in these techniques at an English intelligence centre, and the introduction of internment provided an opportunity to try them out.

The treatment to which the 14 men were subjected had five elements: prolonged wall-standing for 20–30 hours at a stretch, hooding for long periods, deprivation of sleep, a diet of bread and water, and exposure to continuous monotonous noise. A week of this treatment had a devastating effect on the men's mental state. They experienced hallucinations and were reportedly incapable of simple acts of memory or reasoning. Whether this was a useful state in which to interrogate a man seems doubtful, although the security forces later claimed to have obtained vital intelligence from the exercise.

The case of these 14 men became the main

focus of more general public disquiet over interrogation techniques in Northern Ireland. In March 1972 the British government announced that sensory deprivation would no longer be used, but the Irish government nevertheless accused Britain of torture before the European Court of Human Rights. The judgment of the court, delivered in 1978, declared that sensory deprivation did not 'occasion suffering of the particular intensity and cruelty implied by the word torture', but affirmed that it did constitute 'inhuman and degrading treatments', stating that 'the five techniques ... caused, if not actual bodily injury, at least intense physical and mental suffering ... and also led to acute psychiatric disturbances during interrogation.'

The men involved in the case all took civil action for damages in the courts, receiving payments of up to £25,000 each.

the authorities' worst fears. Obstruction of the army's efforts to carry out the arrests started immediately; the approach of the soldiers was greeted with a cacophony of dustbin lids beaten by local residents to warn men who suspected their names might be on the list. Quickly, a more violent reaction developed and the streets of Belfast and Londonderry were the scene of prolonged fighting, in some places lasting several days. Catholic rioters and snipers took on the army with unprecedented ferocity. Protestants seized the opportunity to join in, assaulting Catholic areas, in many cases with firearms. As in 1969 whole streets were burned out. Within 48 hours 23 people had been killed or mortally wounded, 19 of them civilians. In the panic, some 7000 Catholics sought temporary refuge in camps south of the border made available by the Irish government. Within days of the introduction of internment, it was clear that, far from improving, the security situation had worsened sharply.

In the initial army operation on 9 August, 342 of the planned 450 people were arrested. After they had been taken to holding centres

and interrogated, 116 of the original 342 were released – in itself a revelation of the poverty of the intelligence on which the internment list had been based. According to the Provisionals, probably a reliable source on this point, 56 of their members were among those arrested, about half the number of Provi-

sionals whose names had been on the internment list. Many allegations of brutal treatment by the security forces during interrogation of internees were made, and the case of 14 men singled out for special in-depth interrogation, including prolonged sensory deprivation, was to become an international

Left: An early attempt at 'hearts and minds': British soldiers relax with local girls in an army-run club. Such fraternisation, clearly a threat to the Provisionals' grip on Catholic areas, soon ceased in the face of violent intimidation.

cause célèbre. It seems clear that, although crude physical torture in the manner of a South American military regime was ruled out, the security forces were keen to exploit the opportunity offered to obtain the information they needed and were well aware that such information was unlikely to be provided voluntarily. The result was much rough treatment, stopping short of certain loosely defined limits. Many of the recipients of this treatment were totally innocent of any connection with terrorism.

The stories of ill-treatment which soon emerged in the press provoked demands for a public inquiry from Catholic political leaders that found a sympathetic echo in the Westminster parliament. On 31 August the British government appointed a commission of inquiry under Sir Edmund Compton, and a second inquiry was conducted by Lord Parker of Waddington the following year. Both inquiries reached a generally similar conclusion that there had been 'ill-treatment' but no 'brutality'. On 2 March 1972 the British government announced a tightening-up of controls over interrogation.

Catholic outrage

Understandably, Catholic resentment was not appeased by these inquiries. The vast majority of the Catholic population was outraged by the interrogation techniques and by internment itself. Arrests continued into the winter: by mid-December, 1576 people had been pulled in for questioning and 642 of them had been interned, mostly at Long Kesh camp, near Lisburn, and on the depot ship HMS *Maidstone* in Belfast harbour. As can be seen from these figures, the security forces' intelligence remained woefully inadequate, leading to many mistakes. This clumsiness was exploited deliberately by the Provisionals, who on more than one occasion fed the army a false tip-off, so that soldiers arrested someone known by their local community to be harmless, confirming people's worst opinion of the security forces.

It would be wrong to suggest that internment completely failed to harm the Provisionals' organisation. Enough members were interned to have an impact, but it was as nothing to the increase in support for the Provisionals generated in Catholic areas of Ulster and overseas in the crucially important Irish-American community. The immediate effect on the security situation in Northern Ireland is vividly conveyed by the relevant statistics: in the seven months of 1971 before internment there were 13 security-force and 17 civilian deaths, whereas for the five months of the year after internment the numbers killed were 46 and 97 respectively. The number of bombings continued to rise,

Right: The Provisional IRA's answer to fraternisation: a young Catholic girl, accused of friendship with a British soldier, is tied to a lamppost, her head shaved and her body tarred and feathered, as a warning to others. Such attacks, usually carried out by the women's section of the Provisional IRA, effectively ended all contact between the army and local civilians in certain areas.

topping 100 for the first time in August, and the size of bombs grew. By the end of the year the Provisionals were using huge car-bombs to wreck city streets. The predominantly Catholic border areas of the province also became an increasingly dangerous area for the army – between September and November they were fired on 243 times in rural districts. In October the army adopted a policy of cratering roads leading across into the Republic to block the movement of terrorists and arms, but they met vigorous resistance from local people who did their best to render the roads passable again.

Meanwhile, in the urban areas, the mixture of discreet negotiations and force by which the army had maintained some degree of control in the hardline Catholic enclaves broke down completely. Barricades set up around such districts as the Bogside in Londonderry and Andersonstown in Belfast in the immediate aftermath of the events of 9 August could not be 'talked down' again. The army did not acquiesce easily in this state of affairs. On 18 August, for example, they moved into the Bogside and Creggan districts of Londonderry in force at dawn and dismantled the barricades, but faced with sniper-fire and an intensely hostile popular reaction they could not sustain a presence – and the moment the soldiers withdrew, the barricades were rebuilt. Had the army been confronted only by snipers, they might well have followed a policy of penetrating the enclaves and inviting confrontation, since the British sol-

diers were generally far more skilled in the use of their arms than their enemy and almost always inflicted heavier casualties than they received in gun battles. But the army had no answer to the rioting crowds, armed only with projectiles, who assembled whenever soldiers appeared on the Catholic streets. The rioters could not be controlled, and thus an army presence merely fomented disorder. In general, to avoid this, soldiers were ordered not to enter the Catholic areas, which became 'No-Go' areas for the army.

Behind the barricades, the Provisionals held sway. For the first time, armed Provis-

Above: Masked members of the Provisional IRA man a 'security check' at the entrance to the 'Free Derry' No-Go area, Londonderry, 1971. Such shows of terrorist strength prompted the army's move into the No-Go areas in July 1972. Below left: A corporal of the Parachute Regiment, armed with an SLR, takes up position on a street corner in Belfast.

ionals appeared openly on the streets, even manning barricades as regular checkpoints. They imposed their own, often brutal, law and order, imposing severe punishments both on common criminals and on those suspected of informing or associating with the British. Such punishments as kneecapping or tarring-and-feathering did not help the Provisionals' popularity with most Catholics, but fear of the British Army and of the Protestants was strong enough to dictate acquiescence in intimidation. The No-Go areas offered the Provisionals perfect safe bases from which to carry on their bombing campaign.

The introduction of internment also brought a resurgence of non-violent protest by Catholics who rejected the Provisionals' terrorist methods. For the first time since 1969, there were non-violent mass demonstrations, and the Civil Rights Association (NICRA) was resuscitated to organise agitation against internment. Across Ulster, Catholics refused to pay rent or rates in protest, and Catholic representatives withdrew from participation in local government as they had already withdrawn from Stormont.

On the Protestant side of the divided province, the rising tide of violence provoked a militant response. Armed Protestants had intermittently appeared on the streets since the Troubles began – notably in October 1969 and in June 1970 – but the autumn of 1971 saw a marked growth of Protestant paramilitary

strength and an expansion of their activities. The Ulster Defence Association (UDA) was formed at this time, and was soon to become by far the most numerous paramilitary grouping, alongside the already-established Ulster Volunteer Force (UVF). The opinion was widely voiced in some Protestant circles that it was time the majority community adopted the tactics of the minority – that is, imitated the Provisionals. In December 1971, a Protestant group blew up McGurk's Bar in Belfast, killing 15 people; sectarian attacks on Catholics were soon to be one of Ulster's major problems.

Hostility and harassment

The hardening of attitudes in the face of the Provisionals' campaign was not restricted to the Protestant community, however; the British Army was also affected by the course events had taken. Although supported by the UDR and the RUC – the latter had been fully rearmed by 1971 in response to the worsening situation – the British soldiers bore the brunt of both terrorism and rioting. Their attitudes were inevitably affected, not just by the more spectacular incidents – the death or wounding of a comrade – but also by the daily experience of hostility, harassment and abuse from Catholics. Undoubtedly, some soldiers exploited the routine activities of policing the streets – such as spot-checks and searches – as an opportunity to humiliate or inflict pain on

a population which had come to be identified as an enemy. The discipline of British troops in the face of the most intense provocation during street disturbances remained on the whole remarkable, but there were increasingly frequent signs of restraint wearing thin. It was the renewal of the civil rights movement's tactic of protest marches in the teeth of the soldiers' tougher stance that was to lead to tragedy on 'Bloody Sunday' in January 1972.

All marches and demonstrations had been banned in Northern Ireland since August 1971 but the revived Civil Rights Association regarded peaceful protest as a basic human right and refused to respect the ban. In the climate of insecurity created by terrorism, they did not find it easy to generate new momentum for their marches. On Christmas Day 1971 about a thousand people tried to

march from Belfast to the internment camp at Long Kesh but were turned back by the security forces. This was not a march of sufficient size to have much impact. However, on 22 January 1972 some 3000 protesters assembled for a march along Magilligan Strand near Londonderry to the new internment camp opened in the area to take the overspill from Long Kesh. As they advanced along the beach, their path was blocked by a barrier of barbed wire manned by men of the 2nd Battalion, Royal Green Jackets and of the 1st Battalion, Parachute Regiment. Undeterred, the marchers attempted to find a way round the barrier; the soldiers proceeded to break up the march, using rubber bullets, CS gas and their batons. Leading Catholics who were present at the demonstration regarded the army response as unacceptably violent; it redoubled the Civil

Above: Hit in the leg by a nail bomb, a British Para is aided by his colleagues. Left: Magilligan Camp, County Londonderry, created to house overflow internees from Long Kesh. On 22 January 1972 over 3000 people tried to march on Magilligan in protest at internment, but were met by rubber bullets, CS gas and army baton charges.

Rights Association's determination to carry through another demonstration the following weekend.

On Sunday, 30 January, some 6000 marchers assembled in the Creggan estate in Londonderry for a march to the Old Guildhall in the city centre, where they were to be addressed by Catholic MPs Ivan Cooper and Bernadette Devlin, and by the veteran British socialist Fenner Brockway. The civil rights movement had at last regained its ability to command attention: pressmen from around the world were on hand to witness the anti-internment protest, drawn largely by the widely shared expectation that there would be trouble. Protestant extremists had threatened to attack the protesters, and there was always the possibility that the IRA, particularly strongly entrenched in the No-Go area of the Bogside known as 'Free Derry', would put in an appearance. The army, for its part, had decided that the march would not be allowed to follow its planned route but would be turned aside so that it stayed in Catholic areas of the city; they had no plans, however, to attempt to enforce the ban on marches.

The procession set off in easy-going mood, with women and children prominent in the crowd. When the marchers reached the bar-ricade in Waterloo Street set up by the army to prevent them proceeding to the Old Guildhall, their leaders redirected them to Free Derry Corner as the new venue for the speechmaking. As the march moved off to its new destination, however, about 200 stone-throwing rioters attacked the soldiers at the barricade. The army was prepared for just such an event: an 'arrest group' was positioned behind the barricade in Waterloo Street and another barricade nearby. Its role was to move forward at speed once rioters were clearly separated from peaceful demonstrators and make as many arrests as possible. The arrest group was provided by the 1st Battalion, Parachute Regiment, recently involved in the encounter on Magilligan Strand.

Thirteen shot dead

At 4.10pm a company of Paras rushed forward on foot from behind the Waterloo Street barricade and chased the rioters up Chamberlain Street, while other Paras took up positions on the flanks to block any escape. A third unit drove forward in their Pigs (Humber armoured personnel carriers) and

Above: British troops round up suspects during a 'sweep and search' operation in Londonderry, early in 1972.
Above right: The Waterloo Street barricade, Sunday, 30 January 1972; army faces mob.

dismounted behind the rioters. As this unit of Paras left their vehicles on open ground near the Rossville Flats, shooting began. Within 20 minutes, 13 Catholic civilians had been shot dead or mortally wounded and 12 others injured; all the casualties had been inflicted by the Paras, who fired a reported 107 rounds.

The army has always maintained that the soldiers opened fire because they were fired on and that, in accordance with regulations, they shot only at identified targets who were either using weapons or throwing bombs. The Widgery Tribunal set up by the British government to examine the events of the day that became known as 'Bloody Sunday' accepted that the soldiers had been fired on,

but stated that 'none of the deceased or wounded is proved to have been shot whilst handling a firearm or bomb'. Some of those killed were, in fact, demonstrably free of involvement in rioting or any other form of violence. Lord Widgery exonerated the Paras from blame for the deaths, but did allow that some individual soldiers had been 'reckless' in their firing. If true, this was a strange lapse of skill in one of the most highly trained elite regiments of the British Army.

To most Catholics, both north and south of the border, the Paras appeared to have committed straightforward murder, deliberately killing unarmed demonstrators. The sense of shock was intense. In Dublin, a crowd

marched on the British Embassy and burnt it down. More than 20,000 people attended the funerals of the victims. Britain's reputation suffered worldwide from the graphic and predominantly unfavourable television and press coverage of the shootings.

The deaths in Londonderry ended the resurgence of civil rights marches, despite a brave attempt to continue by the most committed, and gave extra impetus to the terrorist campaign. Within a fortnight of Bloody Sunday over 300 terrorist acts were recorded in Ulster and five British soldiers were killed. The Official IRA, completely overshadowed by the Provisional IRA during 1971, was stung into action: they set out to take revenge

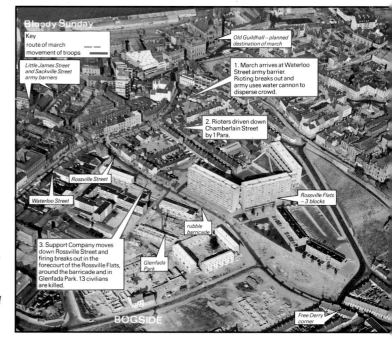

Left: Part of the huge civil rights march (some 6000 people were estimated to have taken part) in Londonderry, 30 January 1972. Most of the protesters were peaceful, accepting the decision to divert the march to Free Derry Corner, but a small proportion were intent on causing trouble; the result of the army reaction to them has gone down in history as 'Bloody Sunday'.
Right: An aerial photograph shows the scene of violence on 30 January 1972 and the course of events leading up to it. Thirteen Catholic civilians were to die that day, in circumstances that did little for the army's reputation for restraint.

Bloody Sunday

Simon Winchester, a reporter with the *Guardian* newspaper, was in Londonderry on 30 January 1972, the day that was to become known as 'Bloody Sunday'. Here he describes the events of that tragic afternoon:

'But suddenly a scream went up. "The soldiers, the soldiers!" someone yelled ahead. I looked around to my left. A line of armoured Pigs was speeding towards us: two 3-tonne lorries were roaring up; soldiers were jumping out and rushing at us. I did immediately what everyone else on the ground did: I ran forward, as hard and as fast I could.

'But then the firing started – ten or a dozen heavy, hard bangs, that two years of street experience taught me were rifle shots, and they seemed to be coming from behind. I dropped flat, tasting the dirty asphalt of the Rossville Flats forecourt, muddying my corduroys as I fell into a glass-strewn puddle. The noise stopped for a second: I was up and on again, heart pounding with fear, breath coming in strained gasps. I got to a line of bunkers under the wall of a block of the seven-storey flats. I stopped and looked around, aware of a huge and panicky crowd all around me. In the courtyard the armoured cars were slowing and turning as more and more soldiers – paratroopers, I could be sure from their camouflage jackets and their rounded helmets – jumped out and took up firing positions. And in the middle of the courtyard lay a man . . . he was badly hurt: a wound in his leg was bleeding heavily, and blood gushed out on to the asphalt where I had lain myself only seconds before.

'Then I rushed on again and into the crowded stairwell of the flats, sheltering for a few precious moments while the firing went on and on. From here I could discern both the hard rifle fire of the army SLRs and what I thought might have been the sharper cracks of .22s and the low steady thudding of a submachine gun. But there was a helicopter chugging overhead as well, and gas guns were still discharging in the background, and men and women screamed and glass crashed and voices were raised in hysterical panic, so it was difficult to be very sure. But gunfire was raging out in the open, and people, it seemed clear, were being hurt.

'I ran on and out of the stairwell, feeling by now terribly alone and vulnerable as I crossed open space. Paratroopers were crouched around the far side of Rossville Street and by another new block of flats at Glenfada Park: beside me, on the west side of the flats, lay two bodies – one a young boy, dressed in jeans, the other an older man in a brown coat. At first I had thought they were sheltering from a rain of rifle fire: I had dropped down, and a

hundred others grouped around a red phone box had dropped as well. But when the firing stopped again we all got up: the two on the ground lay still. They were dead.'

Below: The stark reality of Bloody Sunday: one of the 13 civilians shot dead by the army. A further 12 people were wounded in an incident that shocked the world.

Left: The events of 30 January 1972 caused widespread outrage, especially in the Republic of Ireland, where the British Embassy in Dublin was attacked and set ablaze.

appalling. On 20 March a bomb in Donegall Street, Belfast, killed six people and injured 147. The victims of these outrages were as likely to be Catholics as Protestants. The Provisionals' argument that civilian casualties were a regrettable accident which they did their best to avoid was of little comfort to the nerve-racked population going about its business under constant threat of sudden death or maiming.

Still, the Provisionals' military campaign was apparently achieving its aims. With a high level of recruitment in the wake of Bloody Sunday, funding and arms supplies well established, and safe bases in the No-Go areas, they were able to inflict enormous damage on the economic life of the province and heavy casualties on the security forces. Maudling, the home secretary, had accepted in December 1971 that the IRA could not be totally defeated, defining the objective of British policy as the reduction of violence to 'an acceptable level'. But the level of violence was rising, and there seemed no way the security forces could regain control. Some political initiative was obviously needed – and fast.

Direct rule

The Provisionals were keen to turn their military success into political gains. On 10 March they called a unilateral three-day truce in the hope of drawing the British government into negotiations on a 'peace plan'. The British refused the bait. Their alternative, which would allow them to avoid negotiating with terrorists, was to try to isolate the Provisionals from majority Catholic opinion. This could only mean some move to reduce the powers of Stormont or abolish it altogether, followed by a concerted effort to win back Catholic allegiance. The British government thus informed Faulkner that they intended taking over responsibility for security in Northern Ireland. Unwilling to accept this reduction of their powers, Faulkner's government resigned, and on 24 March Edward Heath announced the suspension of Stormont – initially for one year – and the appointment of a secretary of state for Northern Ireland to run the province. Direct rule from Westminster had come at last.

The first secretary of state, William Whitelaw, expected immediate trouble from the Protestant community. The Protestant backlash had been building up through the early months of 1972. On 12 February William Craig, a former Stormont minister, had

on the Parachute Regiment. On 22 February 1972 they exploded a car bomb in the Paras' Aldershot barracks – the first IRA bombing in England since the 1930s. The operation was a disaster. Instead of killing soldiers, the OIRA caused the deaths of five cleaning women, a gardener and a Roman Catholic chaplain. This tragic fiasco did much to cancel out the propaganda victory presented to the IRA by the Bloody Sunday shootings.

The violence escalates

The growing carnage from the bombing campaign in Northern Ireland also cost the PIRA support among Catholics. By March bombings were occurring at the rate of four a day, and not only property was being damaged. On 4 March a bomb in the Abercorn Restaurant in Belfast killed two people and injured 136; many of the injuries were

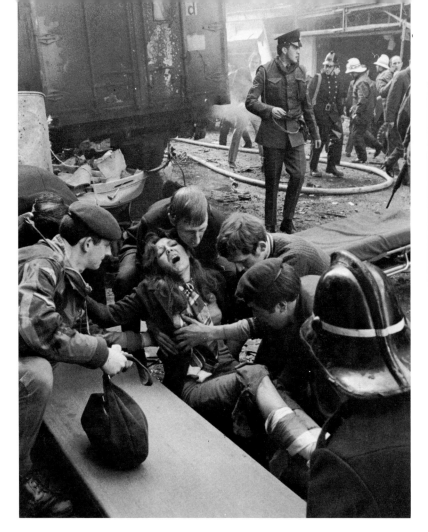

Force levels 1969-72

January 1969	3000 (normal garrison)
October 1969	8000
January 1970	7300
July 1970	11,243
January 1971	7742
August 1971	12,300
January 1972	14,218
July 1972	21,288

Deaths in Ulster 1969-72

	1969	1970	1971	1972
Army	0	0	43	103
RUC	1	2	11	17
UDR	0	0	5	25
Civilians	12	23	114	322
Total	13	25	173	467

announced the formation of the Ulster Vanguard Movement, inviting the press to a dramatically staged parade of uniformed men at Lisburn. His speech was deliberately threatening and included the warning: 'God help those who get in our way for we mean business.' The activities of members of the UVF had already brought them into internment camps alongside their Republican enemies. There was also much talk of the large quantities of arms held by Protestant groups.

Conciliation with the Catholics

Yet the suspension of Stormont, the focus of Protestant power, brought a relatively muted response. Attempts to organise a general strike quickly fell apart, and mass demonstrations led to little positive action. The Protestants felt bitter resentment and indulged in aggressive rhetoric, but the way was open for Whitelaw to pursue conciliation with the Catholics.

A low-profile approach was adopted by the security forces in dealing with the Catholic community. In effect, this involved total acquiescence in the inviolability of the No-Go areas – whereas, as recently as 14 March, a patrol of the 2nd Battalion, Royal Green Jackets had entered 'Free Derry' and provoked an intense gun battle in which two IRA men were killed. Internment was scaled

down; by 8 June, 520 internees had been released. Most Catholics were deeply suspicious of the British government, but the suspension of Stormont and the new security approach received a cautious welcome.

The Provisionals had no intention, however, of halting their campaign of violence. They viewed the prorogation of Stormont as a first victory achieved by their organisation in its armed struggle; by stepping up their operations still further, they hoped to attain their next goal – British withdrawal from Northern Ireland. During April and May, 16 British soldiers were killed in Ulster. The bombing offensive intensified: on the two days of 13–14 April, for example, 40 devices were planted. Car bombs became more frequent. On 10 May the Belfast Co-op, the largest department store in the city, was destroyed. In terms of improving the security situation, direct rule had achieved nothing.

Yet there was a strong pressure for peace building up within the Catholic community. Another foray into terrorist action by the OIRA brought it to the surface. On 19 May they murdered a 19-year-old Catholic British soldier, William Best of the Royal Irish Rangers, who was paying an off-duty visit to his home in the Bogside. Revulsion against this killing was widespread. Local women formed a peace movement and there was outspoken criticism of continuing terrorism from Catholic Church leaders and moderate

Above left: Racked with pain, a victim of the Abercorn Restaurant bombing of 4 March 1972 is lifted carefully onto a stretcher by soldiers and firemen. Planted by the Provisional IRA, the bomb was intended as retaliation for Bloody Sunday, but the indiscriminate nature of the attack alienated moderate Catholic opinion. During this period the people of Belfast went about their business under constant and nerve-racking threat of sudden death or maiming.

Catholic politicians. The OIRA felt bound to declare a truce on 29 May; the PIRA did not. Since the Provisionals were responsible for the overwhelming majority of shootings and bombings, the OIRA truce had little effect on the security situation.

As the violence continued, the British government's low-key approach to security inevitably came under heavy criticism. In protest at the army's failure to dismantle the barricades around Catholic areas, the Protestant UDA erected their own barricades, declaring that these would not be taken down until the No-Go areas were dealt with. UDA members appeared on the streets in paramilitary uniform. These gestures were mainly symbolic – in general, relations between British soldiers and the Protestants were good – but they put more pressure on the government to get results. The murder of Catholics by Protestant extremists was by now common enough to demonstrate that a full-scale armed conflict between the two communities – with the British Army in the middle – was not an impossibility.

The British government's desperate need for a solution to the crisis, parallelled by the pressure on the Provisionals from the war-weary Catholics to seek an end to hostilities, created the conditions for an attempt at a negotiated settlement. The first move came from the Provisionals. On 13 June their leaders Sean MacStiofain, Daithi O Conaill, Seamus Twomey (now Belfast Brigade commander) and Martin McGuinness offered the British a truce if Whitelaw would agree to meet them publicly. The secretary of state immediately rejected the plan, announcing that he would not negotiate with terrorists. Nevertheless, secret meetings were held between British representatives and the Provisionals to see if grounds for a truce and negotiations could be established. One stumbling block was overcome when the government granted the status and rights of political prisoners ('Special Category' status) to internees. This had been the objective of a hunger-strike begun in Long Kesh internment camp the previous month. The British also released Gerry Adams from internment – he had been nominated by the Provisionals as one of their negotiating team.

On 22 June, the Provisionals announced that they would suspend operations at midnight on 26 June, provided the British responded in kind. Whitelaw made it clear that the army would reciprocate, ceasing arrests, raids and searches. Determined to demonstrate that the truce was not dictated by military weakness, the Provisionals continued with their campaign until the last possible moment – a British soldier was shot five minutes before the midnight deadline. But operations then ceased on both sides.

PIRA ceasefire

A secret meeting between the Provisionals and Whitelaw was arranged for 7 July. MacStiofain, O Conaill, Twomey, McGuinness, Adams and Ivor Bell, along with a lawyer, Myles Shelvin, were flown to London by the RAF. They met Whitelaw in a private house in Chelsea; it was the first time that the IRA had negotiated with the British government since 1921. The Provisionals demanded a declaration that British troops would be withdrawn by January 1975, an amnesty for political prisoners, and a recognition that the inhabitants of all Ireland should decide the issue of Northern Ireland. Whitelaw was committed to the Downing Street declaration of 1969 which stated that the constitutional position of Northern Ireland could only be changed with the consent of the majority in the province – that is, the Protestants. Nevertheless, it was agreed that the truce should continue indefinitely and that there would be further negotiations.

Although it was an imperfect peace – notably, the campaign of sectarian killings instituted by Protestant extremists earlier in the year was now gathering momentum and continued unchecked – most people in Northern Ireland were deeply relieved by the break in the endless bombings and shootings.

The sense of disappointment was equally profound when the truce collapsed. On 9 July, only two days after the London meeting, trouble flared on a mixed housing estate in west Belfast. A group of UDA men set out to prevent Catholic families taking up residence in houses allocated to them on the estate; in an effort to avoid trouble, the local army commander decided to prevent the Catholics moving in; his men were soon confronted by a hostile Catholic crowd, shots were fired, and the truce was over.

There followed two weeks of mayhem and massacre. Within eight days 15 British soldiers had been killed and many more wounded. Civilian casualties were heavier. The climax came on the afternoon of 21 July, which became known as 'Bloody Friday'. Within little over an hour, between 2pm and 3pm, 19 bombs exploded within a mile radius of Belfast city centre. The area was crowded with shoppers and office workers, and although warnings were telephoned for all the bombs, the scale of the operation overwhelmed the security forces' efforts to clear threatened streets and save lives. The bombs at Oxford Street bus station and Cavehill Road shopping centre went off

Below: As Provisional IRA violence increased, so did the Protestant 'backlash', manifested here in a march of Ulster Defence Association members in 1972. The crude nature of the 'uniforms' in this show of force belies a very real threat of violence – despite the OIRA and PIRA truces, the numbers of sectarian murders rose dramatically in 1972.

before the places had been cleared, killing two soldiers and seven civilians and injuring 130. Panic and terror seized the crowds in the streets as bombs seemed to detonate on all sides. Television images of the maimed and of the remains of bodies being scooped into plastic bags shocked all who saw them. (Later a number of Protestant paramilitaries were to assert that it was these very scenes on television that provoked them into the business of sectarian murder.)

The Provisionals were unrepentant in their public stance. They accused the security forces of deliberately ignoring the telephoned warnings in order to cause civilian casualties and discredit the IRA, and they 'extended their sincere sympathy' to the relatives of the dead. But in private, even many members of the Provisionals regretted the operation. The effect on Catholic opinion was such that the Provisionals' reputation fell to an all-time low. They had been widely blamed for the breakdown of the truce with the British Army; now they had handed their opponents a propaganda victory on the same scale as Bloody Sunday.

The authorities were determined to exploit the split between the Catholic population and the Provisionals before some other event occurred to swing sympathy back the other way. It was the opportunity which the British Army and government had long awaited. Their objective was to end the No-Go areas, restoring their authority over the whole province and denying the IRA any further safe bases for their urban terrorist operations. The army immediately began preparations for what was to be known as Operation Motorman.

The British adopted the tactic of an overwhelming display of force. They did not wish to engage the Provisionals in combat,

only to occupy their territory. The best way to minimise opposition seemed to be an operation on a massive scale. On 27 July a highly publicised airlift of men and equipment into Northern Ireland began. The British presence was to be boosted by 4000 reinforcements, raising the number of soldiers to a peak of 21,800 men. A number of armoured vehicles were also brought in, although no gun-armed tanks – the image of tanks on the streets was considered too provocative, an unnecessary escalation of the conflict. There were, however, some Royal Engineers' Centurions fitted out as heavy bulldozers, which were to play a major part in the operation.

The army made public both the scale of the build-up and its purpose – to launch an assault on No-Go areas throughout the province. The publicity achieved its desired effect: many of the Provisionals fled south of the border or to some other spot they considered safer, calculating that an attempt to stand and

Above left: A Royal Engineers' Centurion, fitted with a bulldozer blade, clears a barricade in the Bogside No-Go area of Londonderry during Operation Motorman, 31 July 1972.
Below left: A corporal of the King's Own Royal Border Regiment uses heavy steel fencing to protect himself as he covers a patrol moving into a scrapyard in search of terrorists.
Below: Operation Motorman, 31 July 1972: a Ferret scout car, with a Saracen armoured personnel carrier behind, moves past bemused civilians during the army push into the Bogside area of Londonderry. The overwhelming army presence prevented any response by the IRA.

fight could decimate their ranks. At 4.30am on 31 July 1972 British armoured columns poured into the No-Go areas; they met with little resistance. In Londonderry there was some gunfire and rioting which left two people dead, while in Belfast there were no serious casualties. The Centurion bulldozers demolished the barricades efficiently and speedily, and large numbers of troops followed – nine battalions were deployed in Londonderry alone. In a parallel operation, the UDA's Protestant barricades were dismantled, but this was no more than a gesture towards impartiality – they had only been erected to provoke just such a military reaction. The army also occupied hardline areas in country towns such as Lurgan, Armagh, Newry and Coalisland.

Consolidating 'Motorman'

Once inside the Catholic areas, the army prepared to settle in. Large buildings – often schools, then on holiday – were commandeered as temporary barracks. Engineers quickly assembled strongpoints from which soldiers could carry out surveillance of the streets; 16 were established in the Andersonstown district of Belfast alone. Work began almost immediately on more permanent accommodation for the troops in veritable forts. The army obviously intended to stay.

Their task was made easier by another major blow to the Provisionals' popularity on the very day of Operation Motorman, when the small village of Claudy in County Derry was virtually demolished by no less than three car bombs. Nine civilians were killed as the

bombs exploded with no warning – a widely credited rumour suggested that the bombers had attempted to phone a warning but had found the local phone-box out of order. The Provisionals denied responsibility for the Claudy atrocity, but the guilt, deserved or not, stuck to them.

The difference between the Catholic response to internment in August 1971 and to Operation Motorman in July 1972 could not have been more striking. The British troops were not welcomed – there were to be no cups of tea – but war-weariness and demoralisation had taken the fight out of the most hostile communities. Motorman dealt a severe blow to the Provisionals' effectiveness. Constant surveillance, patrols and searches in the Catholic enclaves now denied the Provisionals any safe haven. In the four months before Motorman there were some 500 explosions and almost 6000 shooting incidents; in the four months after, there were 393 explosions and under 3000 shootings.

These figures still represented a level of violence far above anything that could be considered 'acceptable' by the authorities, but the turning point was decisive. Before July 1972, the British government had been forced to follow a political path they did not like – notably negotiations with the Provisionals – in the hope of shoring up security in Northern Ireland. After Motorman, they were able to pursue the elusive goal of involving Catholics in the running of the province without a sense of acting under duress. Never again would the IRA come close to dictating British government policy by sheer military pressure.

4. Sectarian Conflict 1972-1977

The high plateau of political violence in Northern Ireland occurred in the period from 1972 to 1977. In 1972, 467 persons (including members of the security forces) were killed in shootings and bombings. The death toll fell to 250 in 1973 and fell once more to 216 in 1974. However, this was reversed in 1975 when the figure rose to 247, and in 1976 deaths due to political violence numbered 297. In 1977 the toll was 112. Some felt that the 1977 figure finally represented what the British home secretary, Reginald Maudling, had called 'an acceptable level' of violence, back in 1971; or at least indicated that one was on the horizon. That admission was a sign of how deeply ingrained had become the expectation of a long and bloody domestic conflict. The sustained violence of the years from 1972 to 1977 gave no hopeful signs to the hard-headed realist that the Troubles would be shortlived.

Some general comments may be made about the profile of sectarianism and insurgency in this period. Between 1972 and 1977 there was a slow but sure change in the nature of the Troubles. Put simply there was a move away from 'massed ranks' confrontations to 'small group' activity, from the pitched battle to the hit and run. This was part of the general development of the Ulster drama. By 1977, because of war-weariness, frustration or despair, the public as an actor had all but left the stage of political demonstration. The well-organised urban and rural guerrilla bands had taken their place. But it was not the paramilitaries, Republican or Loyalist, who, by 1977, appeared capable of popular mobilisation. It was a small group of idealists endeavouring to end the violence – the Peace People (see chapter 5).

Another feature of these years was the geographical limitation of political violence. Because Northern Ireland is quite small, with a small population, violence to person and property has touched the lives of most people, directly or indirectly. Yet something like 85% of the deaths have occurred in three main areas – the Catholic/Protestant confrontation zones of Belfast and Londonderry, and the border region. So while the sense of terror in this period was all too real, many Ulster people experienced violence just like everyone else in the United Kingdom – on the television screen.

About 60% of all deaths were people who had no direct involvement in the paramilitary groups or the security forces. Of these, Catholics suffered disproportionately from the violence. This is unsurprising since a sustained guerrilla war was being waged from Catholic areas and brought on the heads of the Catholic population some brutal consequences. A better guide to the profile of violence is some estimate of responsibility; this exhibits a clear pattern. Between 1972 and 1977 roughly half the total killings can be attributed to Republican groups and about one-third to Loyalist paramilitaries. This too may be misleading, however; if one includes bombing of property as political violence then the source was overwhelmingly Republican.

Left: Armed with a Sterling sub-machine gun and mounted on an army vehicle, a corporal of the Royal Military Police keeps a wary eye on the hostile streets of Belfast in the early 1970s. The spread of violence forced the army to adopt the role originally undertaken by the RUC – that of protecting the Protestant areas of the city – and led, inevitably, to confrontation with militant Catholics.

The Provisional IRA campaign

Traditionally the Irish Republican Army was a rural army. The Provisionals (PIRA) had their roots in the Catholic working-class districts of Belfast such as the Falls, Ardoyne and Ballymurphy, and in the Bogside in Londonderry. Just over a year after its formation and split from the Official IRA (OIRA), the PIRA had prepared and organised itself for a war, first, against the Stormont administration, and second, against the British state.

The Provisionals simply took over the traditional organisational structure of the IRA and modelled themselves on the military units of brigade, battalion and company. These were ultimately responsible to the Provisional Army Council whose chief-of-staff in this early period was Sean MacStiofain. In Belfast nine of the existing IRA company commanders joined the Provisionals in 1970. So the PIRA had the rudiments of an army structure within which to organise the flood of recruits who joined after internment was introduced in August 1971. Some of those whose names became prominent in or through association with the PIRA in this period include Seamus Twomey, Joe Cahill, and Gerry Adams in Belfast and Martin McGuinness in Derry. The Belfast Brigade had three battalions. The First covered the Upper Falls, Turf Lodge and Andersonstown; the Second was responsible for Ballymurphy, Clonard and Divis; and the

Third operated in east Belfast and in the Ardoyne. By 1972 the PIRA was well organised throughout Northern Ireland with a network of safe houses, arms dumps and contacts. The No-Go areas in Belfast and Londonderry had facilitated the entrenchment of the Provisionals and they always knew that they had a safe haven in the Republic where they could train, recuperate and prepare. Total membership by 1972 was probably about 1500 volunteers, the overwhelming majority of them in Belfast.

The PIRA had the organisation and it had the members to wage war. Now it also had the weapons to do so. At first, adequate finance had been raised in the Republic. The Provisionals did not talk politics, they wanted

Above: The IRA on the streets: hooded and well armed, IRA gunmen mount guard at an entrance to the 'Free Derry' No-Go area, 1972. The symbols of militant Republicanism – flags, poster of Connolly, and Thompson sub-machine gun – are all in evidence. Right: The bodies of two Protestants, killed by the IRA in November 1974. Sectarian violence has been a major feature of the Troubles.

guns. They spoke the pure words of traditional physical-force Republicanism without the complications of Marxism. They proclaimed themselves the true heirs of Easter 1916. This call had elicited an emotional and sympathetic response. Money and weapons came rolling in. In fact two members of the Dublin government, Charles Haughey and Neil Blaney, were charged in 1970 with illegal arms-dealing to help the Catholics in Northern Ireland. Though they were later acquitted, Ulster Protestants suspected that the Republic's government was financing subversion in the North. The money raised in Ireland purchased easily acquired guns on the open and black market. American M1 carbines and Springfield rifles were used in sniper

attacks. In February 1971 five British soldiers were injured in a burst of fire from a Thompson sub-machine gun, a weapon long hallowed in IRA folk memory. Pistols, either newly bought or taken over after the split with the OIRA, were widely circulated. In 1972, however, the most famous weapon of the PIRA campaign first made its appearance. The Armalite assault rifle was to be the new generation's Thompson. It was light, accurate, deadly, and easily transportable. Indeed the Armalite probably gave the PIRA a short-term tactical advantage, being more adaptable and flexible than the weaponry of the security forces. The reputation of the Provos and the Armalite thus became inextricably linked in the minds of Ulster people.

That the Provisionals had firmly established themselves as a force to be reckoned with was made clear in 1973. Under pressure from London, the Republic's government had tightened security regarding the availability of commercial explosives. It had also attempted to control the selling of sodium chlorate which had been used to make fire bombs and explosives. Then, on 28 March, a PIRA gun-running ship, the *Claudia*, carrying five tonnes of arms and ammunition from Colonel Gaddafi in Libya, was intercepted by the Irish authorities. On board was Joe Cahill, the former Belfast commander. Yet things getting tougher did not mean that the PIRA was any less effective. There was enough money and enough surplus weaponry throughout the world, but especially in America, to keep the campaign going. There was some reduction in PIRA activity in 1973 though nothing significant.

The main financial and logistical support for the Provisionals outside Ireland came from the Irish community in the United States. The Irish Northern Aid Committee (Noraid) had been set up in 1970 to collect funds for humanitarian purposes, and it has

been claimed that Noraid funds have been partially laundered to buy weapons or set up deals for arms organisers. However, the Provisionals have taken a somewhat dubious pride in the assertion that they fund the military campaign through bank robberies, protection and extortion, and do not need outside help. Moreover, the security forces agree with this assessment.

Both the PIRA and OIRA engaged in a military struggle against the Stormont regime, though the OIRA chose to call it a defensive campaign. Common cause was found in bringing down the institutional symbol of Protestant majority rule in Northern Ireland. Arguably it was not IRA bombs and bullets that led to the fall of Stormont, but the actions of British paratroopers. The killings on 'Bloody Sunday', 30 January 1972, were the final straw for an exasperated Cabinet in London. Edward Heath's decision to take responsibility for security away from the Unionists in Belfast forced a prorogation of the Northern Ireland parliament on 24 March. This marked a first watershed in Republican militancy.

Formation of the INLA

Two months after the suspension of Stormont, the OIRA declared a ceasefire. One reason advanced was that the leadership feared an outright civil war with the Protestants. The OIRA Army Council called for the putting away of guns and the development of class politics – its opinion was that real political gains had been made since 1969 and that these should be built upon. This ceasefire has been maintained ever since and much energy has been channelled into community politics to which even talk of Irish unity is subordinated. For example, the OIRA was responsible for large graffiti in Belfast announcing 'Sectarianism Kills Workers'. This

approach did not go down too well with all Officials. In December 1974 some of them, led by Seamus Costello, broke away (taking their guns with them) and set up the Irish Republican Socialist Party (IRSP) whose military wing was the Irish National Liberation Army (INLA). A murderous feud broke out between the OIRA and INLA that lasted until the summer of 1975. Five people died and over 70 were injured. The INLA survived, developed an uncompromising Marxist, anti-British, anti-Protestant position, and even attracted some disaffected Provisionals, notably Dominic McGlinchey, at one time 'the most wanted man in Ireland'. Republican violence from 1972 to 1977, however, was mainly PIRA violence.

For the Provisionals the fall of Stormont was only an interim achievement. While there was some talk among the Belfast PIRA about going political and some pressure from ordinary Catholics to end the campaign, the general consensus was to continue the fight. Ireland unfree, they argued, would never be at peace. Britain was the source of that oppression and therefore British rule in Ireland had to be ended once and for all. In a benign mood, the PIRA saw Protestants as true Irish folk, despite being the dupes of the English and the embodiment of England's imperialistic design. They could be forced to see the error of their ways; they could be forced to be free. Anyway, the Provisionals believed that Protestant power had been broken along with Stormont and were not worried about a Protestant backlash – some even welcomed it. The English had created the problem, the English had the power to solve it. They could be demoralised and convinced of the necessity to cut their losses in the North. Established as a non-negotiable demand in the policy document 'Eire Nua' (New Ireland) was the necessity of a declaration of intent by the British government to

Right: British soldiers in helmets and visors clear burning rubble from a riot-torn street in Belfast, 1975. Above right: A building burns in Belfast as local people, by now oblivious to the violence and destruction around them, stroll past. Above, far right: The impact of the crisis on the civilian population took many forms, not least the constant security checks. Here British soldiers search pedestrians as they enter a security zone in Belfast in 1974.

LEESON ST.

withdraw. Put succinctly, the Provisionals' strategy is 'Brits Out'.

Militarily this thinking was translated into the strategy of 'one last push' – 'one last push and we'll throw the Brits out'. This entailed making Northern Ireland ungovernable by causing the maximum disruption, politically, socially and economically. It meant setting ambitious goals for those on 'active service', for implied in the strategy of 'one last push' was an unrelenting engagement against military, political and economic targets. Provo thinking was about an intensive rather than a protracted war. The PIRA was prepared not just to make Northern Ireland ungovernable but to make the British presence there unacceptable to public opinion and to the liberal conscience in Great Britain itself.

The PIRA military campaign was composed of three interlocking elements. The first was the waging of an 'economic' war. This involved a sustained bombing campaign to undermine business confidence and commercial security. PIRA logic was cunningly

simple. Not only would Northern Ireland become a greater financial liability for the British government as its economy slumped, but the Exchequer would also have to stump up the money to pay compensation for damage to property. This financial burden alone, it was calculated, would stimulate thoughts of withdrawal. The centres of many towns, but especially Belfast and Londonderry, were severely bombed. Two things came to symbolise the economic war for those who were its victims. The first was the 'Business as Usual' signs posted up as soon as possible on damaged premises. The second was the Belfast Europa Hotel (since renamed the Forum Hotel) which kept going through the Troubles despite earning the epithet of 'Northern Ireland's most bombed building'. While there were headlines to be grabbed with the 'big bang' strategy, one of the most effective weapons of the economic war turned out to be the simple incendiary device. Small enough to be fitted into a cigarette packet or something similar, incendiaries

could be left in shops near to closing time. Primed to go off a few hours later, they were effective in causing widespread damage to stock and to premises. Their simplicity and convenience enabled the Provos to engage in blitzes with devastating consequences. On Saturday 9 November 1974, for example, incendiaries detonated in three Belfast shopping precincts. Although warnings were given, many shops were gutted, and it took over two hours to bring the fires under control.

Yet despite the undoubted PIRA success in hitting economic targets it is questionable whether the economic war had any significant success at all. The financial burden was not the crucial issue for British politicians, and the strategic economic targets were beyond the PIRA's grasp. Northern Ireland has indeed experienced severe economic problems, but these have been due to the world recession rather than PIRA bombs. By the mid-1970s the town-centre security-gate system was providing acceptable protection to business people and shoppers alike. PIRA frustration was evident when they widened the economic war to include as legitimate targets managers of British and multi-national enterprises. In February 1977, for instance, came the murder of Jeffrey Agate, manager of the Du Pont synthetic fibre plant in Londonderry, and attempts were made on the lives of other businessmen. The subsequent public outrage forced the PIRA to abandon its terror campaign against individuals in the business community.

The urban war

The second element of the PIRA military campaign was the waging of a guerrilla war on several fronts. The urban guerrilla warfare had its own characteristics which distinguished it from that waged on the other main battlefront along the border. The purpose of the urban war was to stretch and harass the security forces with frequent attacks on personnel and disruption by bombing. Part of the tactic was to demoralise Protestants. Terror could be a weapon to weaken resistance and force them to look for peace at any price. If this did not work it might provoke them into confrontation with the British government. This too would serve PIRA ends by spreading disillusionment among Unionists and disaffection in Westminster.

In this early period of the shooting war between the PIRA and troops, intensive gun battles were common. A number of Provisionals would engage a British patrol and a large number of shots would be exchanged. However, PIRA commanders soon recognised that it was playing the British Army at its own game and committing too many men to set-pieces. Discretion was indeed the better part of valour. Shoot-outs were also unpopular with Catholic residents because passers-by were at risk in the crossfire. The victims included the young and the old, such as the eight-year-old girl shot in an hour-long gun battle in April 1972, and the 70-year-old man killed in the Ardoyne the following September. The Provisionals would blame the army for such deaths, but many believed that they had precipitated the violence. Soon

the method of attack changed to the hit-and-run sniper attack. The Armalite was deadly and accurate and could be swiftly broken down and concealed. This allowed small units of about three volunteers to hit their targets and then melt away. It also meant fewer civilian casualties. One popular tactic was to take over a house and hold the occupants prisoner. The PIRA unit could then wait for an army or police patrol to be lured into the street on a bogus phone call. Having made a hit, the Provisionals could make their escape by a planned route.

PIRA units also engaged in the murder of Protestants and the planting of pub bombs in retaliation against Loyalist violence. A myth had grown up that the PIRA would never shoot a Protestant simply because of religion. In these violent years it was an unwritten and largely unheeded rule that no Protestant wished to put to the test. Undoubtedly the most brutal of the PIRA's tactics was the use of the car bomb. Daithi O Conaill, later to become chief-of-staff, encouraged the use of this devastating weapon. It was a true terror weapon designed not just to destroy property but to spread panic. The instability of the explosives used sometimes resulted in premature detonation, which resulted in more PIRA deaths than did security-force operations. In February 1972, for example, a car travelling in east Belfast exploded, killing the four occupants – the security forces counted this as an 'own goal'. Unfortunately it was not just PIRA volunteers but innocent civilians who suffered. PIRA sources claimed that adequate warnings were always given, suggesting that the authorities deliberately ignored them to discredit Republicanism.

Whatever the truth, the consequences were often gruesome and shocking.

On 12 June 1973, for example, Coleraine was hit by a car bomb that killed six people. In both this bombing and that at Claudy the previous July, when nine people died, the incompetence of the PIRA volunteers was blamed for the deaths. In Coleraine a telephone warning was actually received but directed police to the wrong street. Evacuees walked straight into the real car bomb. No one will ever know whether this was planned or not. However, the indiscriminate use of car bombs and their unpredictability damaged the PIRA's cause among Catholics rather than strengthened it. Gradually the Provisionals downgraded it in their campaign of urban disruption.

The border war

The first victims of PIRA's border war were two RUC constables killed by a booby-trapped car in August 1970 at Crossmaglen, south Armagh. This village has become the symbol of the cunning and the viciousness of the border struggle, and the PIRA units that operate in the area have become renowned for their skill. In these early years the Provisionals found it relatively easy to mount gun attacks on British troops from safe firing positions in the Republic. Such attacks could turn into raging battles when army patrols called in reinforcements by radio. Border gunmen took pride in the vaunt of being the best in the organisation. They had greater freedom of movement and if confronted on the northern side of the border could make use of the network of unapproved roads to

Above: IRA recruits under training in the Republic in the 1970s. Despite the Dublin authorities' proven record of anti-IRA policy, some remote areas of the South remained IRA havens.

Right: Map showing the counties and major towns of Northern Ireland, with an inset of the dangerous area of south Armagh that is known to the security forces as 'bandit country'.

make good their escape to the south. British troops were forbidden any 'hot pursuit'.

It was also reported that the PIRA Army Council gave the border priority in the supply of new weapons. After 1971 US Army M16 rifles, Japanese-made Armalites and RPG-7 rocket launchers imported from Libya made their appearance. A report in the Ulster journal *Fortnight* in 1976 revealed that Soviet-made Kalashnikov rifles were in use by the PIRA. The British Army had in fact captured two of these in patrols in the border area. Twenty-nine other Kalashnikovs were intercepted along with more ammunition and weaponry en route for Ireland in December 1977. Rumour had it that the PIRA was buying these weapons from the Palestinians.

However, the border shooting war tended to follow the pattern of its urban counterpart. Classic early battles were those at Dungooly (January 1972) and Aughnacloy (December 1974) where the PIRA and army exchanged thousands of bullets over several hours with

neither side claiming any hits. By the mid-1970s sniping attacks were more common, and gunmen had turned their attention to softer security targets such as off-duty Ulster Defence Regiment (UDR) and Royal Ulster Constabulary (RUC) reservists. Protestants in the border areas tended to rely for protection upon membership of these legitimate forces rather than membership of paramilitary groups. The PIRA's ruthless murders of UDR and RUC personnel were claimed by Unionists as a policy of religious genocide, and there is indeed little evidence that the PIRA made any hard and fast rule about choosing between targets; such murders, on a consistent basis, became part of a very nasty mini-war. To some of these activities the PIRA Army Council in Dublin turned a blind eye. On 18 September 1975, for example, five Orangemen were gunned down in Tully-vallen Orange Hall. A group calling itself the Republican Action Force claimed responsibility. The same group also claimed responsibility for one of the worst atrocities of the

Above: A British soldier on patrol in the border area in a Saracen armoured personnel carrier. Below: A farmer's wife guards her husband, a part-time UDR member, near the border.

Troubles. On 5 January 1976 a minibus carrying 12 workers was stopped by gunmen near Whitecross in south Armagh. The driver, a Catholic, was set free. The 11 Protestant workmen were cut down with automatic weapons; ten died immediately and the eleventh was seriously injured. It is now clear that the Republican Action Force was a cover name for a PIRA unit. The Army Council never disowned the action.

More effective and dramatic than bullets was the bombing campaign against the security forces. It was safer to kill at a distance, and the development of sophisticated detonating techniques provided the PIRA with the means to attack heavily armoured military and police patrols. A favoured tactic was to use culvert bombs placed under narrow country roads. Picking a vantage point, usually close to a convenient escape road across the border, the PIRA unit would wait for a Saracen, Ferret scout car or RUC Land Rover to pass over the culvert, then detonate the bomb and make its getaway.

Another frequently used weapon was the milk-churn bomb. A common feature of Ulster's country roads is the farmer's milk churns left on the verge for collection by dairy workers. Such innocent-looking utensils could be packed with over 200 kilograms of explosives and detonated to ambush a passing patrol.

One of the most bizarre bombing incidents happened in January 1974. A renegade PIRA unit, said to have included Brigid Rose Dugdale, the daughter of an English millionaire, hijacked a helicopter in Donegal and loaded it with two milk-churn bombs. They forced the pilot to fly over Strabane RUC station, where they tossed out the bombs. The explosives neither hit the station nor detonated. Not all such PIRA 'experiments' were failures, however, and weapons like home-made mortars fixed on the backs of lorries successfully hit RUC stations along the border. By 1977 the success of the security forces against the PIRA in Belfast compelled a shift of military emphasis to the border. The impossibility of effectively controlling illegal traffic to and from the Republic gave the Provisionals the advantage they needed.

The bombing campaign in England 1972-4

The third element of PIRA strategy was the bombing campaign in England. It had a two-fold justification for the Army Council. Bombs in England could dramatise the Irish question much more effectively than bombs in Ulster. In this the PIRA was following the Fenian tradition established in the 19th century. Taking the war to England was also designed to encourage the British establishment to cut and run from Northern Ireland. The bombs in England certainly brought attention to the PIRA. With hindsight, however, they hardly advanced its cause.

In fact it was the OIRA who carried out the first bombing attack in England in this period. In revenge for Bloody Sunday they planted a bomb at the Paras' HQ in Aldershot in February 1972, killing seven people, five of them cleaning women. The following year the Provisionals began their own campaign. There were difficulties recruiting bombers from the Irish community in England, so the PIRA sent over its own units. In London in March 1973 two car bombs injured 200

people, and an elderly man died of a heart attack at the Old Bailey as a device exploded. The unit responsible, however, which included the Price sisters, Marion and Dolours, was arrested at Heathrow airport. In August and September there was a series of incendiary attacks on department stores. On 4 February 1974 a bomb in the boot of a coach taking army families along the M62 motorway from Manchester to Catterick killed eight soldiers, two children and a woman, and injured many others. While the Provisionals did not claim responsibility for this it was probably their work. On 5 October bombs exploded in two pubs in Guildford, killing five. In November two more people were killed in pub bombings at Woolwich, near London. On 24 November came the worst outrage of all.

Two pub bombs were detonated in Birmingham, one at the Mulberry Bush, the other at the Tavern in the Town. Nineteen people were killed and over 100 seriously injured. The Provisional Army Council did not accept responsibility for these bombs even though PIRA operatives had been detected earlier in the Midlands. (One such, James McDade, had been killed while planting a bomb at Coventry telephone exchange.) Probably the leadership recognised its mistake, for the bombings brought nothing but condemnation, even from erstwhile sympathisers. The immediate response of the British government was to introduce the Prevention of Terrorism Act which gave the authorities wide powers to detain terrorist suspects or to exclude them from Great Britain. However, the Army Council were not so concerned about the present as about the judgment of 'history'. By 1975 the PIRA leadership seemed to believe history was on their side. On 10 February 1975 an indefinite ceasefire was announced, and it seemed as if the English bombings had forced the British government to make concessions to the Provisionals.

Ceasefire and aftermath

In secret talks with British officials, the PIRA believed it had been given an assurance of British withdrawal. From February to September 1975 only four British soldiers were killed, although sectarian killings were on the increase. However, by the autumn the ceasefire had begun to break down. The PIRA felt that it had been cheated and that the 'peace' had allowed British intelligence thoroughly to penetrate its ranks. A new campaign was launched in England (culminating in the Balcombe Street siege in December) and the violence began again in Northern Ireland. In 1976, the PIRA's greatest coup was the murder of the British Ambassador to the Republic, Christopher Ewart–Biggs. This was clearly revenge for

Left: A Saracen armoured personnel carrier protected by wire mesh patrols the border town of Crossmaglen, a hive of Republican activity.
Top right: The army was not alone on the border: this IRA checkpoint was photographed in April 1982.

Above centre: A Saracen lies on its side, victim of an IRA bomb.
Above: Concrete blocks mark the border in a vain attempt to seal it.
Right: An army patrol leaps from a Scout helicopter as a Sioux acts as top cover.

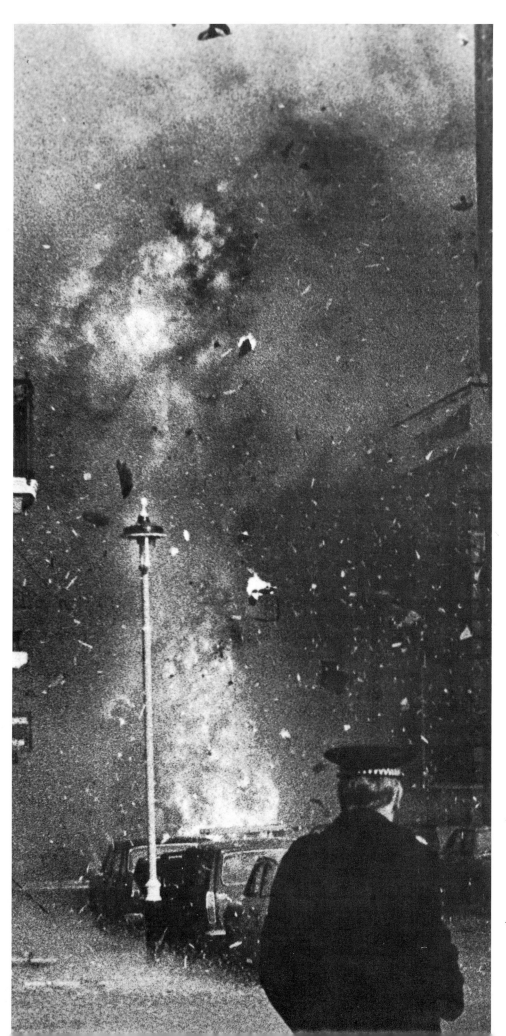

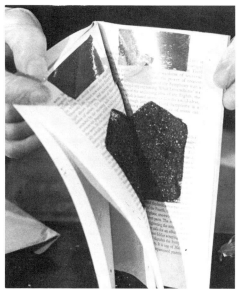

Left: The IRA comes to London: a policeman watches as a car bomb explodes in Great Scotland Yard during the campaign of 1974–5. The enormous force of a car-bomb explosion could cause immense material, physical and psychological damage.

Top: A tool of the bomb-disposal trade: a remote-controlled 'Wheelbarrow' vehicle blasts open the boot of a suspect car on the streets of Northern Ireland. The tracked 'Wheelbarrow' is fitted with an extendable boom, on which are mounted an automatic shotgun and a television camera. These valuable devices have saved many lives – several have been blown to pieces on active service.

Above: An example of a book bomb, a particularly nasty type of anti-personnel weapon favoured by many terrorist groups in the 1970s. Opening the book triggers off a small but potentially deadly explosion.

what the Army Council saw as British perfidy during the ceasefire. It was also a message that the Provisionals were not beaten.

Yet by the end of 1976, the Provisionals did feel that the British were getting the better of them. More efficient intelligence, the use of improved interrogation techniques by the RUC, and war-weariness among Catholics were all putting great strains on the PIRA and causing a steady decline in the numbers of volunteers. The response of the Army Council was to institute a restructuring of the military organisation, which they effected especially thoroughly in Belfast. While the formal structure of brigade, battalion and company remained, the active service units were remodelled on the cellular pattern. Each cell was brought together for specific tasks, then dispersed. It was hoped that the changes would reduce security penetration, protect volunteer identities and be more efficient in the use of manpower. What this symbolised was a change in strategic perception. The 'one last push' strategy had been replaced by an emphasis on a war of attrition. Fatalism rather than optimism became the reigning disposition.

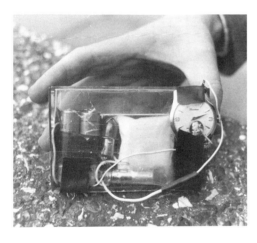

Above: The miniaturisation of terror: an incendiary device, no bigger than a tape-cassette, of the type left in department stores by the IRA. Slipped into the pockets of clothes on sale, such devices would explode hours later, starting fires which could be devastating.

Top right: The bomb-maker's tools: a cache of batteries and timers seized by the police in a raid on a Manchester flat in 1976. All the material on show could be bought quite openly in any hardware shop; only when put together was it deadly.

Centre right: Marion (left) and Dolours Price pose for a tourist snap outside No 10 Downing Street, London. Both girls were later to be found guilty of terrorist offences.

Right: The aftermath of the bomb attack that killed 11 people, eight of them soldiers, on the M62 motorway on 4 February 1974.

The Balcombe Street siege

In the autumn of 1975 a new Provisional IRA offensive was launched in England. A London unit was activated, and it sustained a campaign of bombing and shooting from September until the beginning of December. Possibly the Provisional Army Council believed that the only way for the British government to fulfil its supposed promise to declare a date for withdrawal from Northern Ireland was to resume attacks on English civilians. Bombs were planted at the Hilton Hotel, Green Park tube station and in restaurants in the West End. Among those killed were Professor Gordon Hamilton Fairley when he was caught in a blast meant for Tory MP Hugh Fraser; and Captain Roger Goad, an army bomb-disposal expert. On 25 November a man famous for helping to compile *The Guinness Book of Records* and a strong supporter of tougher anti-terrorist legislation, Ross McWhirter, was shot dead at his home.

London police were thus on their guard, and on the evening of Saturday 6 December were alerted to an incident in Mount Street, Mayfair. A black Ford Cortina was chased from the scene and abandoned near Balcombe Street. The occupants of the car were cornered and forced into a block of flats in the street. They burst into the apartment of John Matthews, 55, and his wife Sheila, 53. Mr

Matthews was tied up and kept that way for most of the siege. This was the beginning of an ordeal that was to last until Friday 12 December, a total of 138 hours.

Heavily armed police immediately surrounded the flats and cut the telephone line to prevent the cornered Provisionals contacting any colleagues. Powerful arc lights were trained on the flat to deprive the gunmen of restful sleep. Having secured their men, Scotland Yard set up an operational command of six top officers including the commissioner, Sir Robert Mark, and the head of the Bomb Squad, Roy Habershon. They were ultimately responsible for the conduct of the siege. Not only had they to consider effective tactics but also the health of the two hostages. However, one point was established immediately: there would be no deals.

Indeed, the police did have crucial advantages. The PIRA unit had jettisoned its automatic weapons and had only handguns. Also they were unprepared for a long siege and had no ready access to food stocks. The police could therefore regulate food supply and use it as a bargaining counter. Because of the position of the Matthews' flat it was quite easy to monitor the conversation and mood of the captors and the police could modify their actions accordingly.

Neverthless it was only on Monday that it

was finally confirmed that there were four gunmen. Until then the police were sure of only three, who were named 'Tom', 'Mick', and 'Paddy'. 'Tom' was the spokesman and refused an offer of food. On Tuesday it seemed as if they were going to 'tough' it out. Food was again refused and the field telephone used to maintain contact with the police was thrown from the flat into the street. On Wednesday the police cut off the flat's electricity, mainly to deny the Provisionals access to television and so to increase the sense of isolation. The atmosphere began to change, and on Thursday food was accepted at last.

Mrs Matthews was released on Friday and another meal was accepted. At the same time a new telephone link was connected and 'Tom' conducted another parley with the officer in charge of operations. Finally, with assurances of no ill-treatment, the men agreed to give themselves up. Leaving their five handguns behind, one by one the captors and hostage emerged into Balcombe Street. It took nine minutes for the surrender to be completed.

The four PIRA men were later each found guilty of six murders and sentenced to life imprisonment for a minimum of 30 years. The siege was a welcome success for Scotland Yard.

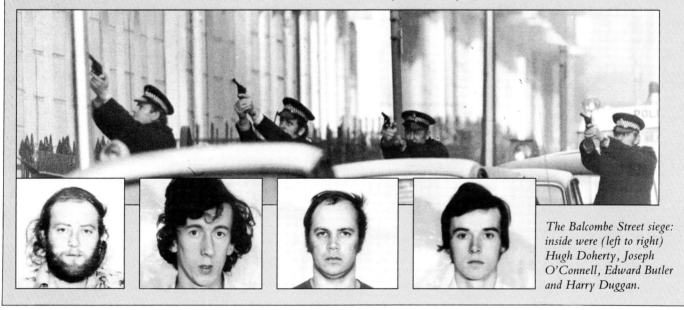

The Balcombe Street siege: inside were (left to right) Hugh Doherty, Joseph O'Connell, Edward Butler and Harry Duggan.

Militant Loyalism

Militant Loyalism, like physical-force Republicanism, is a form of military self-help. Before 1969 militant Loyalism had been tamed and controlled to some extent by incorporation in the B-Specials – a factor overlooked by those who view the old Stormont regime only as a 'repressive apparatus'. After 1969 it became independent of political control and became organised in paramilitary units. These groups were reactive, without any clear strategy other than a defence of Protestantism and a hatred of Republicanism. While the voice of Protestant paramilitarism is aggressively self-confident, its behaviour reflects an angry despair and a deep insecurity. These were greatest during the years 1972–7 and expressed themselves in a long series of sectarian killings and bombings. While the PIRA was a 'primary' terrorist organisation carrying on an insurgent war against the British state and clearly against Ulster Protestants as well, Loyalists were 'secondary' terrorists. Their violence was sustained not so much by internal ideological compulsion as by the external influences of

PIRA activity and the policy response of the British government.

The extent of Loyalist political violence was constrained by some obvious factors. Paramilitaries could not conduct an economic war since they would be attacking their own livelihoods. Neither had they any clearly identifiable 'legitimate' targets. Though there were instances of paramilitaries killing members of the security forces, they brought loud condemnation on the heads of those responsible. For the overwhelming majority of Protestants, the army, RUC and UDR were 'their' forces. As self-professed 'loyal' citizens it was inconceivable for Loyalists to conduct an English bombing campaign. For reasons of simple logistics it was also impossible to take the war to the Irish Republic to the extent to which many paramilitaries would have wished. (A few car bombs were planted in the Republic by Loyalists, notably those in Dublin and Monaghan on 17 May 1974. No warnings were given in either case and 24 people died in Dublin and another six in Monaghan.) However, such overall constraints were not effective in muzzling Protestant gunmen. Over 500 Catholics were killed by paramilitaries between 1972 and 1977.

Protestant paramilitary strategy

Common elements are identifiable in the strategy of Loyalist paramilitaries. The first involved a tactic of 'clearing the decks'. This meant the forced removal of Catholics from Protestant areas by intimidation and worse. A similar process was going on in Catholic areas in Belfast, leading to the largest population movement in western Europe since the Second World War. By 1973 the sectarian pattern of residence was more or less fixed throughout Northern Ireland. Those foolhardy or brave enough to remain exceptions to the rule had to face the prospect of that terror known in Belfast as the 'doorstep murder'. Once the decks were cleared, paramilitaries devoted themseles to 'holding the line'. This entailed prevention of Catholic encroachment into areas taken by Protestants to be their domain. Random murders took place most frequently in north and west Belfast.

A second element was activity designed to 'keep Britain up to the mark' in its obligations to Northern Ireland. Paramilitaries believed that Protestant opinion needed muscle to get concessions once Stormont was prorogued, and that only through determined action could Loyalists be sure that Westminster would not impose a solution on Protestants without their support. The 1974 Ulster Workers' Council (UWC) 'constitutional stoppage' was the high point of paramilitary

Right: The United Kingdom was not the only country to suffer terrorist attacks from groups in Northern Ireland: in 1974 a series of bombing incidents took place in Dublin, probably the work of extremist Protestant groups from north of the border. Here an old woman, her leg shattered in the blast, clings desperately to a rescuing fireman.
Above: A bomb concealed in a shoulder bag. Timed devices such as this one were unreliable, and often detonated prematurely.

success (see chapter 5). However, such power was essentially negative and if overused could fragment that unity of Protestants it was designed to foster. This is precisely what happened in 1977 when the second constitutional stoppage proved a divisive and abysmal failure. A third element was preparation for a 'doomsday situation'. The earliest paramilitary documents, circulated in Belfast in 1971, called for the establishment of an organisation that would be capable of taking over control in the event of British withdrawal. Talk of 'doomsday' was one means of retaining Protestant support for a paramilitary 'longstop'.

The fourth and most significant element of Protestant paramilitary strategy was the campaign of sectarian killing. Two justifications have been claimed for this tactic. First, the killings were to terrorise the terrorists, to eliminate IRA volunteers. Paramilitaries suggested that a distinction was made between active Republicans and ordinary Catholics. Evidence shows, however, that the vast majority of victims shot or bombed by Loyalist squads were innocent of IRA involvement. They just happened to be in the wrong place at the wrong time. Secondly, the killings were designed to instil terror in the Catholic community – in this case there was no need to make a distinction. The logic was as follows. Murdering Catholics would force the minority to disown the IRA in their midst. If it did not it 'proved' the point that all

Catholics were suspect and disloyal. It was a 'Catch-22' situation, and explains why the killings continued even when it was demonstrated that innocents suffered. Indeed, after the 'clearing of the decks', Protestant paramilitaries found it difficult to get intelligence on IRA members and almost impossible to 'hit them where they lived'. From 1972 to 1976 any Catholic was fair game. It seemed the only way the Loyalists could hit back.

After 1976, Loyalist assassinations became more selective and showed every sign of detailed planning. This was clearly the case in the killing of Maire Drumm, former vice-president of Provisional Sinn Fein, the PIRA's political wing, in October 1976. Drumm had gone into the Mater Hospital in Belfast for a cataract operation. A Loyalist gun squad disguised as medical staff shot her dead in a precisely executed murder.

Whereas Republican violence came mainly from one source, the PIRA, Loyalist violence was shared by an 'alphabet soup' of Protestant paramilitaries (so-called because of the confusing complication of their initials). There were at least 12 recorded groupings operating at any one time. In this nether world it is difficult to be precise. It is likely, though, that these groups had overlapping membership and that a number were simply labels of convenience for another organisation or freelance operators. An Ulster Army Council was set up in 1973 to coordinate this Protestant paramilitary factionalism. In 1974 this body was replaced by the Ulster Loyalist Central Coordinating Committee (ULCCC), though it proved as disputatious as it was cooperative. The ULCCC split in 1976.

Protestant weaponry was rather more ramshackle than that eventually possessed by the PIRA. Paramilitaries relied to an extent on homemade guns, although they managed to smuggle in some rifles from Canada and Scotland. Two main organisations were responsible for most of the paramilitary activity. These were the Ulster Defence Association (UDA) and the Ulster Volunteer Force (UVF).

Ulster Defence Association

The UDA emerged in September 1971 as an umbrella organisation encompassing a number of small Protestant vigilante groups which had formed to protect their own areas against IRA violence. The centre of gravity was in west Belfast with the Shankill and Woodvale Associations. Other Defence Associations such as those of east Belfast, Lisburn, and Comber simply subscribed to the umbrella organisation. Formed on military lines, the formal controlling body was a 13-man inner council (some put the number at 20) whose spokesmen were chairman and vice-chairman. While this structure gave apparent cohesion to the UDA, it exhibited the nature of its origin. Each Defence Association throughout Ulster was, in effect, a power base, sometimes with its own ideas about how that 'defence' was to be conducted. This could lead to feuding not just about aims but about personalities.

Popular myths have grown up about a power struggle within the UDA between east and west Belfast over protection money in 1973. While there is some truth in this,

conflict within the UDA was caused by an absence of agreed policy and effective leadership. Charles Harding Smith, the first UDA chairman, had two attempts made on his life before he fled to England in 1976. Ernie Elliot, another of the original west Belfast leadership, was abducted and murdered by a shotgun blast to the head in December 1972. Legend has it that Elliott used to patrol his fiefdom with the writings of Che Guevara in his pocket. He was probably killed for proposing discussions with the IRA. In September 1973, Tommy Herron, the vice-chairman and leading spokesman, was also murdered. It was at one time rumoured that the security forces may have been implicated but it seems likely that he was the victim of another feud. Not until 1976 did Andy Tyrie fully establish himself in authority as UDA chairman. Thereafter he was able to maintain reasonable stability within the loosely structured force.

The UDA provided one of the abiding memories of the early years of the Troubles with its massed-rank parades. UDA men dressed in combat jackets and bush hats, wearing masks or dark glasses, carrying iron bars or pick-axe handles, symbolised Loyalist extra-parliamentary force. And it was not just a show of force. Possibly the majority of sectarian attacks in 1972–5 were carried out by the UDA or those closely associated with it. Despite the fact that UDA leaders do not deny the involvement of their organisation in murder and bombing in this period, the UDA

Below: Protestant paramilitaries show their strength: a UDA parade, designed to intimidate and gain publicity, in Belfast in 1975.

Above: A typical Protestant mural, resplendent with Unionist symbols, reminds passers-by that it was not just Republicans who were interned.

has never been proscribed. It was and still is by far the largest of all paramilitary organisations. At its peak in 1972–4 membership was approaching the 50,000 mark, although only a few were involved in sectarian killing. It was overwhelmingly working class and was concentrated in the Belfast region and Londonderry. By 1977 numbers were down to about 10,000 due to a decline in Republican violence, more effective security policy and the failure of the 1977 UWC strike. UDA leaders also claimed that membership was being restricted to weed out corrupt elements and make the organisation more manageable.

One of the UDA's early successes was to urge the British government to take action against the Republican No-Go areas. The UDA raised barricades in Belfast and confronted the army with a show of strength. The ruse worked, for the army had no desire to fight on two fronts. This put additional pressure on William Whitelaw, secretary of state for Northern Ireland, to launch Operation Motorman in July 1972. Despite the success of Motorman, the PIRA campaign continued and some UDA men decided on direct action. They were fed up with parading and playing at soldiers. They were disgusted at the 'televised destruction of Ulster', as they

put it. On the later admission of Tyrie, the UDA then became heavily involved in sectarian killings, many of which were horrific and brutal.

Most of these killings took place in Belfast as tit-for-tat retaliation for the violence of Republicans. The PIRA responded in kind by killing innocent Protestants. Gunmen would roam the streets in cars looking for likely victims. Once picked up, one's fate was sealed. There would be no witnesses. Between 1972 and 1974 over 200 sectarian murders were committed by both Loyalist and Republican squads, though the main responsibility has been laid at the UDA's door. Early in 1973, Tommy Herron called for an end to the killing, but since there was no coherent UDA policy, either political or military, the respite was shortlived. Then on 1 February 1973 a busload of Catholic workmen was ambushed. A hand grenade killed one workman and injured the rest. Police investigations led to the internment of two Protestants four days later – these were the first Loyalists to be interned. Another 20 had been interned by April and there were fears that paramilitary leaders could be in danger. In these circumstances the Ulster Freedom Fighters (UFF) emerged in May 1973.

Between 1973 and 1977, despite a temporary ceasefire, the UFF was responsible for a large number of sectarian killings. Although the authorities proscribed the UFF as a separate illegal organisation, there is little doubt that it was a *nom de guerre* for militant dissidents within the UDA. The latter spoke for the UFF and issued statements on its behalf. Sometimes the UDA would admit the possibility of overlapping membership, but never accepted responsibility for UFF killings. In that way the main Protestant paramilitary organisation avoided proscription. Since 1977 the UFF has seen itself as an elite commando unit and has been critical of 'cowboy' operators on the Loyalist side who indiscriminately shoot Catholics. However, the UFF was not always so careful. Probably its most famous and gruesome murder was that of Senator Paddy Wilson and his secretary, Irene Andrews. Wilson was a popular and well-respected member of the mainly Catholic Social Democratic and Labour Party. He was also election agent for Gerry Fitt. On 26 June 1973 he and his secretary were found murdered in a disused quarry on Belfast's Hightown Road. Andrews had been stabbed 20 times in the head and body. Wilson had been stabbed 30 times and his throat had been cut. 'Captain Black' of the UFF claimed responsibility.

The UDA's greatest success was providing the muscle behind the UWC strike in May 1974 (see chapter 5). After 1975 and under the guidance of Andy Tyrie, the UDA became an established feature of Ulster Protestant working-class life. It began to devote a lot of energy to business, community and welfare work. It also got involved in politics proper, proposing a strategy of negotiated independence for Northern Ireland.

Ulster Volunteer Force

The modern UVF is a smaller and much more secretive organisation than the UDA. In the late 1960s it was no more than a figment of the imagination of Gusty Spence, its legendary leader and imprisoned hero. By the early 1970s it had recruited some ex-servicemen and a number of idealistic youngsters. The UVF thought itself to be an elite force, dedicated and principled in the way of its illustrious historical namesake formed in 1913. Because it was clandestine it also had an *esprit de corps* not to be found in the open UDA (which UVF men thought undisciplined and corrupt). Maximum membership was put at about 1500. Support for the UVF was concentrated mainly in west Belfast, south and east Antrim, and mid- and south Armagh.

The UVF was intermittently involved in the wave of sectarian killings in 1972–3. It is difficult to calculate its full responsibility, for a number of murders were probably carried out by UVF men acting under a cover name. Under the influence of Spence from inside

prison (and for a few brief months out of prison), the UVF appeared to be moving towards political rather than military activity. To an extent the leadership had a vision of a political settlement based on working-class solidarity, a common cause in the struggle against economic and social disadvantage. The UVF in fact declared a ceasefire in November 1973 and announced its condemnation of sectarianism. It even showed a willingness to talk to the PIRA. Merlyn Rees (who succeeded Francis Pym as secretary of state for Northern Ireland when the Conservatives were replaced by a Labour government in February 1974) rewarded the UVF by lifting proscription in April. In June 1974 the Volunteer Political Party was formed to give expression to the UVF's political ideas, with Ken Gibson as its spokesman. However, in the Westminster elections in October, Gibson managed to poll only 2600 votes in the constituency of west Belfast. This poor

showing brought to a head simmering discontent within the UVF, most of whose members had not joined for political education but to get guns. After November, under a new hardline leadership, the UVF returned to the business of anti-Catholic terror.

By October 1975, Rees was forced to outlaw the UVF again after it had admitted responsibility for a concerted campaign against Catholic targets. The main reason for this upsurge in 1975 was Protestant fears concerning the PIRA ceasefire. There were rumours of a British sell-out, and the posture of the government did not alleviate these fears. Indeed, the UVF offered to end its violence if the government in turn ended *its* ceasefire with the Provisionals. Not only was the UVF now engaged in full-scale sectarian killing, it was also engaged in a feud with the UDA. On top of this, old internal animosities were being settled by the gun. All in all the period 1974–7 greatly discredited the UVF in the eyes of the Protestant community.

Two UVF-linked operations give a flavour of the times. The west Belfast UVF always had a reputation for being hard men. One group, operating freelance and largely outside the formal paramilitary structure, was responsible for 19 killings in north and west Belfast between November 1975 and February 1977. Victims were abducted by car and usually badly mutilated before death. Most were finally dispatched with meat cleavers. Hence the notorious name for the gang – the Shankill Butchers. A second example is the Protestant Action Force (PAF),

Above: A Protestant clergyman addresses a parade of the proscribed UVF. The involvement of the UVF in the sectarian killings of the mid-1970s alienated many moderate Protestants.
Left: The Miami Showband, three of whose members were murdered by the PAF in 1975.

a group recognised as a cover for UVF volunteers in Armagh and Belfast's Tiger Bay area. The PAF was especially active in the 'murder triangle' of south Armagh in 1974–5. In a long line of killings, the most famous was the Miami Showband massacre. A PAF unit dressed in UDR uniforms flagged down the Miami Showband minibus close to the border on 31 July, but while planting a bomb in the van a premature explosion killed two of the PAF unit. Three of the band were then killed. Significantly, the UVF connection with the UDR was not denied but boasted of, and indeed, in August 1975, announcing the establishment of the 'Ulster Central Intelligence Agency', the UVF claimed it was receiving military intelligence from members of the UDR.

In 1976 and 1977, the UVF was more or less neutralised as a paramilitary force by a devastating series of arrests. Informers revealed names and operations of UVF units in east Antrim, Ballymena, Coleraine, Bangor and Belfast. The authorities took the opportunity to smash them. By the summer of 1977 the UVF had declared an indefinite ceasefire, out of necessity rather than choice.

Protestant paramilitaries

Fragmentation, overlapping membership, and names of convenience make it difficult to distinguish with any great certainty the composition of some paramilitary groups. For example, the Ulster Defence Association is linked with a number of organisations which admit to sectarian killings, such as the Ulster Freedom Fighters and the ephemeral Ulster Protestant Action Group. Similarly, the Ulster Volunteer Force has associations with the Protestant Action Force and other freelance gangs. The other main Protestant paramilitary organisations include:

Down Orange Welfare: Never directly associated with shooting or bombing, DOW was formed in 1972 by Lieutenant-Colonel (retired) Edward Brush and was based in northern County Down. Much of its membership overlapped with the Orange Order and was thus 'respectable'. It claimed at one time a membership of 5000. Probably the best analogy would be a Protestant 'Home Guard'. DOW was involved in enforcing the UWC strike in 1974.

Orange Volunteers: The OV claimed a membership of 3000 in 1974 and was led by Bob Marno. It was originally associated with William Craig's Vanguard movement and was active in the UWC strike. It wore a uniform of black anoraks and maroon berets and its individual members probably had links with other paramilitary groups, notably the UVF.

Red Hand Commando: A small and violent organisation that emerged in 1972 and was declared illegal in 1973. RHC probably split in the mid-1970s with one element gravitating towards the UDA and another, more determined group, associating with the UVF. John McKeague, a ubiquitous Loyalist, was always reckoned to be a founding member, though he denied it. When McKeague was murdered in 1982, RHC claimed responsibility though it transpired that the Republican INLA had done it. A number of RHC-linked killings were probably done by freelancers using it as a flag of convenience.

Tara: A secretive Loyalist group linked with members of the Orange Order. At one time it described itself as the hard core of Protestant resistance, though Tara's extremism appears to have been verbal and theological rather than military. Its commander, William McGrath, was jailed in 1981 for homosexual offences committed at the Kincora Boys' Home in Belfast.

Tartan Gangs: Not a paramilitary organisation as such, but groups of youths whose energy was harnessed to supplement the street power of the paramilitaries, especially the UDA. Active from 1971 to about 1976, its name was taken in memory of the three young Scottish soldiers murdered in March 1971.

Vanguard Service Corps: The VSC took the name Ulster Volunteer Service Corps (UVSC) in 1973. It was led by Hugh Petrie, an ex-serviceman, who was one of the leaders of the UWC strike. Mainly its function was to provide protection at the mass rallies held by Vanguard leader William Craig. Observers were quick to label the behaviour of the VSC/UVSC as proto-fascist.

Below: Wall-art commemorates the violent and apparently shortlived Protestant extremist group known as the Red Hand Commando. From time to time the title of this force has been used as a 'flag of convenience' by hard-line Protestant freelancers involved in the assassination of Catholics.

5. The Political Response 1972-1977

After the violence of the summer months in 1969, when the army had been called in to aid the civil power, the British government became reluctantly enmeshed in the complex internal politics of Northern Ireland. Following the meeting of the Northern Ireland premier, Major James Chichester-Clark, and the Labour prime minister, Harold Wilson, at Downing Street on 19 August 1969, London was determined to keep its eye on the Unionist administration in Stormont. By what has become known as 'direct rule by proxy', control at one remove was achieved by sending two senior civil servants to Belfast whose job it was to monitor the progress of political reform agreed at Downing Street and to report to London. British involvement was to be an 'invisible hand' but no less real for all that.

Certain assumptions underlay the political strategy adopted by both Labour and by the Conservatives who came to office in June 1970. The first was that, as far as possible, the Ulster question should be kept out of main-stream political debate at Westminster. Secondly, it was believed that Stormont could be reformed under the appropriate (if distant) supervision of British ministers and civil servants. Indeed the very abnormality of the Ulster crisis in terms of the accepted traditions of postwar British politics encouraged Westminster to see the Troubles as a temporary eruption intruding into more pressing areas of British policy such as the economy or the Common Market. In those early years there was an understandable lack of concentration on Ulster affairs. This was to prove costly, and eventually to force upon London a radical review of the relationship between Stormont and Westminster.

While in retrospect the slide to political chaos and violence in 1972 appears inevitable it did not seem that way in 1969. For the British government at any rate there were some optimistic signs that political stability could be re-established and that conflict could be taken off the streets and returned to the debating chamber. A two-pronged strategy seemed to be called for. There was the necessity, first of all, to fashion a package of political reforms to satisfy Catholic grievances while attracting sufficient allegiance from moderate Unionists. In practice this meant convincing the leadership of the Unionist Party to see 'reason' and not to stand on the dignity of giving 'not an inch'. In this regard, British policy met with qualified success. It was impossible to make reform palatable to all Unionists or even to a majority of Protestants. It did prove possible, however, to convince a reluctant majority in the Unionist government at Stormont. First Chichester-Clark and then his successor, Brian Faulkner, were able to carry the legislation of a number of significant reforms. These included the creation of a ministry of community relations; the creation of the office of Ombudsman for complaints against local authorities; reform of the RUC and disbandment of the B-Specials; and proposals for the thoroughgoing reform of local government organisation and franchise. In June 1971, Faulkner went so far as to suggest a new series of parliamentary committees which would enable the opposition to review policy and suggest changes. In August, the first Catholic to be brought into the Northern Ireland Cabinet, Gerard Newe, was appointed minister of state in the prime minister's office.

Emergence of Alliance Party

There were hopeful developments outside the Unionist administration that further encouraged the British government that their policy of reform would pay off and draw together conciliatory politicians of both sides, Protestant and Catholic. Two new parties emerged in 1970 committed to peaceful constitutional change. In April the non-sectarian, centrist Alliance Party was formed under the leadership of Oliver Napier. Alliance brought together pro-reform Unionists who had supported O'Neill, former

members of the Northern Ireland Liberal and Northern Ireland Labour Parties, and moderate-minded Protestants and Catholics hitherto uninvolved in party politics. The party's central message was one of compromise and cooperation, and it proposed to unite on a common platform of support for the Union and an end to religious discrimination. Originally aiming to win support from the majority of the electorate, Alliance came to see its role as the moderating 'centre' of Ulster politics necessary for the formation of any truly balanced Northern Ireland government.

Formation of SDLP

Also in April 1970, the Social Democratic and Labour Party (SDLP) came into existence under the leadership of Gerry Fitt. It displaced the old Nationalist Party which had come to be seen by Catholics as something of an irrelevance. For the first time, the SDLP provided Northern Catholics with a modern party organisation capable of democratically articulating their views. Previously the Nationalist Party had relied on an informal network of priests and local notables. The SDLP also formulated a programme for social and economic reform – again something distinctly lacking in the inarticulate conservatism of Catholic nationalism. This was the work of the party leadership, which blended the traditional labourist, trade-union thinking of Gerry Fitt and Paddy Devlin in Belfast with the radicalism of civil rights activists such as John Hume, Austin Currie and Ivan Cooper from the west of Ulster.

However, it was not just organisation and policy presentation that made the SDLP a different force from traditional nationalism. There was now a new constitutional emphasis; whereas the Nationalist Party had been straightforwardly anti-partitionist, the SDLP accepted that there could be no change in the constitution of Northern Ireland without the consent of the majority. The new party was prepared to work within the institutions of the province, first of all to achieve social and economic reform, and

secondly to generate popular support for the eventual goal of Irish unity. This willingness to participate in the political process was indeed a dramatic gesture by Catholic political leaders. But Unionist politicians failed to grasp its significance and their insensitivity on this point, however understandable, precipitated the downfall of the very institutions they were pledged to defend.

The second element of necessary strategy was the implementation of a security policy that would satisfy Protestant demands for action against the IRA and placate the anti-reform politicians both within and outside the Unionist government. All things being equal, this appeared to be an evenhanded approach, giving something to both sides. Unfortunately the politics of security did not harmonise with the politics of reform. In July 1971 two

Far left: A Loyalist crowd, angry at the imposition of direct rule in March 1972, protests in front of the Northern Ireland parliament building at Stormont. Any threat – real or supposed – to the political status quo in the province is guaranteed to elicit this sort of response. Below: The last two prime ministers of Northern Ireland: left, Major James Chichester-Clark (August 1969–March 1971), and right, Brian Faulkner (March 1971–March 1972). Neither proved capable of dealing with the growing crisis in the province. Right: A dangerous game: a youngster in Northern Ireland plays at being a gunman. To an army patrol his parka, mask and gun would look real enough, with tragic consequences. The effect of the violence on the young is a cause of some concern.

Catholics – Seamus Cusack and Desmond Beattie – were shot dead by the army during a riot in Londonderry. The government's refusal to hold an inquiry led to the withdrawal of the SDLP from Stormont. In August, the introduction of internment directed against Catholics proved the last straw. It alienated virtually all sections of Catholic opinion and in October 1971 an 'alternative parliament' was set up in Dungannon consisting of opposition politicians under the presidency of John Hume. The internment 'outrage' confirmed the opposition belief that despite the reformist image, Unionist politics remained incorrigibly sectarian. Stormont would have to go. This leg of British policy would no longer stand. Nor did the government's increasingly hard line on security placate the Protestant anti-reformers. The Unionist Party began to

disintegrate from within and to face new challenges from without.

In February 1972 William Craig, ex-minister for home affairs, helped form Ulster Vanguard, a right-wing Unionist ginger group critical of the Faulkner leadership and British policy. In March 1973 Craig's organisation split completely from the Unionist Party to become the Vanguard Unionist Progressive Party (VUPP), which rejected Faulkner's apparent subservience to London and advocated an 'Ulster' solution to the crisis, untrammelled by British restraints. There was also a growing challenge from the Reverend Ian Paisley's Democratic Unionist Party (DUP) founded in September 1971, which claimed to be 'right wing in the sense of being strong on the constitution, but to the left on social policies'. This populist Unionism was critical of the old order and in this period seemed to put an emphasis on greater integration with the rest of the UK. Yet, while concerned for tougher security, Paisley was opposed to internment, and thus showed greater political acumen than most in Unionist politics.

By 1972, then, the Unionist administration in Stormont had precipitated the worst of all possible outcomes – a reform package that no longer satisfied the raised political consciousness of the Catholic minority while at the same time provoking the atavistic hostility of the majority; a security policy that alienated the mass of Catholic opinion while doing nothing to curb the escalating violence. Unable to distinguish between legitimate dissent and subversion, between prudence and principle, Unionist security policy entirely dissipated whatever immediate political gains reform had generated. On 22 March 1972, in the aftermath of 'Bloody Sunday', the British government proposed to Faulkner that Stormont should relinquish control of its law-and-order functions. This was something that Unionists could not accept. On 24 March, Stormont was suspended, and Edward Heath, the Conservative prime minister, announced that under Section 75 of the 1920 Government of Ireland Act, Westminster, as the sovereign parliament, would forthwith assume responsibility for Northern Ireland affairs. Direct rule had been imposed.

Direct rule and power-sharing

Direct rule came as a shock to Ulster Protestants, though the immediate response was muted partly due to a certain demoralisation and disorganisation, partly due to the fact that there was little they could actually do. A symbolic two-day strike was organised by Vanguard to coincide with the last sitting of the Northern Ireland parliament on 28 March. There was also some wild talk about a

Above: A member of the Parachute Regiment cautiously patrols the streets of Belfast, in the neighbourhood of City Hall.

unilateral declaration of independence, but this was bravado, not practical politics. The British government recognised that the suspension of Stormont would be greeted as a victory for the Catholics and tried to soften the blow for the majority by reiterating and reaffirming Northern Ireland's position within the UK. Later, provision was made for regular referendums to be taken to test support for the British connection. This was calculated to try to take the border out of politics while at the same time satisfying Protestant opinion. A poll was held on 8 March 1973 and confirmed what was already known – that there was a Protestant majority in favour of the Union. Of those who voted 98% supported it. Most Catholics, however, boycotted the poll, but the percentage of the total electorate in favour was still 57%.

Under the Northern Ireland (Temporary Provisions) Act which became law on 30 March 1972, responsibility for the government of the province passed into the hands of the secretary of state for Northern Ireland, who was to have a seat in the British Cabinet. The first Northern Ireland secretary was William Whitelaw, a respected and senior member of the Conservative government. He was initially assisted by two ministers of state and a parliamentary under-secretary, who were responsible for the administration of policy through the Northern Ireland Office. The NIO was staffed by civil servants seconded from Whitehall and operated sep-

arately from the existing civil service at Stormont. An advisory commission of 11 prominent Ulster figures was appointed to represent local views though this was a mere formal concession to popular participation. The procedure for legislation was to be by Orders in Council, a convenient constitutional device which had the advantage, from the government's point of view, of keeping Northern Ireland affairs more or less distinct from the normal business of the House of Commons. What amounted to government by decree was justified by the temporary nature of direct rule. Once the administrative and political machinery was in place, Whitelaw set about his task of effecting a workable settlement for devolved government.

Concession and compromise

To improve the political atmosphere the secretary of state began to release some internees, to show Catholics that political gains were to be had through cooperation. This was balanced by Operation Motorman on 31 July 1972, the clearing of Republican and Loyalist barricades in Belfast and Londonderry and the army occupation of Republican 'No-Go' areas. What characterised this early phase of direct rule was the tactic of balance, a calculation of concession and compromise to effect a positive response from Protestants and Catholics. Despite this evenhandedness, direct rule increased political uncertainty. The Provisionals believed that they could get rid of the British once and for all, and Loyalist paramilitaries responded with a campaign of sectarian killing. The direct rule team appeared to be presiding over a barely disguised civil war. Nevertheless, Whitelaw persevered, and virtually kept open house at Stormont Castle. He engaged in an exhaustive round of private talks with all parties and legitimate interest groups. He even went so far as to hold secret discussions in London with representatives of the Provisional IRA. Whitelaw's pervasive optimism, bluff good humour, and willingness to find something positive in even the most cranky of political proposals earned him the name of Willie 'Whitewash'. It was a name that expressed the profoundest suspicion of Whitelaw's motives.

After six months of the new approach there was precious little evidence that the conditions for political reconstruction had been established. When the secretary of state called a round-table conference of the local parties at Darlington, County Durham, on 25–7 September 1972, only three bothered to turn up. Paisley's DUP and the SDLP refused to participate. Those which did, the Official Unionists, Alliance and the Northern Ireland

Eireann authority following the broadcast of an interview with Sean MacStiofain, the Provisional IRA chief of staff. The reporter was gaoled. Nevertheless the informal British approach raises suspicions of behind-the-scenes manipulation.

A valuable contrast in political impact is provided by the coverage of the two Loyalist strikes in May 1974 and May 1977. The leaders of both the Ulster Workers' Council (UWC) strike and the power-sharing Executive believe that the radio and television coverage of the 14 days in May 1974 was crucial to the Loyalist victory. The UWC had learned from the miners' struggle against the Conservative government in 1973–4 and knew the value of a good press. Due to the confused response of the Northern Ireland Office (NIO) and Executive and their hesitation in providing spokesmen to confront the strikers, radio and television reporters came to rely upon the UWC for information. This contributed to its authority and credibility and led critics to claim that the BBC had become the strikers' news service. UWC leaders came across publicly not as rebels but as the men in control of Northern Ireland's destiny.

In 1977, however, the situation was completely reversed. Rather than stressing support for the action, news reports emphasised the numbers working as normal. Instead of day-to-day bulletins about the run-down of the economy and power supply, in 1977 discussion focused on the long-term damage to jobs and business of such 'constitutional stoppages'. The field was not left free for spokesmen of the strikers. The NIO argued its case forcefully and got across its message that the stoppage was a sinister challenge to order and stability. National broadcasts were universally hostile. On BBC's *Nationwide* on 4 May, Bernard Falk's report set the tone by ridiculing and lambasting the strike. These points are not meant to suggest that the BBC and ITV alone determined the course of events; in 1974 and 1977 there were significant differences of circumstance. But they do illustrate the immense difficulties for the media in balancing the claims of responsibility, objectivity and honesty in the divisive political culture of Northern Ireland.

Left: A Ford Anglia, suspected of containing a terrorist bomb, is blown up as a precaution by an army remote-controlled 'Wheelbarrow' device (note wire trailing from the car, bottom left). Photographs such as this, dramatic and violent, are meat and drink to the media, but are not necessarily representative of life in Northern Ireland, large areas of which appear unaffected by the Troubles.

sharing, but only by the narrowest of margins. The SDLP also agreed to forgo the demand for the immediate ending of internment. Eventually, on 22 November, an Executive-designate was agreed. It was to consist of 11 members – 6 Unionists, 4 SDLP and 1 Alliance – plus 5 non-voting members – 2 SDLP, 2 Alliance and 1 Unionist. Faulkner was to be chief executive and Fitt to be his deputy. However, there was yet one more hurdle to leap. Agreement had to be reached on the Council of Ireland. This was achieved on 6–10 December 1973 at Sunningdale, Berkshire. Modelled on the institutions of the EEC, the Council was to be composed of two tiers; a 14-strong Council of Ministers and a 60-member Consultative Assembly. Initially it was to be charged with the review of economic cooperation in Ireland. Sunningdale proved the last straw for the Unionist Party, who rejected the settlement at a meeting on 4 January 1974. Faulkner then resigned the leadership of the party, renamed his supporters in the Assembly the Unionist Party of Northern Island (UPNI) but carried on as chief executive. Despite all the obstacles and difficulties the Executive was in place by January. Whitelaw appeared to have achieved his Irish miracle and returned to Westminster to deal with the deteriorating industrial relations situation facing the Conservative government. Francis Pym took his place – but not for long.

The general election

As the Executive struggled to establish its credibility, its position was undermined by a decision taken in London. In February Edward Heath called a general election. To the dismay of the power-sharing parties it was clear that in the province the election would be used as a referendum on the Executive's

Right: William Whitelaw, Conservative secretary of state for Northern Ireland, 1972–4. Below: The Sunningdale talks, December 1973.

short existence. In the highly charged political atmosphere of the campaign it was impossible to make a fair assessment of its performance. The language of the campaign was full of emotional terms like 'betrayal' and 'sell-out'. Too much had happened too soon and this worked to the advantage of the anti-Executive forces. These Loyalists – DUP, VUPP and the Unionist Party – allied themselves under the umbrella of the United Ulster Unionist Council and won 51% of the vote and 11 of the 12 Westminster seats. The UUUC claimed that this was a mandate for changes and immediately began to agitate for new Assembly elections, an end to power-sharing and the abolition of the as yet unconstituted Council of Ireland.

Such claims did not alter the fact that the UUUC did not have a majority in the Assembly. On 14 May 1974, the Sunningdale agreement was accepted by a vote of 44 to 28. Loyalists, however, asserted a legitimacy higher than an Assembly vote. They shifted their opposition to extra-parliamentary action. That same Tuesday evening, 14 May, Harry Murray, a shop-steward at the Belfast shipyard of Harland and Wolff, announced to the press that the Ulster Workers' Council (UWC) was calling a strike against the Executive. On behalf of the UWC he demanded that new elections be held, for no

majority had voted for power-sharing with Republicans nor for a Council of Ireland. The 'constitutional stoppage' that was to end Whitelaw's carefully balanced settlement had begun.

UWC strike and aftermath

This idea for a 'constitutional stoppage' or general strike was an initiative of Protestant worker leaders and it was one that was only hesitantly and reluctantly adopted by even the most militant of Loyalist politicians. Preparations had been made well in advance, however, and the UWC was clear about what it was doing. The aim was not just temporarily to paralyse the Ulster economy and force the hand of the British government. The strike was also designed to illustrate the power and solidarity of Protestant opposition to imposed solutions that might satisfy London's sense of balance but did not address the problems of Loyalist insecurity. In particular there was a determination to scuttle the 'Irish dimension'. The UWC strike may thus be seen as an effectively organised boycott of British policy. Yet the eventual success of the UWC strategy which, after 14 days, forced the collapse of the Executive, did not just depend upon the skilful manoeuvres of the strikers. It depended equally upon the response of the new Labour government in general and the new Northern Ireland secretary, Merlyn Rees, in particular. This response showed that both Rees and prime minister Harold Wilson misread the situation and miscalculated the efficacy of the UWC tactics. Loyalist will finally proved stronger than that of the British government.

Rees, acting on the advice of the army, was reluctant to confront the UWC with a serious show of force. The army also advised against attempting to use troops to operate vital services. (In any case, the army did not possess the expertise to run the power stations, controlled by the UWC.) The view of the military was that it was courting disaster to confront the mass industrial action of the strikers while fighting the IRA at the same time. As it happened, the Provisionals engaged in no offensive action during the strike, which led some Catholic politicians to claim that the troops' non-intervention proved that the military supported the Loyalist aims of the strike. Despite such a conspiracy theory, the answer appears more prosaic. The army treated the strike as a logistical and policing problem, not as a challenge to the authority of the government. British policy therefore found no adequate focus, to the advantage and the relief of the UWC. Later, members of the strike committee admitted that outright violence between Loyalists and the forces of the Crown would have meant the collapse of

support for the stoppage. Protestant opinion would not have stood for it. As it happened, however, the 17,500 troops in Ulster were not used as strike-breakers despite plaintive appeals from the Executive.

During the stoppage the UWC was organised by a coordinating committee headed by Glen Barr, a young Vanguard Assemblyman with paramilitary connections. The composition of this committee was a coalition of leading Unionist politicians, paramilitary leaders and worker representatives. Paisley, Craig and Harry West, leader of the Unionist Party, rubbed shoulders with Andy Tyrie of the UDA and Ken Gibson of the UVF, and with Billy Kelly of the power workers, Hugh Petrie of Short Brothers' aircraft factory and Harry Murray of the shipyard. Later, workers and paramilitaries were to feel that the politicians had jumped on the bandwagon and used the strike for their own ends. Whatever bad feeling arose subsequently there was enough consistency of purpose to present a united front throughout the 14 days. It had been planned to use as little intimidation as possible, though paramilitary muscle was overtly and covertly employed to prevent people getting to work and to make sure shops and factories stayed closed. Roadblocks were set up all over the province and in Protestant districts of Belfast the UDA established virtual No-Go areas within which its men paraded in mass ranks. As the impact of the strike widened, it took on a credibility of its own. The UWC became a sort of alternative government, controlling petrol supplies, organising food distribution and permitting safe conduct for essential supplies and services. Its spokesmen were given extensive air time on radio and television, a fact that outraged both Rees and the Executive.

In the events of these crucial days there were few casualties and few dramatic showdowns between the security forces and strikers. On 22 May there seemed the likelihood of serious trouble when troops and paramilitaries faced each other across barricades on the Sandy Row and Shankill in Belfast. However, discussion between army commanders and paramilitary leaders led to peaceful removal of the obstructions. The UWC did not really need shows of force. It had control of the electricity power supply. This was the trump card. The slow, deliberate running-down of the grid exerted increasing pressure on the authorities. Rees was faced with the total breakdown of all services, including sewage, with the concomitant threat to public health. The British government's nerve broke first. It did not have the will to call the UWC bluff. The ill-fated Executive resigned.

Victory went to the UWC. What the 'constitutional stoppage' proved was that no

political agreement was possible against the organised will of significant sections of the Protestant population. Yet this power was negative. The UWC had no authority to determine a new settlement. That responsibility passed back into the hands of the secretary of state and the British government. The reaction of London was initially one of despair and exasperation. Certainly this was the tone of Harold Wilson's famous television broadcast of 25 May, in which he accused Loyalists of being 'people who spend their lives sponging on Westminster and British democracy and then systematically assault democratic methods'. Obviously there was some calculation in this outburst, some final attempt to shame the UWC into calling off its strike. Nevertheless it illustrated a feeling of frustration. Northern Ireland's problems were becoming a tiresome distraction. Even if it wanted to, though, the government could not ignore the crisis. Merlyn Rees had to begin all over again the painful process of trying to piece together a political settlement.

Convention replaces Assembly

The Assembly was prorogued and on 4 July the government issued the White Paper, *The Northern Ireland Constitution*, the main provisions of which were incorporated into the Northern Ireland Act of 17 July 1974. There was to be an elected Northern Ireland Constitutional Convention again, with 78 members whose function was to formulate a report on the form of devolved government 'likely to command the most widespread acceptance throughout the community there'. This report would be sent to the secretary of state who would then submit it to parliament for approval or rejection. The Convention approach represented something of a retreat for the British government. Rather than try to generate an agreement by the Whitelaw approach of 'creative initiative', Rees was forced to opt for an 'internal settlement'. The Convention's logic was to encourage locally elected representatives to mould their own compromises and establish their own political proposals. This was a false prospectus for at least two main reasons. First, the British government already had a preconceived notion of what would be an acceptable outcome of the Convention. It was still looking for some form of power-sharing and had set its face against majority rule. Secondly, since May the political lines had hardened against compromise. Loyalists, in the full flush of the UWC victory, were in no mood for making concessions. They had their eyes on the restoration of the old Stormont order. On the other side, the SDLP had been left in an exposed political position with the collapse of the Executive, and felt betrayed by the British

Above: The Ulster Workers' Council strike, 1974: a picket blocks a road in Belfast. As the province ground to a halt, neither the security forces nor the politicians in London could break the deadlock.
Above right: Protestant crowds celebrate the collapse of the power-sharing Executive. The actions of the Loyalist majority in Northern Ireland in 1974 effectively defeated one of the more promising political initiatives and gave notice that similar attempts in the future would also be blocked.
Right: Schoolboys view the aftermath of a terrorist bomb blast, Belfast, 1974. By 1985 a whole generation had grown up hardened to violence.

government. It was understandably wary of involving itself in a Convention likely to be dominated by Loyalists, and was suspicious of British intentions. The SDLP spokesmen, while making clear their support for power-sharing, began to lay greater stress on the 'Irish dimension' despite the knowledge that it was the insistence on the Council of Ireland that had precipitated the Protestant reaction against the Executive. To the dismay of its labourist leaders like Fitt and Devlin, the SDLP was becoming 'greener', more traditionally nationalist. Thus from the outset the whole Convention exercise appeared a half-hearted affair and very few believed anything positive would come from it.

Elections to the Convention did not take place until 1 May 1975. It was the seventh poll in just over two years and confirmed the collapse of the political centre. With a lower turnout than normal in Ulster elections,

victory went to the UUUC alliance of DUP, VUPP and Official Unionist. The UUUC took 55% of the vote and 46 seats. SDLP won 24% of the poll and 17 seats; Alliance 10% and eight seats. Faulkner's UPNI did poorly, with a vote of only 8%, and gained five seats in the Convention. The result meant, as expected, that the UUUC could resist all moves towards power-sharing. Only once during the labours of the Convention did there appear a chance of breaking the deadlock. William Craig, leader of Vanguard, suggested a form of 'voluntary coalition' with the SDLP for the duration of one parliament to cope with the Ulster 'emergency'. Though Craig's proposal had the support of Andy Tyrie's UDA, his Convention party split 9–5 against, and the initiative was decisively rejected by the UUUC. The Convention report of 7 November 1975 called for a return of devolved majority government with

minority representation on parliamentary departmental committees but not in Cabinet. On the advice of Rees, Westminster rejected the report, and even an extension of the Convention's life in 1976 did nothing to produce anything acceptable to the British government. Direct rule continued.

Another development in December 1974 and early 1975 distracted attention from the rather sterile debates of the political parties. The Provisional IRA declared a ceasefire (officially termed a 'truce'), which led to speculation that some secret agreement had been reached with the British government about withdrawal from Northern Ireland.

Politics of the ceasefire

The British government had tried before to reach an understanding with the Provisionals about the realities of the Northern Ireland situation. On 7 July 1972, during a brief ceasefire, a six-man PIRA delegation, including Daithi O Conaill and Gerry Adams, had been flown to London to a secret meeting with William Whitelaw. The secretary of state's aim seems to have been to encourage the Provisional leadership to move towards political activity. He and his officials were looking for an end to hostilities in return for political concessions. On the other hand, the PIRA delegation were looking not for sweet words but for a commitment on the part of the British government to remove its 'occupation forces' from Ireland. The ceasefire had broken down within two days of the London meeting.

The second and sustained ceasefire had rather curious origins. After the embarrassment following the revelation of the Whitelaw talks, formal British policy was to have no direct negotiations with the PIRA leadership. An intermediary for the second round of talks was therefore necessary; this turned out to be a group of Protestant clergymen headed by the Reverend William Arlow. A preliminary meeting had been held on 10 December 1974 between leading Provisionals and the clergymen at Feakle, County Clare. Shortly afterwards Arlow established contact with officials at the NIO. Sympathetic noises were made by Rees and a ceasefire was called over Christmas and the New Year. After further consultation between NIO officials and Provisional Sinn Fein, the political wing of the PIRA which had been legalised in 1974, an indefinite ceasefire was announced in February 1975.

The motives and expectations of both sides still remain controversial and unclear. From what evidence there is, it appears that the Provisionals believed that the British government was preparing to wash its hands of Northern Ireland. The Convention, they thought, was a 'put-up job', the inevitable failure of which would provide London with the excuse it needed to withdraw. This was an analysis that the British representatives did nothing to contradict. It seems that in the discussions of January and February the NIO encouraged these ideas without giving any positive commitment. Ambiguity was in its interests. Undoubtedly the PIRA was convinced that a ceasefire would be one important condition facilitating such a change in British policy. For Rees and his team the immediate advantage was an end to the insurgent campaign. It was hoped that this would enable a normalisation of the political situation and a prolonged ceasefire might build up Catholic opinion against any new military action. A second consideration was that the PIRA might decide to go political. In the meantime a period of peace would enable the security forces to build up intelligence and perhaps

Left: A common Belfast scene – a British soldier, armed with a 7.62mm Lee Enfield sniper's rifle. Above: Merlyn Rees, Labour secretary of state for Northern Ireland, 1974–6.

exploit tensions within the Republican movement. Another possibility is that Rees intended the ceasefire to encourage the politicians in the Convention to reach an agreement. If so this was a serious miscalculation. The SDLP, as the legitimate representative of Catholic opinion, was outraged that the NIO had gone behind its back to deal directly with the gunmen. The UUUC in turn was loud in its denunciation of any 'understanding' between Her Majesty's Government and the 'enemies of Ulster'.

To monitor the ceasefire, 'incident centres' were set up in Catholic areas of Belfast, Londonderry and other towns. These centres, manned by Provisional Sinn Fein activists, were in direct contact with NIO officials to ensure that no infringement of the ceasefire would get out of hand. For many Loyalist paramilitaries these developments seemed to presage a 'sell-out' by the British. Sectarian killings of Protestants and Catholics increased while security force casualties dropped dramatically. As the year went on, the ceasefire, such as it was, began to break down. On 11 November the NIO withdrew from the incident-centre arrangement. In January 1976, Harold Wilson, far from announcing any new initiative, declared that a united Ireland was a proposition that no British government could impose upon the people of Northern Ireland. The ceasefire was at an end. On balance the government probably emerged from the affair with immediate advantage. After 1976, the PIRA was not able to mount a campaign of pre-ceasefire proportions. Divisions, conflicts and confusions had also been exposed in its ranks. The Provisionals bitterly and ironically levelled accusations of 'perfidi-

ous Albion' against the NIO. On the other hand the government had stored up for itself the mistrust of all the established political parties.

Direct rule 1976–7

In September 1976 Merlyn Rees left Northern Ireland to become home secretary and was replaced by Roy Mason. As defence secretary since 1974, Mason was already familiar with the security problems in Northern Ireland. He made no urgent attempts to foster agreement on devolved government, accepting that the end of the Convention meant that direct rule would have to continue for the foreseeable future. Instead Mason set about improving the machinery of direct rule and the effectiveness of security policy. In order to achieve a 'normalisation' of the situation Mason continued two lines of policy initiated by Rees in 1975–6. These were the 'criminalisation' of terrorism and the 'Ulsterisation' of the security forces.

By 5 December 1975 the last internee had left the Long Kesh internment centre (renamed H.M. Prison Maze in 1972), and the criminalisation strategy got under way. After 1 March 1976 no one convicted of terrorist offences was granted the special category status conceded by Whitelaw in 1972. Special category, also known as political status, enabled prisoners to organise their regime on a compound or 'prisoner-of-war' basis. They did no prison work, had free association with one another, could wear their own clothes and had other privileges such as more frequent visits. This status had been criticised as a serious mistake in the official Gardiner Report of 1975. A committee chaired by the former Lord Chancellor, Lord Gardiner, had been asked to examine anti-terrorist legislation in Northern Ireland in the context of civil liberties and human rights. It reported that political status contributed to the romanticisation and even encouragement of political violence. After March 1976, those convicted of terrorist crimes served criminal sentences in the new 'H-Block' cells constructed at the Maze and Magilligan prisons, and had to conform to normal prison routine. A new emphasis in security policy was now conviction by confession. The interrogation centres at police barracks, in particular Castlereagh in Belfast, became pivotal points of the criminalisation strategy. They also became a focus of a PIRA propaganda campaign claiming that torture and unusual punishment were being used to exact confessions.

Ulsterisation entailed reducing the policing role of the regular army and increasing the presence of the RUC and UDR. Under a new chief constable appointed in May 1976, Kenneth Newman, the RUC was reorganised and re-equipped with modern weaponry. Both the police and police reserve were granted increases in recruitment levels, as was the full-time complement of the UDR. This constituted an all-round tougher approach to security which also involved more widespread use of the Special Air Service (SAS) Regiment in undercover operations. Security was to become the dominant theme of Mason's tenure of office.

There were a number of developments that worked in his favour. The first was the emergence of a new peace movement. It arose as an emotional response to the death of three

Catholic children in west Belfast on 10 August 1976, killed by a PIRA getaway car which was being chased by an army patrol. The Peace People, led by two Catholic women from Andersonstown, Betty Williams and Mairead Corrigan, and a journalist, Ciaran McKeown, were the focus for a spontaneous outpouring of sympathy from both Catholics and Protestants. Emotional rallies were held in Belfast and elsewhere. The movement's purpose was symbolised by the meeting of mass demonstrations of Catholics and Protestants, former neighbours, but divided by the Troubles. The Peace People represented a reaction both against the killing by paramilitaries, Republican and Loyalist, and the intransigence of party politicians. Committed to non-violence, peace and justice, they were naive enough to believe that these goals could be attained by non-political means. They thought that goodwill was enough and tried to avoid specific and concrete proposals. This vagueness was the Peace People's initial strength and their ultimate undoing. However, in the first year of Mason's tenure of the NIO, the movement contributed to a less violent political atmosphere.

The second factor in Mason's favour was the significant diminution in Loyalist killings. This was due to at least two reasons. One was the body-blow delivered to the UVF in 1976–7. A number of informers helped to smash much of the organisation's network throughout Northern Ireland. Another was the increasing politicisation of Andy Tyrie's UDA, which had become fascinated with the prospect of a negotiated independence for Northern Ireland. To everyone's surprise, much of the original thinking on the

Northern Ireland problem over the next five years was to come from such UDA men as Glen Barr and John McMichael.

The 1977 UUAC strike

A crucial political victory for Mason came in May 1977 when he faced down another Loyalist strike, engineered by the United Unionist Action Council. The prime mover of the UUAC was Ian Paisley, who had the support of most paramilitaries. Ostensibly the strike was designed to force a change towards a tougher security policy, although it was also judged to be an attempt to blackmail the government into conceding devolved majority government. The UUAC tried to recreate the success of the UWC in 1974 but was unable to win over or coerce the Protestant workforce. It was generally seen as 'Paisley's strike' and was thus too party political to command widespread Loyalist support. In particular, the power workers refused to come out and the strike fizzled out after ten days. This failure also meant that Mason had an easier time with Loyalist politicians. Angered by Paisley's *démarche*, the Official Unionists left the United Ulster Unionist Council and the coalition disintegrated. Mason was able to work on the principle of divide and rule and did not have to face the same obdurate Unionist bloc which had confronted Rees.

So by the end of 1977 the record of direct rule was ambivalent. On the one hand there was a definite improvement in security and an observable return to what passed for normality in the life of Belfast and other towns. On the other, the political *impasse* remained – compromise appeared as far-off as ever.

Below: The 'H-Blocks' built at the Maze prison (formerly Long Kesh) in 1976.

Right: Betty Williams (left) and Mairead Corrigan, leaders of the Peace People.

6. The Security Forces 1969-1985

The security forces deployed in Northern Ireland during 1969 were formidably experienced in counter-insurgency work. This makes it all the harder to explain why they failed to prevent the IRA developing as a major insurgent force in the first three years of the Troubles. However, a closer look at Ulster's indigenous forces – the Royal Ulster Constabulary (RUC) and the B-Specials auxiliary police – shows that their knowledge, expertise and direction were seriously deficient. The British Army, on the other hand, with its impressive record of colonial counter-insurgency operations in Malaya, Kenya and Borneo, was ensnared by a tight but vacillating political control which never allowed it to develop a coherent campaign. Only when negotiations between the British government and the revived IRA had broken down in 1972 were British politicians convinced that there was no political 'quick fix', and the security forces freed from an almost monthly change in the conduct of operations.

It would be wrong, however, to blame political miscalculation for all the province's troubles when misconduct and ineptitude on the part of security for s made such a substantial contri n. This was particularly so during th mer of 1969 when the RUC and the B-Specials appeared to inflame rather than pacify the spreading revolt. Part of the trouble was that they were simply not numerous enough: there were only 3400 RUC men and 8000 B-Specials. When serious disorders began the RUC were quickly exhausted, and the training and equipment of the B-Specials was hardly suited to riot control. But it was also true that neither force was impartial and they simply could not be fully accepted by the province's minority population.

The RUC at the time was not quite as massively Protestant as was widely believed. In fact in 1969 it was some 11% Catholic, a not insignificant figure given the historical polarisation between the two communities. Indeed there had been a perceptible blurring of the battle-lines through the 1960s as prosperity coupled with the IRA's renunciation of violence encouraged tentative moves towards reconciliation. This 11% was not so much remarkable for the RUC's acceptance of Catholic recruits as for the willingness of so many Catholics to adopt such a strong anti-nationalist stance. However, the exhaustion and increasing panic of the summer of 1969 strained mutual tolerance beyond breaking point. Most RUC men believed they were

Left: A patrol of the 17/21st Lancers, equipped with a Ferret scout car and a Saracen armoured personnel carrier, halts by the roadside in a rural area while the officers confer with helicopter-borne plain-clothes police.

witnessing a nationalist uprising along sectarian lines and reverted to traditional sectarian behaviour. On 19 April, in response to rioting between civil rights protesters and Protestant extremists, they staged what can only be described as a punitive raid on the Bogside in which they hoped to cow the population by cracking the nearest few heads with their truncheons. On the night of 14/15 August the RUC again panicked, driving Shorland armoured cars into the Catholic Divis Street and Falls Road area in Belfast and killing three people with indiscriminate machine-gun fire. Both exercises were futile and served only to infuriate the Catholics more. One of the first priorities in the Troubles would obviously be changes in the RUC.

The B-Specials

Even more urgent, however, were changes in the B-Specials. This force was entirely Protestant in composition and owed its origins to the volunteers raised to fight Irish Republicanism in 1920. In the violence of 1922 they had gained a reputation for brutality and anti-Catholic bias which had become something of a legend. There were no medical or educational tests for recruits, who were often bigoted and not apt to acquire high standards of discipline. They were popularly reckoned to be uniformed thugs (somewhat gleefully by the Protestant community) and their deployment on riot duties in 1969 was almost an act of desperation in the Northern Ireland Stormont parliament's struggle to maintain control. Indeed the province's government was so nervous that they might perpetrate a headline-catching massacre that they were not authorised to draw arms but issued, at first, with batons only. The arrival of this much-vaunted shock force on the streets of Londonderry on 14 August was bathetic: ill-equipped and in ill-fitting uniforms they were unable to keep step as they waved to friends on their march through the Protestant areas towards the rioting. Their assistance did not enable the RUC to restore order and, although they later drew their weapons, the Specials were fortunately unable to make much use of them because, by then, the British Army was on the streets.

In their favour it should be said that the efforts of both the RUC and the B-Specials were hampered by inappropriate training and weaponry. The Specials were more of a territorial army reserve than a police force – in times of emergency they were supposed to set up roadblocks and guard key installations with their armoured cars and rifles. They were ready for a rural guerrilla campaign such as that of the late 1950s but completely unprepared for riot control. Nor were the

RUC much better off with their small riot shields which were little use against stones and none against petrol bombs. Although they had CS gas and gas guns, there was often a delay in supplying the cartridges, which usually appeared some hours after a riot had reached full pitch. Both forces were unequal to their task in equipment and attitude, and ripe for the reforms that came at the end of 1969. The disbandment of the B-Specials was closely followed by the establishment of the Ulster Defence Regiment (UDR), while the RUC underwent extensive changes.

While all this went on the British Army was left, virtually alone, to hold the ring and restore order. Its failure to do this was a testimony to the genuine popular pressure behind the revolt but also to military shortcomings. Of all armies the British was one of the most experienced in countering disorder and insurgency. It had faced rioting in one part of the globe or another throughout the 20th century and had recently assisted in putting down the 'Red Guard' riots stirred up in Hong Kong by the Chinese Cultural Revolution with the aid of mobile barricades, CS gas and wooden baton rounds. In Hong Kong the fierce security-force reaction to rioting had been spearheaded by the Hong Kong Police and the Gurkha soldiers of the garrison, who tended to employ an uncompromisingly tough and unrestrained approach, but this sort of thing was out of the question in Ireland. With the eyes of the international news media upon them and with their political masters a mere hour's commercial flight away from them, the soldiers were very restricted in what they could do.

Riot control

The conciliatory tactics adopted in the face of this uncertainty failed to stop the momentum of continuing disorder. For a few months the soldiers found favour with the minority Catholic population, and sentries on the 'Peaceline' between the two communities were welcomed with mugs of tea. However, they were inching their way towards inevitable confrontation as protests, marches and other gatherings nearly always ended in riot. Much of the time soldiers came under attack only as they tried to prevent mobs from one community attacking the other, but, however restrained their reaction to this, it was bound to sour relations eventually. One of the most worrying aspects of the deteriorating situation from the point of view of the security forces was their apparent ineffectiveness in the face of rioters.

The tactics they employed were 'toothless', in the absence of any effective technique to use against stone-throwing mobs. The small

shields, steel helmets, and unprotected vehicles of the early days soon gave way to long shields, plastic helmets with visors, and one-tonne Pigs (Humber armoured personnel carriers), Saracens or Land Rovers, but this only increased the army's defensive capacity. The wooden baton round used in Hong Kong was considered too dangerous for deployment in Ulster, so offensive tactics were confined to the use of CS gas and snatch squads. The basic tactic was for soldiers to be protected from the hail of stones until the rioters ventured too near. Then the snatch squads, composed of selected men stationed just behind the front rank, would race out from behind the line of shields and try to arrest their antagonists. Because lightly clad youths in trainer shoes who have a 40-metre start are rarely caught by the fastest soldier running in boots and encumbered by a light shield this was not widely effective. The rioters were also astonishingly resilient in the face of virtual drenching with CS gas and they soon began to throw things more lethal than stones – petrol, nail and blast bombs.

The army's growing frustration was reflected in the increased hardening of response allowed to soldiers. After the riots of Easter 1970 Lieutenant-General Sir Ian Freeland, GOC (General Officer Commanding) Northern Ireland announced that petrol bombers would be shot dead. In practice this rarely occurred and was impracticable in the case of nail or blast bombers as soldiers could not distinguish such missiles from stones until they landed, with spluttering fuses, in their ranks. In June 1970 the rubber bullet was

introduced and used with a will, although it was too inaccurate and short-ranged to be very effective. These defects were overcome by the introduction of the plastic bullet in 1973 and, although both rubber and plastic rounds were dangerous enough to be controversial, they were preferable to lead.

Long before the first British soldier of the present Troubles was killed on active service in Ireland in February 1971 the security forces were under potentially lethal attack. They had developed an armoury of riot-control weapons to tackle their immediate problems – 'Salamander' water-cannon and a military bulldozer (vulgarly known as a 'Paddy-Pusher') designed to force crowds back, as well as the rubber bullet and better protection for men and vehicles – but these were nearly all vulnerable to high-velocity weapons. There had been gun battles of one sort or another even before the army arrived on the streets of Belfast, so one of the first priorities of the peacekeeping operation was the conduct of searches for weapons. Searching is not an activity which can be unobtrusively or discreetly carried out, but there was considerable evidence that it was often intended to cause maximum inconvenience and damage by irritated soldiers relieving their feelings of frustration. It was certainly very unpopular, and when it was used almost as a punitive measure during the infamous Falls Road curfew of July 1970, served to finalise the break between the army and the minority community.

A single significant and dreadful event – the murder of three very young Scottish

Above: The strain of urban confrontation: a distressed young soldier of the Royal Highland Fusiliers is gently led away by an avuncular NCO, while the warrant officer on the right displays grim determination.

soldiers who had been drinking in a city-centre bar – finally made it clear that the army would have to treat whole areas of the province as hostile territory. Right up to this moment on 10 March 1971 the army had been carrying on an uncoordinated, disorganised 'hearts and minds' campaign among both communities. It took the form of organising youth clubs, sporting events and discos which were ostensibly designed to woo the disaffected, rioting youths but served rather as recreation for the soldiers by enabling them to meet local young women. Few of these contacts survived into 1971 and they proved largely valueless from an intelligence-gathering point of view.

Off-duty dangers

As a result of restrictions on their off-duty movements the soldiers faced a cheerless life during a tour of duty in the province. From the escalation of the Troubles in 1970 very large numbers of them were deployed in Ulster – anywhere between 10,000 and 20,000 men – and there simply was no suitable accommodation for them. They slept crowded into unused factories, shops and even coaches in living accommodation that was sometimes so insecure that they were forced to wear their flak jackets at all times.

Above left: A Royal Highland Fusilier snatch-squad in action: as a ringleader is seized, irate women are kept at bay.
Left: The plastic round, introduced to replace the controversial rubber bullet.
Above: British troops on patrol have become part of everyday life for the people of Northern Ireland.
Below: Troops search suspects at a checkpoint.

During 1971 at least they still took civilian clothes with them on a tour of duty so that they could spend off-duty hours in city-centre bars and discos. IRA attacks on off-duty and unarmed soldiers made this practice very unsafe. At the same time the IRA publicly tarred and feathered girls from the minority community who consorted with soldiers – this effectively snuffed out the last link between the army and the disaffected areas.

While the situation deteriorated the army had been relying on the police and Special Branch for intelligence-gathering. As a result of the Hunt Report published in October 1969 the RUC had been reformed, disarmed (though only temporarily) and put under the command of a London police chief, Sir Arthur Young. Despite the changes the RUC was simply unable to operate normally in the Catholic areas, as a highly publicised incident in January 1971 made clear: two RUC men were rescued from a mob in Clonard, west Belfast, by soldiers who apparently forbade them to re-enter the area as they could not guarantee their protection. This meant that the RUC was limited to the fruits of the low-grade intelligence-gathering of the army's foot patrols and to the results of interrogation of prisoners by the Special Branch. High-grade sources of information within the nationalist community had dried up. However, the RUC still played a useful role collating and storing all information on each 'parish' and passing it on as each new army unit arrived to take over security duties. Most soldiers seemed impressed by the extent of the RUC's knowledge in each 'parish' but its limitations became exposed when internment began in August 1971.

The 1971 bombing campaign

The lead-up to internment had been a heightening of the IRA campaign which included business and commercial premises as 'legitimate' targets from April 1971. There were 37 serious explosions in that month, 47 the next and 50 in June. This blitz continued in tandem with the rioting and shooting attacks on the security forces and added considerably to the impression of escalating disorder. The urban centres – particularly that of Londonderry – soon looked as though they had been under aerial attack and there was an inevitable toll of civilian casualties. Security-force moves to counter this latest threat included an upgrading of bomb-disposal capabilities and a campaign to increase civilian vigilance. These measures gradually became effective as most

Left: Isolated within a potentially hostile community, the army in Northern Ireland has to import its entertainment. Above: Map of Northern Ireland in 1981, showing the main areas of army activity and the RUC boundaries.

shops and restaurants began to employ their own security officers to search customers and keep an eye out for car bombs. In addition to this, important town centres were cordoned off to traffic and all shoppers were searched before entering.

Effective countermeasures to the bombers took time to work and there is no doubt that, by midsummer 1971, the security forces were hard-pressed and looked it. Internment had been effective in the past and the Stormont government wanted to revive it, although the British government and army were more dubious. By August the situation was desperate enough to warrant almost any new initiative and on 9 August the troops detained 342 men. Of these 116 were released within 48 hours but new arrests were continuously made as the month wore on, and army battalions in sensitive areas were given a daily ration of men to be 'lifted'. However, the operation of internment could be assessed as ineffective almost immediately because violence escalated rather than decreased throughout August and opposition to the security forces intensified.

It was a fairly obvious conclusion that internment did not seriously hurt the IRA – the reason for this was faulty intelligence.

With hindsight it is now reckoned that most of those interned in August 1971 were nationalists who had long been on the RUC books; most of the new, active recruits to the Provisional wing of the IRA were not known to the security forces. The result was a long, hard look at intelligence-gathering and the entire counter-insurgency campaign, which probably took place at the Lisburn army headquarters in December 1971. The result of this policy was a programme to try to isolate the IRA from the Catholic community by continuing political reforms and also to lessen the indiscriminate nature of internment by gathering more hard intelligence about the various insurgent groups.

Intelligence-gathering

The difficulty facing army and police intelligence at this time was that the nationalist community had succeeded in establishing No-Go areas behind barricades. Not even the low-grade intelligence gathered by alert foot patrols or concealed observers in Observation Posts (OPs) emanated from behind the barricades. There was still much that could be done. The staff of the intelligence section at Lisburn was greatly increased and cooper-

ation at all levels improved. Army units maintained close contacts with local Special Branch personnel and all sources of information were fed to Brigade Intelligence Sections for collation. Street registers of all the nationalist areas were built up and records kept of their families, associates and way of life. In this way a complete picture of IRA organisation was gradually built up.

The rather bizarre structure of the security forces' main opponent before 1976, the Provisional Irish Republican Army, quickly emerged. The PIRA lived in a grand world of battalions, brigades and armies, with commanders, chiefs-of-staff, intelligence units and adjutants. Indeed the bulletins they put out on meetings of their 'Army Council' would not have disgraced the 'Court and Social' column of *The Times*. However, there was a genuine unit sheltering behind this façade and this was composed of a variable number of volunteers – during 1971 and 1972 the Provisional companies were numerically very strong indeed. At battalion and brigade level there were officers of one sort or another – typically a commander, adjutant, quartermaster, as well as intelligence, explosives, training, recruiting and finance officers – but the individual companies raised in each area were largely autonomous and security-force units realised that their prime duty in their 'parish' was to wear down or destroy their local company.

The first difficulty was that of gaining information on the whereabouts of individuals and this was met in a controversial way. Although it was repeatedly denied for some while, armed, plain-clothes patrols were introduced to Republican areas during 1972.

Bomb disposal

British bomb-disposal experts have neutralised over 3500 explosive devices in Northern Ireland since the start of the present Troubles. Known as Ammunition Technical Officers (ATOs), they are members of the Royal Army Ordnance Corps (RAOC), and their training at the School of Ammunition in Warwickshire includes stringent tests of their mental fitness to cope with the strain of their task as well as technical instruction. The RAOC has been coping with unexploded bombs since the blitz in 1940 and its skills have been finely honed in a number of counter-insurgency campaigns since then.

When the Provisional IRA's bombing campaign began in earnest in 1971 comparatively primitive methods were used. Commercial gelignite attached to an alarm clock was popular, but, because members of the public often succeeded in moving these bombs from their premises to safe ground, an anti-handling device was soon incorporated. However, even when microswitches sensitive to movement were added it was still possible for alert ATOs to neutralise the explosives, so there was a further refinement of PIRA technique. The bombers began to concentrate on remote-controlled devices – detonated by electronic signal or command wire – and these proved much harder to combat. For a time it was possible to blow up bombs which responded to an electronic signal by broadcasting a powerful signal over the whole radio spectrum. This made such bombs useless for ambushes until the PIRA's experts introduced a detonator that only fired in response to a pulsed and tone-coded signal. So continues the constant struggle between the bombers and the ATOs to produce ever more sophisticated detonation techniques and the counter to them.

While the terrorists always have the initiative in the battle of developing technique, the security forces can put pressure on them by attacking their supply lines. The PIRA has never been able to get enough commercial explosive and many of its members were killed in the early 1970s, using unstable explosive mixes made from household products. Now the bomb-making operation is in the hands of technical experts who manufacture explosive and sophisticated triggers in well-equipped laboratories.

There are about 250 ATOs in the British Army who are qualified to work on bomb disposal in Northern Ireland. 312 Ordnance Disposal Unit, under the command of the Chief Ammunition Technical Officer – known as Cato – coordinates their work. When the bombing campaign was at its height in the early 1970s, up to 15 ATOs were operating in the province. The job is highly dangerous – six ATOs were killed in 1972 – although advances in disposal techniques have made it progressively safer. The most important development has been the introduction of 'Wheelbarrow' robots to help ATOs tackle bombs from a distance using remote-controlled TV cameras with handling devices and 'pig sticks' which disintegrate explosive charges by firing bullets of water into them at high speed. The robots can now handle 60% of all explosive devices. The army have also developed an Explosives Ordnance Disposal Suit – something like a bulky space suit – reinforced with ceramic armour which gives protection while approaching or walking away from a bomb.

In addition to dismantling devices, ATOs play a vital intelligence role. Forensic techniques are used which can identify individual bomb-makers, and dossiers are built up on changing methods and patterns of attack. One particular threat is from radio remote-control devices, such as that planted by the PIRA in Lord Mountbatten's fishing boat at Mullaghmore harbour in August 1979. Another is the delayed-action bomb. The device which exploded in the Grand Hotel in Brighton in October 1984 is believed to have been planted up to a month in advance. In combating these types of device specific bomb-disposal techniques are less important than forensic expertise and the gradual accumulation of intelligence concerning bombs and bomb-makers.

Below: Bomb-disposal experts of the RAOC pose with the tools of their dangerous trade. Of particular interest is the remote-controlled tracked 'Wheelbarrow'.

BEWARE OF STRANGERS
S.A.S.
(A Licensed Killer Squad of the British Army)
MAY BE OPERATING IN YOUR NEIGHBOURHOOD

AN S.A.S. MAN MAY:—
• DANCE YOU IN THE BALLROOM
• OFFER YOU A DRINK TO WIN YOUR CONFIDENCE
• VISIT YOU AS A SALESMAN
• JOIN YOU AT THE CATTLE MART
• HOLD A JOB IN YOUR AREA

SO THAT HE CAN ARRANGE TO KILL OR KIDNAP YOURSELF OR YOUR FRIENDS

EXERCISE CARE WITH ALL STRANGERS
• AVOID POLITICAL DISCUSSION WHEN STRANGERS ARE PRESENT

(Issued by Citizens United for Border Security).

Far left: IRA propaganda warns local people to be on their guard against strangers who might be undercover members of the Special Air Service. The deployment of the SAS to south Armagh in 1976 had a powerful impact.
Left: Kenneth Littlejohn, tried for armed robbery in Dublin in 1973. He claimed that he and his brother Keith were working for MI6 but this was never proved.
Right: Captain Robert Nairac, tortured and killed by the IRA in south Armagh while working undercover. He was awarded a posthumous George Cross in 1979 for his bravery.

These were called Military Reconnaissance Forces (MRF) and the best-known one is probably the group which ran the 'Four Square Laundry'. This was a genuine laundry operation whose primary source of information was the crew of a delivery vehicle who observed the population at close quarters. However, intelligence could also be gleaned from the laundry itself. A woman whose husband was gaoled but who produced a man's dirty laundry might be hiding a Republican on the run, and scientific analysis of clothing could indicate traces of blood, gunpowder or explosives. At some stage the IRA penetrated the cover of this MRF and the laundry van was attacked on 2 October 1972. The driver, who was officially admitted to be a member of the British armed forces, was killed.

There were other allegations about under-cover activities – some of them rather far-fetched. It was alleged but denied in parliament that the army had established two brothels in Belfast with the aim of collecting information. It was certainly true that women were employed in MRF (one of the crew of the Four Square Laundry van was a member of the WRAC, and another was employed in Operation Lipstick, selling cosmetics from door to door in 1973) but this suggestion seems to have come from the wilder shores of fantasy. More concrete is the admission by a British officer commanding a battalion operating in the Falls Road in September 1972 that 'plain-clothes patrols do operate the district, but their work is reconnaissance'. There has been much speculation as to the sort of troops who made up the MRF, and the

IRA has always accused the SAS of involvement. The British authorities have been non-committal but it is generally assumed now that the MRF were volunteers trained by the SAS. There was also a special detachment of ten 'turned' IRA men established in the spring of 1971.

Considerable publicity surrounded the Littlejohn brothers, Kenneth and Keith, after they were arrested in October 1972 following a bank robbery in Dublin. They claimed that they had been working for MI6 as *agents provocateurs*, bombing police stations and robbing banks on both sides of the border with the aim of implicating the IRA and provoking a security crackdown by the Dublin government. The brothers also asserted that MI6 had ordered them to kill several leading members of the IRA, hide their bodies and then spread the rumour that they had absconded with the organisation's funds. Both men were disowned by the ministry of defence and sentenced to a total of 35 years' imprisonment. In 1974 they escaped from Dublin's Mountjoy gaol, and although Keith was caught immediately, Kenneth was on the run for 18 months before being recaptured. During this period he gave several interviews to the press, in which he elaborated the details of his alleged involvement with MI6. The Littlejohns were eventually released in 1981, years before they had served their full terms.

Interrogation techniques

In addition to these rather shadowy activities the security forces obtained much information from interrogation of detainees and prisoners. To this end they conducted a controversial experiment in which a number

of detainees were subjected to long periods of hooding, being made to stand against a wall and inflicted with 'white noise' to disorientate them. The experiment was probably not a great success in that more orthodox methods of interrogation were almost equally effective. Moreover, the PIRA were presented with a propaganda coup when these techniques were denounced by the European Court of Human Rights in 1978. Apart from this episode the use of interrogation and of informers produced a stream of information which allowed the security forces to build up a picture of the forces ranged against them.

Once the army had re-established its control of the No-Go areas with the massive and successful Operation Motorman in July 1972 it was able to use its new avenues of information. The 'lifting' of IRA men was undertaken with far more accuracy and the level of violence began to show a decline. It was still very high, however, and though the security forces had passed the nadir in their campaign, they did not look likely to, nor did they expect to achieve a military victory. The other part of the struggle – the promotion of political reform – was accordingly advanced in an attempt to wean the Catholic population away from supporting the IRA. The Stormont parliament had been superseded by direct rule from Westminster in March 1972, and an attempt to satisfy the aspirations of the minority had been introduced with the power-sharing initiative. This was destroyed by the success of the strike organised by the Loyalist Ulster Workers' Council in May 1974. There is no doubt that the security forces were taken by surprise by the solidarity of the strike, and their inactivity was blamed by the nationalists for its success.

By this time a considerable part of security-

though most UDR soldiers were only part-time. (In 1984, for example, the regiment numbered 7000, of whom 2700 were full-time.) By 1973 this new force was beginning to take some of the strain off the shoulders of the army and RUC by manning checkpoints or OPs and guarding police stations – particularly in rural areas and at weekends. However, it also provided easy targets for the insurgents, and, by the end of 1984, 147 UDR personnel had been killed, many when off-duty.

There have been two main reservations about the UDR – the standard a part-time force can achieve and its vulnerability to infiltration by Loyalist paramilitaries. In fact every battalion in the regiment has a full-time company, and a high standard of training and operational dexterity has been achieved. The UDR has also gained the distinction of serving the longest period of unbroken duty in the British Army, a total of 15 years by the end of 1984. Occasional links with Loyalist paramilitaries have been turned up and stamped out but the regiment needs constant vigilance to avoid any part of it degenerating into a sectarian force. A number of UDR men based at Drummad barracks in Armagh were charged with sectarian murders in 1984.

The tide turns

Since its inception the UDR has not been used for riot control but this became of less importance after 1973. Even by the end of 1972 the constant pressure of street disorders was beginning to slacken just a little in the wake of Operation Motorman. In 1973 soldiers who returned to tour Ulster began to notice that, while they felt they had had the entire strength of the Catholic enclaves ranged against them on previous tours, some sections of the minority population were no longer hostile. It was not as though support for the security forces had grown, but rather that many had had enough of the constant violence and insecurity and had withdrawn their active support for the nationalists. Experience had also given the security forces better riot-control techniques so that the situation continued to improve. The process has never been continuous and there is always a danger of rioting recurring (the hunger strikes of 1980–81, for example, saw a considerable revival of street disorders) but the large-scale and incessant disturbances of 1971 and 1972 appear to be a thing of the past.

During the 1970s the security forces were gradually allowed to gain domination over the urban Catholic enclaves. By 1978 Brendan Magill, the Sinn Fein leader, admitted that the PIRA had lost control in Belfast: 'which is thick with undercover British operatives. There are three British Army

Above: A tense moment on the streets of Belfast: the occasion is the funeral procession of hunger-striker Joe McDonnell on 10 July 1981. Trouble broke out when RUC and army personnel attempted to arrest a group of hooded IRA men who had fired a volley over the grave.

force strength on the ground in emergencies was provided by the Ulster Defence Regiment. The new force began to form on 1 January 1970 and was seven battalions strong on the official Vesting Day, 1 April. The new force was equipped and run very much as a territorial army unit, and was supposed to be non-sectarian. In its early days, it achieved a very creditable representation of Catholics amounting to a maximum of 18% of its

strength – about the same proportion as former B-Specials who enrolled. As anti-British feeling hardened and the IRA practised intimidation, however, the UDR's Catholic content fell to 3% and there have been accusations that it is not as impartial as it should be. In an effort to regulate its activities, the commanding officer, a brigadier, is advised by a six-man civilian council consisting of three Catholics and three Protestants.

By September 1972 the UDR had been expanded to 11 battalions (later reduced to nine) and, in August of the next year, women were recruited to form a WUDR. As the largest regiment in the British Army, the UDR was a sizable reinforcement of the security forces' numerical strength, even

The SAS

The Special Air Service Regiment is the chief source of Britain's 'special forces'. Servicemen wishing to join the SAS face a very severe selection test which the majority of them fail. If they pass they frequently face a drop in rank to join the regiment, but the appeal of an organisation which seems to epitomise a fighting elite is so strong that there is no lack of volunteers. Once in the SAS volunteers become part of the cult of mystery by which their postings and ranks are never revealed and which makes them distinctly camera-shy. Despite this the regiment is one of the most famous special forces units in the world, chiefly because of its spectacular successes in countering international terrorism.

The regiment was founded by Captain David Stirling as an irregular desert raiding force in 1941. It enjoyed great success operating behind enemy lines in the desert and, later in the Second World War, in Italy, Greece and northern France. After the war it was disbanded but in 1947 was re-established as a Territorial Regiment, 21 SAS (previously known as the Artists' Rifles). In 1952 during the Malayan campaign a regular unit, 22 SAS, was raised from the various special forces operating in the peninsula. The regiment has never looked back and has fashioned a unique role for itself in reconnaissance and irregular warfare. It added to its battle honours in the successful counter-insurgency campaigns in Borneo and Dhofar (Oman).

Although it is not part of the infantry, 22 SAS has an infantry battalion structure in which its operational Sabre squadrons correspond to rifle companies and its Base squadron corresponds to a headquarters company. Despite this it is usually committed to combat in patrols of various sizes depending on the nature of the task – it is believed that patrols in Northern Ireland usually consist of four men. All SAS personnel undergo rigorous and continuous training and are expected to develop skills in subjects such as linguistics, demolition, signalling and first aid as well as skill at arms and physical fitness. The intensity of their training is legendary and has helped to give them the reputation of supermen – which has its advantages.

The SAS was first deployed in Northern Ireland for a few weeks in the late summer of 1969 when D Squadron of the regiment were based at Newtownards, County Down. Their main duty was to keep a watch along the coast of Down and Antrim for possible gun-running operations. After these men had been withdrawn, the SAS did not formally operate in the province again until 1976, although from time to time individual soldiers were seconded for various security and intelligence duties.

At the beginning of 1976, in response to an upsurge of violence in south Armagh, the prime minister, Harold Wilson, announced that SAS troops were to be employed in Northern Ireland for 'patrolling and surveillance' tasks. During the year the regiment scored a number of successes in south Armagh. Although probably fewer than 20 soldiers were initially involved, an immediate effect of their deployment was a sharp reduction in Republican terrorist activity. Over the first ten months of the year only two members of the security forces, both off-duty part-time members of the Ulster Defence Regiment, were killed in the area. Both the SAS's expertise in covert operations and the undeniable psychological effect of their reputation exerted a powerful constraint on the Provisionals in south Armagh. But it was not all plain sailing for the SAS. An embarrassing incident occurred in May 1976 when eight members of the regiment were arrested by a Garda (police) patrol 500 metres inside the Irish Republic in County Louth. The men were charged with firearms offences in Dublin. Although it was believed that the soldiers had deliberately crossed the border, the official explanation was simply that the difficulty had arisen out of a 'map-reading error'.

Since the mid-1970s SAS personnel have continued to serve in Northern Ireland, although because of the secretiveness of the regiment it is impossible to state the exact numbers involved. Their role in the province, however, has been diluted by the provision of SAS-type training for soldiers from other units. Not all covert operations in Northern Ireland are conducted by the SAS, yet because the regiment has such a formidable reputation, the army seems content to let people believe that these troops are extensively employed throughout the province.

Below left: The SAS in training. Although obviously posed, this photograph gives an indication of their equipment; in many cases it is less orthodox than that shown here.

helicopters in the air for most of the time in constant touch with plain-clothes units on the streets. There are soldiers staked out in hiding places throughout the city and suburbs. This makes operations much more difficult than was thought conceivable a few years ago.' His complaint explained why by 1976 the IRA had been forced to recognise some sort of defeat, which led it to reorganise its command structure (see chapter 7).

The war on the border

However, the security forces found it much harder to counter the rural guerrilla campaign. From the beginning of the Troubles the army had established itself in dangerous border areas – most notably south Armagh, where the four posts of Bessbrook, Crossmaglen, Newry and Forkill achieved much notoriety. The difficulties there were immense. The rambling border with the Irish Republic was 480 kilometres long, the secur-

Right: An army Observation Post, heavily fortified against bombs and truck-mounted mortars, disfigures the corner of a Belfast street.

ity forces of the South were not at first present in great strength, nor were communications with them good. The countryside was also very wild and it was impossible to keep up continuous surveillance of such a vast area. Under these conditions the natural advantages for an insurgent are so great that it is not practically possible to destroy his operational capability completely. Nevertheless continuous patrolling and the frequent use of helicopters enabled the security forces to cover a great deal of ground while overt and covert OPs provided a check to terrorist activity. Even so the PIRA was able to inflict heavy casualties on the 2nd Battalion, Parachute Regiment in the Warrenpoint ambush of August 1979, and this was only one of a continuing catalogue of less spectacular but successful attacks.

For the security forces the years 1976 and 1977 brought about great changes in the conduct of the campaign. In January 1976 the SAS was officially deployed in south Armagh after a series of killings there. By April 1977 a powerful new computer had replaced the manual filing system of intelligence. By the beginning of March 1976 internment was at an end, as was special category status for both Republican and Loyalist prisoners. All this marked a conscious policy decision to withdraw the army from the front line of the counter-insurgency campaign and replace it by the RUC (now re-armed) and the UDR. All these moves came under considerable political attack but had all been largely achieved by 1982.

The first of these changes to have effect was the deployment of the SAS. In fact the announcement that it was to be involved in Ulster caught the regiment by surprise and it is now believed that only a dozen men were ready to leave for Armagh at the time. However the SAS reputation gave this force a disproportionate credibility so that the border

area became much quieter for several months. In their operations in rural Ireland the regiment laid much stress on surveillance. The particular expertise of SAS men was used to man OPs for three weeks at a time without relief. Their armoury of modern surveillance equipment included the ZB 298 radar with which they could detect movement at 3000 metres and distinguish the blip made by a cow from that of a man. They also used infra-red alarms and sophisticated night-vision equipment. Their activities are believed to have resulted in a number of successful ambushes of insurgents together with better control of the border areas.

Photographic evidence

The ending of internment closed the chapter on a political mistake but also fundamentally changed the rules of the conflict. Whereas wanted men had simply been 'lifted' before 1976 the onus was now on the security forces to obtain convictions of insurgents by presenting evidence to courts of law. Photography was found to be an enormously useful tool in this process, and the amount of effort expended in covertly photographing

criminal activity could be described as unprecedented in a counter-insurgency campaign. It went some way to disproving Republican assertions that the security forces adopted a 'shoot on sight' policy.

The ending of internment was not greeted as a liberal move by the PIRA. From the beginning of the Troubles the Provisionals had scored many propaganda successes by distorting the actions and motives of the British government and the security forces. In the wake of any disturbance it would be alleged that the security forces had over-reacted, not acted soon enough or attacked peaceful individuals. Officers interviewed on the streets by television crews immediately after incidents were not always sufficiently articulate, so a certain amount of training was laid on. Fairly soon it was common for every unit engaged in Northern Ireland to have one of its officers appointed to Public Relations duties, and an Information Policy Unit was established at Lisburn headquarters. The insurgents were equally active in disseminating their viewpoint. In the early days when large areas of the province's cities were safe for them, their leaders held press conferences and issued bulletins. They also had the services of

A Westland Wessex helicopter arrives to pick up an SAS surveillance team which has been guided to the landing zone by other soldiers. The team has probably been occupying a camouflaged 'hide' close to the border in south Armagh for some days, monitoring movements and building up a picture of possible terrorist activity.

Sinn Fein, their political wing, for making statements or enunciating policy. Their greatest and most determined propaganda battle followed the ending of special category status which they strove to have restored by means of a hunger strike campaign during 1980–81. A strenuous and reasonably successful effort to neutralise this was made by the Press and PR Officers of the Northern Ireland Office and the security forces. Since 1973 both sides have been well aware of the value of good public relations.

All this has been part of evolving a more efficient security campaign. By 1977, computers had been introduced for storing and collating information. Since then the security forces have had nearly instant access to the 500,000 or so files which are registered on the system. This has meant a faster reaction time: for example, security forces manning a vehicle checkpoint can find out from the computer who owns the car they have stopped, whether it is stolen, and whether its occupants have connections with wanted men. Naturally enough there have been objections to this on the grounds that it is too redolent of Big Brother. From the counter-insurgency point of view, however, it is simply a question of deciding that slow-reacting, ignorant security forces are inferior to those equipped with modern information-processing systems.

Modern equipment

The difference between the security operation in the early 1970s and that in the 1980s is very marked. In the early days there was uncertainty in the conduct of operations, inadequate intelligence, and vacillating political control as well as a manpower commitment so great that it strained the British Army's ability to keep its Rhine Army divisions up to strength. Now there is a much leaner, sharper force, spearheaded by the RUC and UDR, familiar with a host of new weapons and techniques that have become available for counter-insurgency operations. For riot control there are better shields, helmets, visors, armoured vehicles and baton rounds. For weapons and bomb searches there are mechanical detectors, trained dog sections, portable explosives 'sniffers' and the 'Wheelbarrow' robots. For surveillance there are television cameras, infra-red alarms, night-vision equipment, radar which can identify human movement or give the direction of incoming rounds, helicopter-borne 'Nitesun' illuminators and computerised data collection.

The human element, the raw material of the security forces, has also changed over the 16 years of the Troubles. At the height of the Troubles strained resources meant that gunners and engineers were undertaking foot patrols and riot control whereas now infantry duties are undertaken by trained infantrymen only. All British Army soldiers are given 'work-up' training in extraordinarily complete replicas of Ulster streets or countryside constructed in Germany or Britain before being sent on a tour of Ulster duty. The tours themselves are of either two years or four months. The two-year tours are for regiments joining the regular Northern Ireland garrison and they take their families with them to reasonably secure and comfortable barracks in the province. Despite this advantage the two-year tour is a harsh option because garrison soldiers are very much involved in security duties while they and their families are constantly exposed as targets for attack.

Bandit country

Patrolling the area around Crossmaglen in south Armagh has consistently been one of the army's most nerve-racking tasks. Here Captain A.F.N. Clarke recalls the first day out in the Armagh countryside for a unit of the 3rd Battalion, Parachute Regiment in 1976:

'I check my equipment for the fiftieth time. Map, compass, belt and pouches, codes, personality check-list, stolen car list, ammunition, rifle and lastly my radio operator to see whether he has everything. . . .

'The clatter of the Wessex becomes deafening as it swoops over the top of the police station and around the football pitch to descend onto the helipad. As it touches down we race out and throw our kit in, clambering after it. The shorter the turn-around the better, and within a few seconds we are airborne and moving tactically along at low level, swinging round trees and hills, dropping into little gullies, dodging power lines and telephone wires.

'We are moving down towards Cullaville right on the border with the Republic. The Wessex swings round in a tight turn, drops, flares and touches on the soggy turf. As soon as the wheels touch we are off and running. Guns into fire positions, my section commanders and I showing them the route. There's no time to notice the tight feeling in your stomach, or the nervous playing with the safety catch.

' "OK, Corporal Menzies, move off."

'I look over to the right and see the third patrol in position on the side of a small hill, to give cover to our two patrols that will be moving. Bill, Corporal Menzies, is moving slowly away towards the road. First objective a vehicle checkpoint on the Crossmaglen-to-Cullaville road.

' "Right lads, let's go."

'We follow, fight our way through the blackthorn hedge and position ourselves on the road. It's an eerie feeling standing there knowing that there are hidden pairs of eyes watching us and logging every move we make for future reference.

'Having talked about it in the Mess the night before, we reckon that the chances of getting hit on the first day are pretty small, because the opposition don't know how we are going to operate, and, being far more professional than the cowboys in Belfast, they will not do anything until they are sure of a kill.'

Right: The 'bandit country' of south Armagh: a foot patrol, spaced out in case of sudden sniper attack and well equipped for rural rather than urban duties, moves through the border town of Forkill. With the Provisional IRA particularly active in the border area, the army presence is essential, and although the duties are tedious, the British regiments have proved effective.

Left: The Queen inspects an Ulster Defence Regiment guard of honour during her Silver Jubilee visit to Northern Ireland in August 1977. The visit was seen by many Unionists as a reaffirmation of the links with Britain, but from the nationalists' point of view it was a political affront.
Right: Roy Mason visiting troops in Northern Ireland in his capacity as minister of defence (1974–6). As secretary of state for Northern Ireland (1976–9), he was responsible for the safety of the Queen during her visit. During his term of office he took over an improved security situation.

advisory council. This was never meant to be more than an interim arrangement and was replaced in January 1974 by William Whitelaw's painstakingly constructed power-sharing Executive. But the Executive collapsed after less than five months.

In May 1974 the province reverted to direct rule, enlivened from time to time by a political 'initiative' of one sort or another in which successive secretaries of state have attempted to find an acceptable scheme for a devolved administration. The British government has always maintained that direct rule is only a temporary expedient, yet after more than a decade it has begun to acquire an air of permanence. Like partition, which few in 1921 believed would last very long, the apparently unsuitable short-term arrangement of direct rule has survived longer than anticipated in the absence of any practical alternative. In October 1984 a public opinion poll commissioned by the *Belfast Telegraph* showed that direct rule was acceptable to over half the community. For the meantime, therefore, it will continue.

'The long way'

Just as the British administrators ensconced at Stormont Castle, next to the Parliament Buildings, settled in for a long stay, the PIRA was at the same time preparing itself for a long-term campaign. The 1975–6 ceasefire had left the organisation weakened and divided. The Royal Ulster Constabulary (RUC) were also having increasing success. In the two years 1975–6 over 2000 persons, mostly Provisionals, were convicted of terrorist offences. At the end of 1976 the PIRA leadership, therefore, began a rethink which led to major

changes in policy and organisation. The strategy of the movement was henceforward to be directed towards what one leader called 'the long way'. On the military side this involved the development of a smaller, more tightly organised body of guerrilla fighters than hitherto, dedicated to a long campaign of attrition. The reorganisation into a cellular organisation necessitated a sharp reduction in the number of volunteers. At the end of the 1970s one assessment put the PIRA's active strength at approximately 300, with perhaps ten times that number of sympathisers who could be relied upon to provide safe houses, lookouts and transport. (By contrast, in 1972, the total strength of the IRA was between 1500 and 2000.) Each cell or 'active service unit' contains about four people, works directly with one commander, and the members of a particular cell do not know the identity of members of other cells. This improves the organisation's security and its efficiency as a terrorist machine, but tends to cut the PIRA off from its wider circles of passive supporters within the nationalist community. Public support is vitally important to both Protestant and Catholic paramilitary groups since it bestows on them a legitimacy which they would not otherwise possess.

The PIRA sought to counter this problem with a second major change in policy. Along with the new 'streamlined' military organisation, the open political wing – Provisional Sinn Fein – would be developed as a radical political party and seek to involve itself in trade-union, community, housing and unemployment issues. In this way it would hope to mobilise mass support for the Republican movement in general. The leadership of the political wing was taken over by activists who

were already well known to the authorities. One of these was Gerry Adams, who played a crucial role in developing the new policies. In the early 1970s he had commanded the PIRA in Belfast, and in 1973 was one of the triumvirate who ran it after Sean MacStiofain had ceased to be chief of staff.

Below: Poster urging the people of west Belfast to vote for Gerry Adams in the June 1983 general election. His election as MP was an embarrassment to the British establishment.

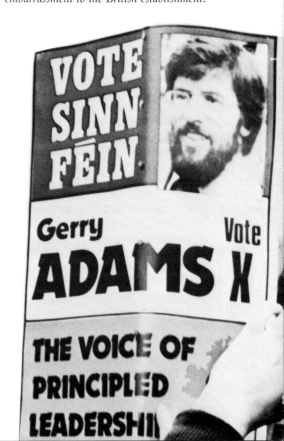

Terrorist tactics and security policies

The 'new model' Provisionals have adopted a number of different tactics over the years but have continued consistently to attack the security forces. In the border regions of Counties Fermanagh, Tyrone and Armagh many Protestants are part-time members of either the Ulster Defence Regiment (UDR) or the RUC Reserve. Living within the community itself these people are particularly vulnerable to terrorist intimidation and assassination. From 1971 to the end of 1984, 147 UDR soldiers (of whom 120 were off-duty at the time) were killed by IRA gunmen and bombers. Since virtually all these victims were Protestant the campaign against local members of the security forces has been characterised by some Loyalists as a deliberately sectarian policy of 'genocide'. The RUC are equally at risk. In November 1983 a bomb composed of gelignite, bolts, nails and other scrap metal exploded at the Ulster Polytechnic. Two policemen attending a day-release social studies course were killed, 14 RUC officers were injured, together with 20 other students and a lecturer. The bomb had been planted in the ceiling of the room some time before it was detonated. On 28 February 1985 a mortar attack on Newry RUC station left nine officers – two of them . policewomen – dead, and injured 30.

Other IRA targets have included prison warders, prominent businessmen and local politicians. On 21 January 1981, the 86-year-old Sir Norman Stronge, former Speaker of the Northern Ireland House of Commons,

and his son James, a member of the RUC Reserve, were killed at their home on the south Armagh border. The Provisionals said it was a 'direct reprisal' for Loyalist attacks on 'nationalist people'. In November the same year PIRA gunmen shot dead the Reverend Robert Bradford, Official Unionist MP for South Belfast – an action which provoked a strong Protestant reaction and calls for improved security. Several days afterwards, the Provisionals in south Armagh apparently decided, on the spur of the moment, to match their Belfast colleagues' action by assassinating the Reverend Ian Paisley, who was on a visit to the area. But the PIRA's cellular organisation made it impossible to gather a team of gunmen quickly enough to mount the attack. The new arrangement has sacrificed spontaneity to security. The Provisionals have therefore increasingly come to concentrate on well-planned attacks – bombings or ambushes – which they hope will have dramatic results. For these major operations a 'one-off' special cell is drawn from a comparatively large pool of personnel and is disbanded afterwards.

Operations outside Northern Ireland come within this category. From time to time the PIRA mounts bombing campaigns in England. In October and November 1981 there were attacks in London on an army barracks in Chelsea (a civilian was killed and 23 soldiers injured), in Oxford Street (where a bomb disposal expert was killed), on Lieutenant-General Sir Steuart Pringle, Commandant General of the Royal Marines, with a car bomb, and at the home of the Attorney-General, Sir Michael Havers. Just

before Christmas 1983, a car bomb outside Harrods department store in Knightsbridge killed two police officers and three shoppers and injured 90 others. The PIRA afterwards admitted responsibility but claimed that the action had not been authorised by the Provisional Army Council. The PIRA's most ambitious operation in England so far was the bomb attack at the Grand Hotel, Brighton, in October 1984, where the target was British prime minister Margaret Thatcher and members of her government. There are two principal aims behind these operations. The first is to persuade British public opinion that continued British presence in Northern Ireland is too costly to maintain for ever. Bombings in Britain, however, generally provoke public support for tougher security policies and a restoration of the death penalty. The second aim is perhaps the more import-

Above: Police and soldiers stand amid the carnage caused when a troop of the Household Cavalry was caught by a bomb in Hyde Park on 20 July 1982.
Top right: The remains of the car bomb that exploded outside Harrods in 1983.

Right: One response to terrorism in Britain has been to raise specially trained police units, capable of countering the threat of politically inspired violence. Here marksmen of the elite C11 squad arrive at the scene of the Libyan People's Bureau siege in April 1984.

Mullaghmore and Warrenpoint

On 27 August 1979 Lord Mountbatten's boat, *Shadow V*, was blown up by a Provisional IRA radio-controlled bomb in Mullaghmore harbour, near his holiday home in County Sligo in the Irish Republic. Lord Mountbatten, his 15-year-old grandson, Nicholas Knatchbull, and a 15-year-old Irish boy, Paul Maxwell, were killed; the Dowager Lady Brabourne died the next day. Also seriously injured were Lord Brabourne, his wife Patricia (Mountbatten's daughter) and son Timothy.

Two hours before the explosion two men in a car had been picked up at a police roadblock 110 kilometres away at Granard in County Longford. In November 1979 Thomas McMahon and Francis McGirl stood trial for the murders. McMahon was gaoled for life, but McGirl was found not guilty both of murder and of being a member of an illegal organisation (the PIRA).

On the same day in August, 18 men, mostly from the 2nd Battalion, Parachute Regiment, were killed in two explosions at Warrenpoint, on a stretch of road separated from the Republic only by the narrow waters of Carlingford Lough. The first bomb, detonated from across the lough as an army convoy was passing, killed six soldiers. The second bomb exploded half an hour later, and was even more devastating. It was cunningly planted in the only area of cover available to the survivors of the first explosion and the reinforcements who quickly arrived on the scene. The second explosion was followed by gunfire from across the lough, but in replying to this the Paras succeeded only in shooting dead an English tourist.

The PIRA was roundly condemned by the world's press for the Mountbatten killing, but the synchronisation of the Warrenpoint and Mullaghmore operations – although almost certainly unintentional – also earned it a massive publicity coup. Moreover, in striking at the Parachute Regiment, members of which had shot and killed 13 civilians on 'Bloody Sunday' in 1972, the PIRA could attempt to justify the carnage as legitimate revenge; as a slogan painted on a Falls Road wall put it: '13 gone not forgotten, we got 18 and Mountbatten.'

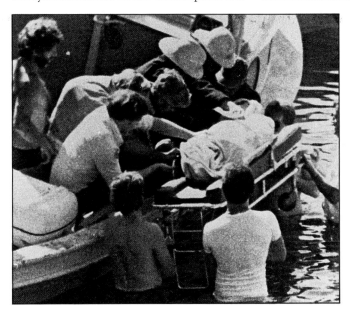

*27 August 1979: a day of unforgettable violence.
Left: Rescuers lift a body from the sea after the killing of Lord Mountbatten at Mullaghmore.
Below: The twisted wreckage of an army truck in which six members of the 2nd Battalion, Parachute Regiment, died at Warrenpoint. The second bomb killed a further 12 soldiers. Although such attacks were shocking, particularly when they occurred simultaneously, the Provisional IRA could never hope to sustain the pressure over an extended period.*

ical terms. A second step in the process was the abandonment of 'special category status' announced in March 1976. This status had been granted by William Whitelaw in mid-1972 to prisoners who were members of paramilitary organisations. They were allowed particular privileges, including a large degree of autonomy within prison, and they were not required to work or to wear prison clothes. In effect the status recognised a distinction between 'political' crime associated with the civil disturbances and so-called 'ordinary' crime. But from 1976 the government determined to remove the distinction, partly for practical reasons, since the status made it difficult for the prison authorities to exercise discipline, and therefore to ensure security. There was also a crucially important political and psychological point to the policy change. By categorising Republican and Loyalist terrorists with 'ordinary' criminals, the government sought to deglamorise the paramilitaries. A common criminal, classed with robbers and rapists, is a much less romantic and emotive figure than a nationalist guerrilla or political freedom fighter. The criminalisation policy was therefore fiercely opposed by the paramilitary groups themselves.

The first people to be denied special category status were convicted in the autumn of 1976. These prisoners refused to wear prison clothes or to work. The authorities insisted that they should submit to ordinary prison discipline and would not allow them to wear their own clothes. The prisoners thus wrapped themselves only in blankets and the protest generally became known as going 'on the blanket'. By the end of 1977 over a hundred men in the 'H-Blocks' at the Maze and Magilligan prisons were participating in

the action. In March 1978, with no sign that the government was prepared to make any concessions, the campaign was stepped up to include the 'dirty protest'. The prisoners smashed up the furniture in their cells, refused to use any toilet facilities and began to smear cell walls with their own excreta.

The hunger-strike campaign

The relatively low-key blanket and dirty protests gradually gathered strength until in 1980 some 300 protesters (out of a total prison population of 2500) were involved. Outside the prisons the Republican 'H-Block Information Centre' mounted a publicity campaign in Ireland and elsewhere to secure support for political status. When the authorities refused to move on this issue, in October 1980 the protesters at the Maze began a series of selective hunger strikes. This is a particularly emotive weapon in the Irish nationalist's armoury and it has been used at intervals throughout the 20th century against both British and Irish governments. Typified as an act of selfless moral courage, the hunger strike can generate emotional public support to an extent that violent action can never do. It also raises acute difficulties for the authorities, who are put on the defensive and, if they refuse to concede the strikers' demands, run the risk of appearing callous and intransigent. Towards the end of 1980 there was a wave of Catholic sympathy for the protest and a series of big demonstrations both north and south of the border. Only as the first striker neared the point of death was an unexpected compromise over prison clothing reached and the strike called off on 18 December.

In the New Year, however, the agreement

broke down and on 1 March 1981 Bobby Sands, the Provisional commanding officer of the Maze, began a solitary fast. At intervals of about a fortnight other prisoners, carefully chosen from a wide spread of home districts so as to achieve maximum emotional impact, joined the strike. Early in April Sands's protest was given a massive boost by his election as MP for the border constituency of Fermanagh and South Tyrone. On 5 May he died after 66 days without food. Nine more hunger strikers starved themselves to death between 12 May and 20 August 1981.

Each death was marked by bouts of rioting in Belfast and Londonderry, although the Provisional leadership reined in terrorist action a little lest violence should undermine the widespread popular support which the H-Block campaign had received. (Nevertheless, on 19 May five soldiers of the 1st Battalion, Royal Green Jackets were killed near Camlough, south Armagh – the most serious single attack since the Warrenpoint massacre.) The campaign soon brought results: two H-Block candidates, Paddy Agnew and Kieran Doherty, who was on hunger strike, were elected to the Dublin parliament in the June general election. Also in June, the House of Commons passed a bill preventing a convicted felon from standing for election to the British parliament. The Republicans countered by putting forward unemployed schoolteacher Owen Carron as 'proxy political prisoner' candidate for Fermanagh and South Tyrone, at the by-election in August caused by Sands's death. Carron was duly elected as an MP, but in keeping with Republican practice on both sides of the border he did not take up his seat. Yet in the face of the British government's steadfast

Left: Rescuers sift through the rubble of the Droppin' Well pub, Ballykelly, blown up by an INLA bomb on 6 December 1982. The pub's dance floor was packed with civilians and soldiers of the Cheshire Regiment, the latter on a two-year tour of the province. Seventeen people were killed and over 60 injured in the blast.

refusal to concede political status, the hunger strikes gradually ran out of steam. The campaign was called off in October after the remaining six strikers' families, strongly supported by Catholic Churchmen, announced that they would request medical intervention if a striker neared death. The new secretary of state for Northern Ireland, James Prior, who succeeded Atkins in September, helped the Provisionals save a little face by offering some minor concessions on prison conditions.

The chief legacy of the hunger strikes, other than bitterness and increased community polarisation, was the Provisionals' move towards a more political stance. The by-election victories in Fermanagh and South Tyrone demonstrated the potential of electoral campaigning. They did not, however, plan to lay down their guns. At the Provisional Sinn Fein ard fheis (annual conference) in Dublin in November 1981, the organisation's publicity officer, Danny Morrison, dramatically outlined a double strategy. 'Who here', he asked, 'really believes we can win the war through the ballot box?' This was received in silence. 'But', he continued, 'will anyone here object if with ballot paper in this hand and an Armalite in this hand, we take power in Ireland?' The applause was loud and long.

On the political side Provisional Sinn Fein has challenged the constitutionalist SDLP for leadership of the nationalist community. Enthusiastically espousing 'community politics' – especially in west Belfast – and developing radical social and economic policies, Sinn Fein has built up a strong electoral base. The party polled 10% of the votes in the October 1982 Assembly elections and 13% in the 1983 general election, when Gerry Adams won West Belfast on an abstentionist ticket. In Fermanagh and South Tyrone, however, Owen Carron failed to be re-elected. The nationalist vote was split between Sinn Fein and the SDLP, and a Unionist won the seat. But in the 1984 European elections Sinn Fein's share of the vote increased no further and the SDLP (with 22% of the vote) was the leading Catholic party. Although SDLP supporters undoubtedly subscribe to the ideal of a 32-county Irish republic, many party followers are strongly influenced by rural and conservative values. Gerry Adams's radical politics – 'Republicanism', he says, 'is a philosophy in which the nationalist and socialist dimension are the two sides of the one coin' – hold little attraction for this important section of nationalist opinion. A further problem which arises from the Provisionals' two-pronged strategy is the comparative incompatibility of

Above: Masked members of the INLA pose beneath an appropriate slogan in Belfast. Founded in 1974, the INLA has a reputation for violence in excess of that of the Provisionals. Below: Mrs Bernadette McAliskey (née Devlin), still active in politics despite being shot by Loyalist gunmen in 1981. A founder member of the IRSP, she denied links with the INLA.

political and military action. While they are committed to violent methods, their constituency of political support will remain largely limited to the hard Republican core of the Catholic community – who do not constitute enough votes to defeat the SDLP.

The INLA

On the extreme left wing of the Republican movement are the Irish National Liberation Army (INLA) and their political wing the Irish Republican Socialist Party (IRSP). The emergence of these groups reflects, as did that of the Provisionals in 1969, the difficulties which any Republican party faces when, however conditionally, it abandons the 'physical-force' approach. The IRSP was founded in December 1974 by a group of socialist-minded Republicans who disagreed with the Official IRA's 1972 ceasefire. The INLA was set up at the same time. Although Seamus Costello – a veteran of the IRA's 1956–62 campaign – was both chairman of the IRSP and chief of staff of the INLA, the membership of the two organisations did not entirely overlap. Mrs Bernadette McAliskey (formerly Devlin), a founder member of the IRSP, but who left the party in 1975, always denied that it had a military wing. The IRSP strove to promote distinctly socialist policies and saw itself as part of a wider international struggle for a Marxist revolution. In recent years, with the leftward trend of Provisional Sinn Fein, the IRSP has lost momentum and is

now of no practical importance.

The INLA, however, has had considerable impact. It is much smaller than the PIRA – the active strength is estimated at being less than 100 – but has gained a reputation for unpredictability and shocking violence. Indeed, Provisionals have been known to refer to INLA members as 'wild men'. Like the PIRA the INLA has an Army Council, but the younger organisation has never adopted a cellular structure, retaining a more traditional series of tiny 'brigades'. The group first came to prominence when a bloody feud erupted with the OIRA in 1975. At much the same time, moreover, recruits were gained from the PIRA during its ceasefire. Relations with the OIRA have always been uneasy, and it is believed that the Officials were responsible for shooting Costello dead in 1977. The PIRA seems more tolerant towards the INLA, however, especially since the hunger strikes. Three of the ten who died were INLA men.

The INLA's most spectacular attack was the car bomb which killed the Conservative Northern Ireland spokesman, Airey Neave, at the House of Commons in March 1979. The organisation was proscribed in the United Kingdom three months later. The INLA has also attacked local politicians. In March 1981 they shot and seriously injured Belfast city councillor Sammy Millar, a prominent member of the Ulster Defence Association (UDA). Their most serious strike against the security forces came on 6 December 1982, when a bomb planted in a disco at the Droppin' Well pub in Ballykelly, near Londonderry, exploded without warning. Twelve off-duty soldiers of the 1st Battalion, Cheshire Regiment and five civilians died; 66 people were injured. They do not hesitate to engage in sectarian assassinations. In a particularly horrifying incident in November 1983, INLA gunmen burst into a Pentecostal Church in Darkley, County Armagh, during a service and fired on the congregation with automatic weapons. Three men were killed and seven injured.

One man implicated in the Darkley attack – he was supposed to have supplied one of the weapons used – was the so-called 'mad dog' Dominic McGlinchey. Over a 13-year period McGlinchey is estimated to have been responsible for 28 murders, 30 bombings and 11 armed robberies. He began as a Provisional, but apparently came to believe that the PIRA was not active enough, and he emerged as INLA chief of staff early in 1982. For two years he operated mostly in the Armagh–Tyrone border area and earned the description of 'Ireland's most wanted terro-

Left: The remains of the car in which Conservative MP and Opposition spokesman on Northern Ireland Airey Neave was killed.

rist'. He was on the run in the South as well as the North and was eventually captured in County Clare after a dramatic week-long chase by the Irish police. Although he had previously claimed that he would never be taken alive, McGlinchey surrendered after a brief shoot-out in March 1984. He was almost immediately handed over to the RUC – the first suspect to be extradited from the South after claiming that his alleged offence was a political one. On Christmas Eve 1984 he was sentenced to life imprisonment for the murder in March 1977 of a 63-year-old woman, mother of an RUC reservist.

Loyalist activity

The pattern of Loyalist activity in recent years has generally been one of response to Republican actions. This is true of both the political parties and the paramilitaries. Andy Tyrie made this point explicitly about his own group when he declared in January 1981 that the UDA was a 'counter-terrorist organisation'. Often, however, this merely means shooting innocent Catholics as a reprisal for some PIRA outrage. For example, a Catholic was shot dead and one was fatally wounded as an immediate response to the murder of the Reverend Robert Bradford in November 1981. Loyalist extremists, nevertheless, are not always simply reactive. A UDA statement in 1980 announced that the group would 'use every means at its disposal to eliminate those who pose a threat to the state of Ulster and all its people'. Who constitutes such a threat is decided by the paramilitaries themselves. Prominent Republicans are occasionally attacked. In January 1981 three Loyalist gunmen shot and seriously injured Bernadette McAliskey and her husband in front of their children. Mrs McAliskey had been playing a leading role in the H-Block campaign. Gerry Adams was wounded in a shooting attack in Belfast city centre on 14 March 1984. The assailants were almost immediately arrested and responsibility for the attack was claimed by the Ulster Freedom Fighters (UFF), a front for UDA terrorists.

Later in 1984 the UFF admitted two other killings, including that of Paddy Brady, a well-known Provisional Sinn Fein worker, in November. The Protestant Action Force (PAF) has also been active. Like the UFF it seems to vacillate between straight sectarian assassinations and attacks on people connected with the Republican movement. In November 1983, for example, PAF gunmen murdered Adrian Carroll, the brother of an INLA man who had been shot dead by the police the previous year. The PAF is a cover-name for the illegal UVF, who, nevertheless, sometimes claim responsibility for actions on

Left: Newtownards, 23 November 1981 – a show of force by Protestant paramilitaries, members of Ian Paisley's 'Third Force'.

their own account. One cause which the Loyalist paramilitaries have supported is the so-far unsuccessful campaign of Loyalist prisoners to be separated from Republicans within Northern Ireland's gaols. During the summer of 1984 Loyalists in Magilligan prison intermittently went on hunger strike. Various public demonstrations were organised on their behalf, and on 12 September the UVF brought Belfast traffic to a standstill with 23 bomb hoaxes.

This campaign, however, never began to match the scale of Republican popular support for prison protests and it illustrates the extent to which Protestant paramilitary activity is largely peripheral to the political aspirations of the majority community. Since Protestants for the most part regard the existing administration and state structures in Northern Ireland as legitimate, most political activity is channelled through political parties. But even these from time to time become frustrated with the apparent unresponsiveness of the Northern Ireland Office. After the assassination of Robert Bradford, Ian Paisley launched a campaign for the introduction of stricter security measures. He claimed that he could mobilise 30,000 Loyalist vigilantes into a 'Third Force', to supplement the official security effort, and also make Northern Ireland 'ungovernable'. In the event he did neither. Several thousand Protestants mounted demonstrations towards the end of the year and journalists were treated to a gathering of hooded men waving gun licences at the dead of night. The existing Loyalist paramilitary groups refused to co-operate with the new venture and the Third Force came to nothing.

While over the years the Reverend Ian Paisley has flirted with paramilitary organisations, the UDA has mirrored this tendency by dabbling in politics. The leader of the organisation, Andy Tyrie, was involved in setting up the New Ulster Political Research Group in 1978, which developed plans for an independent Northern Ireland. More recently Tyrie and his second-in-command, John McMichael, have concentrated on building up an 'Ulster Defence Force', which is intended to provide a cadre of officers for organising Loyalists in case of 'a possible day of confrontation' with either Republicans or even a British government planning to withdraw from the province. In McMichael's words, the UDA must 'get down to the nuts and bolts of preparing the Ulster Protestant community for a head-on collision to decide whether in fact it will survive as a people on this island'.

Diplock courts and supergrasses

On the legal side, the Troubles in Northern Ireland have put great strains on the judicial process. At an early stage it was found virtually impossible to maintain a conventional system of trial by jury because of the problem of intimidation, both of witnesses and jurors. In 1973 the government adopted the recommendations of a Commission chaired by Lord Diplock and for the duration of the emergency established a system of non-jury trials for specifically terrorist offences – the so-called 'Diplock courts'. In the Irish Republic a similar non-jury 'Special Criminal Court' has operated since 1972. In order to compensate for the reluctance of witnesses to give prosecution evidence, the new courts also established the easier admissibility of confessions and this consequently put considerable pressure on the police to extract such statements from suspects.

During the late 1970s there was a growing number of complaints about police interrogation techniques. In 1975 there were 180 allegations of ill-treatment. In 1977 there were 671. In May 1978 an Amnesty International report detailed 78 cases of alleged abuses. The government responded by setting up the Bennett Committee into Police Interrogation Procedures, which reported in March 1979. The committee noted that some injuries sustained by prisoners while in police custody were not self-inflicted. The chief constable admitted that it was undoubtedly possible that there were some 'bad apples' in the RUC. Bennett proposed a number of safeguards, such as the installation of closed-circuit television cameras in interview rooms, and independent medical examinations. Since their introduction the number of complaints alleging ill-treatment has markedly declined.

Another development in the courts has been the use of 'supergrasses' – informers often granted some immunity from prosecution in return for giving evidence against former colleagues. In the first supergrass trial to be concluded (during April 1983) 14 Loyalists received life sentences for over 60 crimes. In August the same year 35 persons were convicted on the basis of statements made by Christopher Black, a former Provisional. One of the most important informers was another ex-Provisional, Robert Quigley, whose information led to the arrest of over 70 people during 1983. In May 1984 nine men and women from Londonderry convicted on his evidence were sentenced to a total of a thousand years' imprisonment.

Below: Protest outside the Belfast court in which a 'supergrass' trial is taking place. The controversy surrounding such trials still rages.

Sometimes, however, the system works differently. In November 1983 a judge dismissed the uncorroborated evidence of a former INLA commander, Jackie Grimley, against seven men. Grimley, who had been a police informer even before he joined the INLA, had a record of 40 criminal convictions and various psychiatric disorders. In December the following year the Northern Ireland Lord Chief Justice, Lord Lowry, stopped a supergrass trial of 35 defendants who faced more than 180 charges on the word of former Provisional Raymond Gilmore. The judge explained that the informant was 'unworthy of belief'. The defendants had originally been arrested in August 1982, since when Gilmore had himself been held in police protective custody. The long delays between arrest and trial – common in supergrass and other cases – is seen by some as an informal method of internment.

The practice of using supergrasses has been vigorously opposed by both Republicans and Loyalists. The technique has certainly damaged the terrorist organisations. By mid-1984 it was estimated that about 450 persons had been charged on supergrass evidence. In 1983 the wife and stepfather of informer Harry Kirkpatrick were kidnapped by the INLA in an effort to persuade Kirkpatrick and other potential informers to stay loyal to their terrorist colleagues. Both people were later released unharmed. The use of supergrasses, however, and the conviction of persons on the sometimes uncorroborated evidence of paid informants, does run the serious risk of undermining faith in the whole judicial system if the practice is misused. In April 1983 the Northern Ireland secretary of state appointed Sir George Baker to review the law relating to terrorist offences. A year later Baker recommended the retention of the Diplock courts and the continued use of supergrass evidence, although he was

extremely critical about the length of time some people had to wait between arrest and trial. 'Justice delayed', he remarked, 'is justice denied.'

The restoration and maintenance of law and order is only one strand in the British government's threefold approach in its Northern Ireland policy. In the sphere of security, the government believes that the province will be best served by giving primary responsibility to the Royal Ulster Constabulary. The eventual hope is that the army – both regular soldiers and the UDR – can eventually be 'phased out' of providing military aid to the civil power. Successive secretaries of state, however, have recognised that security cannot be treated in isolation and that attention must also be paid to two other vital areas: the repair of the province's social and economic fabric and the development of a stable local political framework.

Economic and political developments

Northern Ireland remains one of the most disadvantaged parts of the United Kingdom. In 1984 unemployment consistently exceeded 20%. The proportion of jobless, moreover, varies throughout the province. It is still true that commerce and industry are dominated by the Protestant community. Despite the introduction of equal opportunity legislation and the work of a Fair Employment Agency, the survival of traditional employment patterns, the reluctance of companies to invest in Catholic parts of Northern Ireland – which tend to be the most turbulent – and that of Catholics to travel to Protestant areas for work, mean that it is easier for a Protestant to find work than a Catholic. The unemployment rate in Strabane, County Tyrone, on the border with Donegal, is commonly twice that of the provincial average. In parts of west

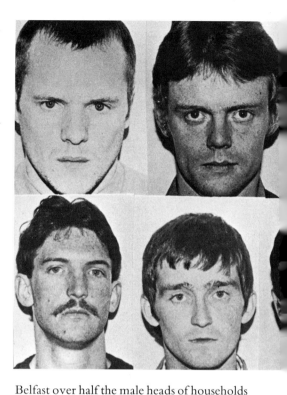

Belfast over half the male heads of households are without work. The effects of the Troubles in discouraging inward investment, and the impact of world economic recession leading to the closure of local factories owned by multinationals, has done much to negate the successes of the old Stormont ministry of commerce in attracting jobs to Northern Ireland. One estimate puts the job losses resulting from the violence between 1970 and 1980 at nearly 40,000.

There is, however, a continuing effort being made to create employment. The most famous example of this was the ill-fated Delorean Motor Company. In August 1978 the then secretary of state for Northern Ireland, Roy Mason, announced the establishment, with generous government assistance, of a major car factory to manufacture a futuristic gull-wing sports car, the brainchild of American motor magnate, John Z. Delorean. This was hailed as an economic coup which would provide over 2000 badly needed jobs. Although the factory was built – on the fringes of west Belfast – and went into production in record time, the venture proved to be a disaster. By 1982 the company had collapsed leaving debts of £100 million, and 2500 Protestant and Catholic workers had been laid off.

Government support is still offered to companies setting up in Northern Ireland. An Industrial Development Board operates at international level, while the Local Enterprise Development Unit encourages small-scale local investment. The two largest industrial employers in the province – plane and missile manufacturers, Short Brothers, and shipbuilders, Harland and Wolff – are state-

Left: Prime ministers Margaret Thatcher of Britain and Garret Fitzgerald of Ireland confer at a summit meeting on 7 November 1983. Anglo-Irish cooperation over security is essential if the Provisional gunmen are to be countered; however, talks with Dublin on any matter are viewed with deep suspicion by Loyalists in the North. One reason for this is that the Republic's constitution is fundamentally offensive to Unionists – Article 2 openly lays claim to the 'whole island of Ireland'.

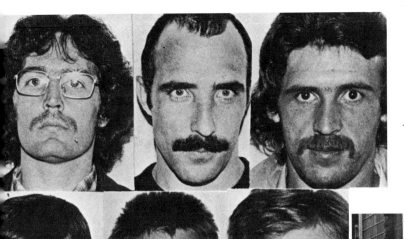

Left: Ten of the Provisional IRA prisoners who escaped from the Maze in a mass breakout in September 1983. The success of this elaborate escape plan was a propaganda boost for the Provisionals' cause and an acute embarrassment to the prison service.
Below: Exuberant Republican graffiti celebrates the Maze breakout. Of the 38 prisoners who escaped, however, 19 were quickly recaptured.

owned and both have in the past been heavily subsidised by the government. Both the companies are sited in east Belfast and employ a predominantly Protestant workforce. This has put orders for Short Brothers at risk. In March 1984 they won a £470 million order for their '330' aeroplane from the United States Air Force only after overcoming strident opposition from Irish-American groups who accused the company of discrimination against Catholics. Job prospects in one sector have expanded during the Troubles. Since 1969 some 12,000 new jobs have been created by employment in the security forces, private agencies and security-related services. These, however, are jobs which few would be sorry to see disappear. The stimulation of the Northern Ireland economy remains an important government aim. It reflects both a continuing belief that part of the province's problems stem from economic and social deprivation, and also an apparently unquenchable hope that support for terrorism can be bought off with jobs, that violence can be 'killed with kindness'.

Talks on power-sharing

The third strand in British policy consists of political initiatives and the attempt to secure a political structure in which the Protestant and Catholic communities can share power. London insists that a devolved administration will not be restored in Northern Ireland without some cross-community power-sharing. This is easier said than done. After the collapse of the 1977 United Unionist Action Council 'constitutional stoppage', Roy Mason started talks with the local political parties to see if some agreement on devolved government could be reached. But the politicians proved to be as intransigent as ever and the initiative was abandoned. Mason thereafter gave up attempting political progress and concentrated on making direct rule as congenial as possible by increasing investment in job-creation schemes, housing and community leisure facilities – a modern-day version of the ancient palliative 'bread and circuses'. Mason's successor, Humphrey Atkins, launched his own initiative early in 1980 when he arranged a conference to discuss possible new political structures. Since the secretary of state insisted that power-sharing was essential, the Official Unionists, led by James Molyneaux, boycotted the talks. Ian Paisley's Democratic Unionist Party (DUP), ostensibly the more extreme Unionist party, surprisingly took part, but found it could not agree with the other main participants, the SDLP, and the conference came to nothing.

The next constitutional initiative was the 78-seat Assembly set up by James Prior in October 1982. This again aims at eventual power-sharing, but it is based on a notion of 'rolling devolution'. Assuming the local parties can come to some sort of accommodation with each other, responsibility for local matters could progressively be devolved to the Assembly. In the meantime the body was given a scrutinising and advisory role in an effort to make direct rule more accountable to Northern Ireland opinion. From the start, however, the Assembly was crippled by the absence of any nationalist representatives. Sinn Fein members refused to take their seats on principle and SDLP members abstained, largely through fear of losing popular support and being outflanked by their Republican rivals.

On the Unionist side, while the DUP were prepared to work within the new institution, Molyneaux's party (who under the influence of Enoch Powell have increasingly come to favour complete integration with Great Britain) only reluctantly participated. In November 1983 as a protest at the lax security in border areas which had made possible the INLA Darkley attack, they withdrew entirely from the Assembly. Unhappy at being bracketed with the abstentionist nationalists, some Official Unionist members broke the boycott in February 1984 and in May the party formally resumed its place in the Assembly. However, as long as the Official Unionists offer only lukewarm support, the DUP resolutely opposes power-sharing, and even the constitutional nationalists refuse to attend at all, the future does not look very bright for the Assembly, although it has done some good work in testing and investigating government policy and giving local opinion some sort of platform.

The two main Unionist parties have also used the Assembly debates and committee work to consolidate their respective followings. The Official Unionist Party and the DUP are constantly challenging each other for leadership of the Protestant community. So far the honours are largely divided. The Official Unionists have the better party organisation and seem to be able to win more

seats at elections, such as the October 1982 Assembly poll and the general election of June 1983. The DUP, however, are sustained by the massive presence of Ian Paisley, who demonstrated in the European elections of June 1984 that he remains Northern Ireland's most effective single vote-winner by gaining over a third of all the first-preference votes cast.

Both the Official Unionists and the DUP oppose the formal involvement of the Dublin government in any constitutional arrangement for Northern Ireland. In recent years, nevertheless, one clear development has been an increase in Anglo-Irish consultation and cooperation, which was powerfully boosted by the shocked reaction in the South to the Mountbatten murder in August 1979. But cooperation has not developed entirely smoothly. The spread of H-Block agitation into the Republic strained relations, and a much more serious rift occurred during the Falklands crisis in 1982, when the Dublin

government broke away from the EEC policy of support for Britain and refused to back economic sanctions against Argentina. Gradually the governments repaired the links and at a meeting in November 1983 Mrs Thatcher and the Taoiseach (Irish prime minister), Dr Garret Fitzgerald, reaffirmed their joint commitment to defeat the men of violence.

Much of the Anglo-Irish security cooperation is at a day-to-day and unspectacular – albeit vital – level, such as regular meetings between the RUC and the Irish police and the sharing of radio channels in border areas. The Dublin government, however, has also made some notable moves to counter Loyalist accusations that the Republic is a 'safe haven' for terrorists. In 1976 the Irish parliament introduced a Criminal Law Jurisdiction Act which allowed persons to be tried in the Republic for offences committed in the United Kingdom. The first convictions were secured in December 1981, when two Provi-

Below: Sinn Fein leader Gerry Adams (left) and Martin Galvin of the American group Noraid acknowledge the applause of the crowd at a rally in Belfast on 12 August 1984. Noraid is widely believed to supply arms and ammunition for the IRA to use in Northern Ireland. For this reason, Galvin was refused an entry visa to the province, but managed to enter illegally. His appearance on the platform led the RUC to attempt to arrest him.

Above and right: Scenes of confrontation and riot as the RUC move forward in an unsuccessful attempt to apprehend Martin Galvin. Sean Downes (in red jacket) can be seen running towards the RUC officers, stick in hand, and then at the moment of impact as the plastic bullet hits him.

Far right: Sean Downes lies dying, despite medical aid. The shocking wound inflicted by the plastic bullet can clearly be seen on his chest. The tragic events were captured by TV cameras. In April 1985 RUC reserve constable Nigel Hegarty was charged with unlawfully killing Downes.

sionals who had escaped from Crumlin Road prison in Belfast were sentenced to ten years' imprisonment in Dublin. In July 1982 Gerard Tuite was convicted on evidence supplied from Scotland Yard for possessing explosives in London. The Republic has also begun to extradite suspects to Northern Ireland. Dominic McGlinchey, who was swiftly handed over after his capture in March 1984, is the most notable example. Yet there are still people in the Republic who are prepared to shelter terrorists on the run. When 38 Republican prisoners escaped from the Maze in a deeply embarrassing breakdown of security in September 1983, it was believed that most of the 19 men not quickly recaptured had taken refuge in the South.

Security cooperation

Cross-border security cooperation remains largely satisfactory. It even extends beyond Ireland itself. In September 1984 a trawler, the *Marita Anne*, carrying a cargo of arms from the United States for the Provisionals, was intercepted off the west coast of Ireland. The haul included 90 rifles, 60 machine guns, 71,000 rounds of ammunition and other munitions. The operation was uncovered through cooperation between the Irish, British and US intelligence services. The US freighter *Valhalla* which brought the arms across the Atlantic before handing them over to the *Marita Anne* had been tracked across the ocean by an American 'spy' satellite. A British RAF Nimrod aircraft subsequently followed

the trawler until the Irish Navy stopped it.

The undoubted effort and expense – one estimate puts the direct cost of the Troubles to the Irish Republic at over IR£1000 million – Dublin has devoted to security reflects the fact that terrorist violence is unacceptable on both sides of the border. Yet the main political parties in the South share one aim with the Provisionals: that of a 32-county Irish republic. Where they differ is in the nature of that republic and also in the means of achieving it. One criticism of southern Irish nationalists is that as partition became institutionalised, and as the two parts of Ireland developed separate structures, economies and identities, Dublin politicians never seriously considered how to end partition nor how to persuade the Protestants in the North to abandon the Union. In May 1983, however, the three chief parties in the South – Fine Gael, Fianna Fail and Labour – together with John Hume's SDLP, set up the 'New Ireland Forum' for 'consultation on the manner in which lasting peace and stability can be achieved in a new Ireland through the democratic process'. After a year's deliberations the Forum reported in favour of a unitary all-Ireland state, rather than a federal arrangement or some system of Anglo-Irish joint authority over the North. This was scarcely calculated to please Unionists. The report, nevertheless, recognised the strength and sincerity of Unionist opinion and specifically spoke of the necessity to 'achieve Irish unity in agreement' – in other words, partition could only be ended by consent. This is not likely to be given by

Northern Ireland's Unionists in the foreseeable future, but the significance of the Forum lies principally in the fact that it was the first systematic and rigorous examination of the partition problem by southern Irish politicians since the establishment of their state.

Unionists in Northern Ireland do not see partition as a problem. For them it is a positive advantage, and they believe they have nothing to gain by throwing in their lot with Dublin. Yet the continuance of terrorist violence forcibly brings home to them the important role which the southern government must play in maintaining law and order. The recent political successes of Provisional Sinn Fein, moreover, demonstrate the strength and vitality of Republican aspirations within Northern Ireland itself. These factors have influenced some Unionist thinking. The Official Unionist response to the New Ireland Forum is contained in a document entitled 'The Way Forward', which proposes administrative devolution and a bill of rights, and gives modest recognition to the aspirations of the Northern minority. This is more than would have been conceded before the Troubles began, but will hardly satisfy even the moderate nationalists, whose immediate political aspirations have themselves grown over the past 15 years. Both the Forum report and the Official Unionists' response indicate some stirring from traditional entrenched positions, but the very slightness of that movement also demonstrates just how intractable the problems of Northern Ireland remain.

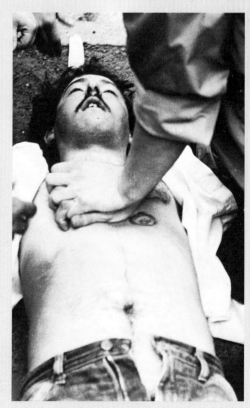

Conclusion

The Northern Ireland Troubles are a rich source of black humour. One example concerns a group of visiting Americans who were treated to a long and detailed lecture on the local situation. At the end one of the visitors complained that he found the whole thing 'very confusing'. 'If you're not confused,' replied the lecturer, 'you don't understand.' This counsel of despair, however, encapsulates an important truth, that Northern Ireland's problems are complex, deep-rooted and enduring. They are certainly not susceptible to the kinds of simplistic solutions offered by the extremists of both sides.

The fundamental difficulty stems from the fact that, while the island of Ireland is a geographical unit, sections of its population have very different national aspirations. Nationalists, North and South, believe passionately in an independent Irish state, whereas the Unionists of Northern Ireland assert that their civil and religious freedoms and their historic culture can only be secured by remaining within the United Kingdom of Great Britain and Northern Ireland. Any solution which fails to accommodate both these sets of aspirations – to some degree at least – will provoke violent opposition from one side or the other. In the present circumstances, and for as long as the British parliament at Westminster remains the ultimate political authority for Northern Ireland, extremist groups within the long Irish tradition of 'physical-force' nationalism will continue to operate both in the province and Great Britain. If, on the other hand, the British government decided that the province should be taken out of the United Kingdom, this would be resisted violently by militant Loyalists.

Independence for the North?

The option of detaching Northern Ireland from the United Kingdom and giving it either some independent or semi-independent status, or, alternatively, amalgamating it with the Republic of Ireland, is not one which recent British governments have ever seriously considered. One reason for this is the historic legacy which has left Northern Ireland within the United Kingdom, and which includes the maintenance by successive British governments of the pledge given in 1949 (and confirmed in the Northern Ireland Constitution Act of 1973) that 'in no event' will the province cease to be a part of the United Kingdom without the consent of the majority of its population. For London to change its policy on this point would also mean conceding defeat to the Provisional IRA and its twin strategy of 'ballot box and Armalite'.

Since the early 1970s, therefore, British policy has consistently been aimed at establishing some kind of devolved administration based on power-sharing between Unionists and nationalists. In the absence of such a structure emerging, London will persevere with direct rule. Although this is not particularly popular – either with the British government or the local population – opinion polls in the province consistently show that it is among the least unacceptable options. In the circumstances of Northern Ireland today, this amounts almost to a positive recommendation.

So long as direct rule continues there will be an irreducible amount of Republican violence. Those who today are fully committed to the Provisionals' military campaign will be satisfied with nothing less than the establishment of a 32-county Irish state and the replacement of the present Dublin regime by a more radical and Republican one. Their extremist politics, espousal of violence, and condemnation of the Dublin government for tolerating partition mean that they pose a threat to political stability in the South as well as the North – as has been the case since 1922. In 1982 the Chief Justice of the Republic described Sinn Fein as 'an evil and dangerous organisation whose object is to overthrow the state and its institutions if necessary by force'.

The authorities in Dublin are faced with the dilemma of how to deal with militant and violent Republicans, who yet have as their principal aim the central desire of the Irish

Index

Figures in italics refer to illustrations